Immersion Travel USA

Immersion Travel USA
The Best and Most Meaningful Volunteering, Living, and Learning Excursions

Sheryl Kayne

The Countryman Press
Woodstock, Vermont

ISBN 978-0-88150-802-4

Cover design by Johnson Design, Inc.
Cover photos from Getty Images
Book design and composition by Hespenheide Design

Published by The Countryman Press, P.O. Box 748, Woodstock, Vermont 05091

Distributed by W. W. Norton & Company, Inc., 500 Fifth Avenue, New York, NY 10110

Manufactured in the United States of America

10 9 8 7 6 5 4 3 2 1

To Naomi and Irving Rappoport

of Boynton Beach, Florida, and

Fairfield, Connecticut,

in loving and appreciative gratitude

for their confidence, encouragement,

generosity, and most comfortable

home where this book was born,

written, and completed—

thanks to you both.

Contents

Acknowledgments

I appreciate the assistance received from the organizations and businesses highlighted throughout the text. Thank you to each and every person who contributed stories, information, and support. It has been immensely rewarding to interact with so many people and share the concept and enthusiasm for *Immersion Travel USA.* Every day for the past nine months, I've had the privilege of meeting someone new—in person, over the telephone, or via the Internet—who has made me stop what I was doing and say, Wow! There are so many wonderful opportunities all over the country that allow immersion travelers to experience the fascination and grow, contribute, and participate in meaningful ways.

Thank you to my literary agent Lisa Hagan, Paraview Literary, Inc., for making the perfect match with the talented, insightful, and creative staff at Countryman Press, and to my public relations powerhouse, Ann-Marie Nieves.

Thanks to my children, Elanit and Aviva, and their husbands, Adam and Mark, and to my mother, Ruth Wolff, for adjusting to my needs, having total confidence in me, and always cheering me on. Thank you to my dear friends Meryl and Louis Rosenfeld, Anne Federici, and Bill Rappoport for their faith, patience, support, and understanding. Thank you to my writing allies, Marsha Temlock and Stacey Wolf, for their reading, rewriting, and brainstorming. And special thanks to my personal first-round editor and friend, Beverly Ehrman, whose persistence, skill, and know-how is reflected on every page of this book.

It has been said that a good librarian can help a writer build bridges wherever she wants to go. Thank you to the Westport Public Library in Connecticut for its multitalented staff and comfortable conference rooms, which provided the quiet, nourishing place I needed to research and write this book.

The Beginning: Welcome to Immersion Travel

Never be afraid to try something new.
Remember, amateurs built the ark.
Professionals built the Titanic.

—DREW CAREY

Welcome to a new way of thinking about and experiencing travel. I had always loved to travel, but hated being a rather ordinary kind of tourist, staying in hotels for a few nights and buzzing through major sites at the speed of Superwoman. I wanted to experience the

What Is Immersion Travel?

Immersion travel means taking an active part in where you visit in order to learn about the culture, traditions, and characteristics of each particular place.

phenomenal difference between visiting a location for a time-limited vacation and integrating myself into the community as someone who belonged there. I needed to see, hear, smell, touch, and taste where I went, really getting to know the people and place. At the time, I didn't know that what I wanted to experience was immersion travel.

A New Approach

Immersion Travel USA represents an innovative approach to vacations, sabbaticals, and leisure time. Immersion travel has traditionally meant traveling abroad to learn a foreign language and immerse yourself in the culture of your destination. Throughout this book, that concept is applied to traveling in the United States.

Every section of the country is different, with its own culture and particular ways of life. We may predominantly share English as the official common language, but each community has its own distinguishing features, habits, traditions, and qualities that make it unique and appealing.

Follow Your Passion

Learn how to choose and plan trips of all kinds to expand your horizons, fulfill your dreams, complement your life, and give something back by working, learning, or contributing. Immersion travel is for everyone at every age and stage of life.

Life-Changing Experiences

Throughout this book you will find personal stories about travelers who discovered their passions through different experiences. Kathleen fell in love with dogsledding on a weekend trip and now has 37 Alaskan huskies and teaches people how to mush. Chuck and Dona were so thrilled after attending the National Storytelling Festival that they

Have fun with local children while volunteering. *Leaders Today*

Immersion Travel

Don't just visit, get involved!

sold their home in New Jersey and opened a bed & break-fast in Jonesborough, Tennessee. Immersion travel can change your life.

A Little Bit of Time Goes a Long Way

The immersion excursions you'll find here are perfect for a nearby hour's drive, a weekend getaway, or a cross-country vacation or sabbatical. An immersion excursion can be your travel destination or a way to enhance an already-planned trip.

It doesn't matter where I go or who I meet, everyone wants to know how to make adventures like mine happen. The first question is always, How in the world did you find this job? People are intrigued by my ability to place myself in interesting situations, often doing unusual things. I've volunteered and worked as a cook on a ranch, removed pesky spotted knapweed from the wilderness in exchange for fabulous pastries at a local bakery, and performed living history vignettes about women of the Gold Rush six miles south of Denali National Park, Alaska, among many other endeavors. A few of my future goals are to become a trained volunteer in animal rescue, drive one of the classic red tour buses in Glacier National Park, and work as a naturalist on a whale-watching boat.

What would you like to do? Well, I'm writing this travel book to help you figure that out and to show you how to see the United States my way, through immersion travel.

Immersion Travel Tips

Here are a few things you can do to meet the locals and learn more about your surroundings, to transform your visit into an immersion experience:

- Talk to people. Introduce yourself to shopkeepers. Ask where the locals go and what's important to them.
- If working, volunteer. Call the Town Hall or Chamber of Commerce and inquire about activities needing volunteers.
- If volunteering, look for activities in the community that will enable you to meet more people. Check community bulletin boards, often found in the post office, library, or community center, and read the local newspaper to become informed about local events.
- If you see a community activity such as a potluck supper or beach barbecue, call and ask if you can attend.
- Stop at the public library to see if there's a book club or program you can attend.
- Contact a religious, professional, political, sports, or hobby group you are affiliated with in your town to find people of similar interests when you travel.
- Explore the community by geocaching, an activity that uses a Global Positioning System receiver to facilitate a high-tech treasure hunt.

How to Use This Book

I'm sure you've already realized that this is not your usual travel book. This is an adventure, resource, and idea book with activities that can be added to an already-planned trip or used to create an immersion excursion around an activity.

Because it's divided into activity and interest areas that make it easy to use, you don't have to read through the whole book to discover what you want to do. As you browse, you'll find more and more fascinating possibilities:

Helping: Volunteer in great locations with phenomenal people.

Learning: Education, self-help, and alternative lifestyles.

Working: Explore internships and short- and longer-term job opportunities.

Caring: Immersion travel for animal lovers, caretakers, and activists.

Playing: Enjoy the great outdoors, sports, and the arts.

Travel to interesting locations, like Cathedral Rock near Sedona, Arizona. *S. Wolf and E. Lamadrid*

Immersion Travel

Immersion travel will change the way you see your world and yourself in it.

Personal Stories

This is my favorite part of the book. Many of the entries are accompanied by a personal story of someone's experience within that program or with a similar activity. A few are composites of experiences from a number of travelers. Some are reflections from professionals in related fields, but most are shared experiences of immersion excursions.

I have been collecting travelers' stories for many years. Some are from people I met once on a train, or boat, or plane, or perhaps from an overheard conversation, and others came to light during my research for this book. I think of the stories as having a great cup of coffee with one hundred of my best friends. Each story has something to say that you usually don't discover from reading a travel book. There are insights into what to look for when selecting a trip and what it feels like to achieve a goal. Some stories are funny, while others are filled with practical and thoughtful advice. I love putting myself in other people's shoes to consider the possibilities from a new perspective; I'm sure you will too.

The majority of the activities featured can also be found in other locations around the country. For example, in Chapter 4, Caring, you'll find whale-watching out of Friday Harbor in the San Juan Islands, off the coast of Seattle, Washington. If this listing sparks your interest, but Washington State isn't in your travel plans, do some research on other opportunities around the country to decide where you could go. There is whale-watching off the coasts of Hawaii, California, Massachusetts, and

Alaska, and in many other locations. Perhaps you'll do what I've done: set a personal goal to go whale-watching in every possible spot in the country.

But you don't need to be on a commercial whale-watching boat to enjoy this activity. Also in Chapter 4, you'll discover that you can sit on a Florida beach in the Palm Bay area and collect important scientific information on the North Atlantic right whale. Anyone and everyone can do it. There's nothing like catching some rays and simultaneously contributing to the protection of an endangered animal.

State fairs are popular summer events. In Chapter 5, I have selected the Wisconsin State Fair, which highlights six major areas of interest: agriculture, commerce, industry, entertainment, government, and sports. With textile, craft, culinary, and horticulture exhibits, a pavilion featuring Wisconsin food and agricultural products, thousands of animals, midway rides, and a daily parade, there is something for everyone.

But other state fairs are equally compelling. The Iowa State Fair is known for its butter cow, and has one of the largest livestock shows in the world. The Association of Connecticut Fairs sponsors quilt, baking, photo, and ox pulls. The Kentucky State Fair, the largest air-conditioned fair in the country, features a world championship horse show. The Indiana State Fair features a pioneer village and an antique tractor show. The Ohio State Fair sponsors an auctioneers' bid call competition. State fairs reflect the culture, history, industry, tastes, habits, interests, and lifestyles of the people in the state.

The Selection Process

This is the first time a listing of immersion travel trips within the U.S. has been collected in one easy-to-use resource. It is a guidebook that will not only inform you of specific things to do and places to see but also spark your imagination and open up new doors of possibility. Each listing met specific criteria to be included in this book.

Whenever I heard or read about an activity that made me want to shout, Awesome! Wow! I'd love to do that! Sounds like fun!, I knew I was onto something great. Then my research began. The organization or vendor needed to have been in business for a minimum of two years. The travel experience offered had to involve helping, learning, working, caring, or playing with meaningful excursions in the great outdoors, sports, and the arts.

Whenever possible, I reviewed specifics about the product offered with people who had participated in the activity. Prices, stipends, and fees were evaluated with comparative pricing information. Web sites, sales, and promotional information were reviewed for clarity and usability; however, this material was provided by the business or organization itself and not necessarily gleaned through personal experience.

Immersion Travel USA is here to help you:

- Plan and enjoy exciting travel vacations that can help pay for or subsidize your expenses. And so you'll know at a glance, entries are labeled where applicable: FREE, STIPEND, WAGE, or TRADE.
- Create immersion excursions for singles, couples, family, friends, large groups, and travelers with special needs.
- Locate one all-encompassing immersion travel adventure or link together a few different experiences.
- Apply your talents and interests to try out a multitude of possibilities.
- Reconsider how you view travel and vacations.

Journal Writing and Guest Books

Keeping a journal while traveling is a great way to maintain a record of your immersion excursions. Adjusting to new people, places, and things teaches you a lot about yourself. Your journal will provide a personal record of your growth that can become a cherished part of your overall experience and be helpful in planning future immersion excursions. I also carry a guest book with me all the time and offer it to those I meet. Most people share contact information (e-mail or postal addresses), while others take a whole page to write a note, story, or even an invitation to stop by and visit when in their neighborhood.

I've found that people of all ages tend to write from the heart, sharing comments and thoughts they might not be comfortable expressing aloud. A guest book is the perfect way to keep track of the people you meet. You can buy one in a dollar store or stationery store or online at www.immersiontraveler.com, where you will also find journals and journaling techniques.

What You Need to Know to Plan Immersion Excursions

I always dreamed about being a cook on a trail ride. I'd pack up the horses with my supplies, ride out to a beautiful clearing, and serve a six-course meal prepared over an open fire. When I started researching available horse-packing and cooking jobs, I learned that horse packing is not something I could jump right into without any experience. It's a finely tuned art. However, I did have experience cooking professionally (20 years earlier) that I was able to translate into a job as a breakfast and lunch cook at Stehekin Valley Ranch, in Stehekin, Washington, which offered horseback riding in the wilderness.

What Do You Want to Do?

Make a list of what you'd like to do or where you'd like to go, along with your time availability and possible budget guidelines. Then browse through the chapters for suggestions to find what fits your list. There are many immersion excursion options with nominal or no fees where the primary expense is getting there. The goal is to affordably merge what you want to do and where you'd like to do it with the skills you have to offer and what you want to accomplish.

Online Applications and Phone Interviews

A standard online application asks for your education, experiences, and references. Since these positions are probably not related to what you ordinarily do for your day job, it's wise to adjust your résumé to include interests and abilities that apply to the position you are seeking. Don't allow lack of experience to dissuade you from trying.

Call the people who will serve as your references. Let them know what you're applying for, why, and what information you'd like them to share and emphasize.

Many smaller seasonal employers do not use a formal application, but ask instead for a cover letter and résumé. Use the cover letter to sell yourself and focus on why you want the position you're applying for and what you'll bring to it. Most interviews are conducted over the phone.

Telephone interviews stress listening and speaking skills. Prepare a list of questions on working conditions, room, board, job expectations, other workers, and additional pertinent points before placing your call. If you receive a call before you are fully prepared, request another appointment to talk. Never accept a job on the first interview; always set up a second time for additional questions to give you time to think, and to talk to other

Learn new skills, such as how to capture the landscape on canvas, at the John C. Campbell Folk School in North Carolina. *John C. Campbell Folk School*

Immersion Travel

The places you go and people you meet will change the way you choose to travel.

people about it. Since you'll become part of the community, make sure that the job is something you can do and want to do and that it is in a place where you want to be.

Don't hesitate to ask for the name and contact information of someone who has participated in the program you're considering. That is a great way to assess the trip from a different point of view.

I underestimated the physical demands of my professional cooking job in Stehekin, Washington. In retrospect, I should have volunteered a few days of my time in a local soup kitchen or a friend's catering business to more accurately assess the demands of professional cooking. Physical and emotional preparation are just as important as packing your bags.

When taking on a new helping, working, caring, or learning adventure, there are three major adjustments to consider: the place, the people, and the work. The goal is to do as much homework as possible to avoid surprises. The more you know about where you are going and what you will be doing, the easier the transition.

Be clear about what you need and don't need to be comfortable. Ask what "rustic accommodations" mean rather than waiting until your arrival. That way you might still enjoy an activity, but decide to stay in a nearby hotel.

When Considering Visiting, Volunteering, or Working

Getting the information you need and asking the right questions about a place you haven't visited before can be difficult. I recommend exploring the Web site and calling the place directly to follow up with questions and get a referral. Always try to speak with at least one person who has visited the place you are planning to visit.

When a listing grabs your attention and you begin to think, Gosh, I could do that, use these questions as a standard guideline:

- What is the program being offered?
- What is the time commitment?
- What ages are most appropriate?
- What are the fees for room and board and are they negotiable?

- Are there program fees? Stipends? Wages?
- What is a typical day like?
- Are there certain skills you need to possess or learn in order to participate in a certain activity?
- What happens if you arrive and don't like what you are asked to do?
- Are there safety or health issues to be considered?
- Is the facility handicapped accessible?
- What are the work hours?
- Will there be ample time to visit nearby places of interest?

Travel Visa Information for Non–American Citizens Visiting the United States

This book is for everyone—people living in the United States as well as guests from other countries. You are invited to experience America in a new and different way by involving yourself in the places you visit and by allowing yourself to get to know and appreciate the people, sites, and activities unique to each region of the country.

Millions of foreign visitors travel to the United States each year as tourists or to visit family and friends. People also come for specific purposes including business, education, training, or to participate in volunteer programs conducted by charitable organizations. Most of these visitors need B-1/B-2 visitor visas to enter the country.

According to the U.S. State Department Web site (www.travel.state.gov/), foreign citizens must apply for a visa at a U.S. Embassy or Consulate abroad. Citizens of certain countries may be able to travel without a visa on the Visa Waiver Program (VWP) if certain criteria are met. The B-1/B-2 visa is for people traveling to the United States for business or tourism for fewer than 90 days, and you must have a round-trip ticket, fly on certain air carriers, and meet additional requirements.

Visa applications take time. It's best to plan ahead so that you'll have the time you need to determine if a visa is needed and for the application to be processed. You can contact the U.S. Embassy or Consulate via the Department of State Web site, www.state.gov//travel/tips/embassies/embassies_1214.html; U.S. Immigration Support, www.usimmigrationsupport.org/visa_h2b.html; or by calling the Visa Services public information line in Washington, D.C. (202-663-1225).

Tourists can stay six months on a B-2 tourist visa, but cannot work or receive payment of any kind, which is fine for many of the volunteering, caring, learning, and playing activities in this book.

There is a J-1 exchange visitor visa for government-approved educational and cultural programs. You meet the criteria for a J-1 Exchange Visitor Visa if you are coming to the United States as a student, scholar, trainee, teacher, professor, research assistant, medical graduate, or international visitor participating in a program of studies, training research, or cultural enrichment specifically designed for such individuals by the U.S. Department of State through its Bureau of Educational and Cultural Affairs.

Activities covered by J-1 Exchange Visitor Visa programs include:

- Au pair and nanny
- Summer camp counselors and staff
- Postgraduate students
- Government visitors
- Medical students coming to the U.S. as residents or interns
- Foreign scholars sponsored by universities as temporary faculty
- Business and industrial trainees

There are also H-2B Work Visas that were created to allow people to come to the United States temporarily for mainly nonagricultural jobs, in which U.S. workers are in short supply. Up to 66,000 H-2B Visas are issued every year, targeted at skilled and unskilled workers.

The following documentation is required for *all* visa applicants:

- Passport, valid for at least six months after your departure date
- Visa application form
- A photograph, 5 cm by 5 cm, with your signature in English on the back
- Certificate of Eligibility for Non-Immigrant F-1 Student Status (Form 1-20 A-B)
- Affidavit of financial support form and evidence of support
- Evidence of English language ability
- Documents that demonstrate (1) the purpose of your trip and (2) provide proof of your intention to leave the U.S. after your temporary stay.

It's not unusual to meet foreign students traveling to the United States to work in and tour the national parks during the summer season. There are programs in Europe and the United States that specialize in arranging work, visa, and major logistics for a fee; however, you do not have to be a student to apply for many of the working positions found in this book. You can apply directly to the business or organization listed, and then contact your embassy for further directions.

Getting There Is Half the Fun

It used to be that people traveled by car to save money on airfare. That has changed with soaring gasoline prices and competitive discounted airfares. I spent almost three times as much money driving to Denali National Park from Weston, Connecticut, as I would have on an airline ticket, but getting there often sets the stage for the rest of the trip. I wanted to meet the challenge of driving to Alaska all by myself, and I did. It was an empowering trip I will never forget. And since my Alaskan job was a four-month commitment, I felt that the benefits of having my car during that time would far outweigh the initial travel costs, and they did.

Driving

- Plan the route.
- Know lodging for the itinerary.
- Estimate gas costs and availability.
- Pack for the end destination and keep a travel bag handy.

Commercial Flights

There are advantages to air travel, but the downside is security concerns, long lines, and luggage limitations. If you're traveling solo or with another adult it's not so bad. If you have children, it can be another story. Younger kids need drinks, snacks, and entertainment planned for any flight over an hour. As a rule I did not allow my daughters candy except on long flights. A bag of M&Ms guaranteed an hour's worth of counting, nibbling, and sorting activities.

The number of people traveling in your party affects the costs. Depending on the part of the country you'll be traveling to, sign up for airline newsletters and frequent-flier benefits. Also consider credit cards that give airline bonus miles. For Denver, Colorado, the least expensive carrier is often Southwest Airlines. For Richmond, Virginia, Delta Airlines runs weekly specials. When Jet Blue began service, the price of a round-trip ticket dropped drastically.

Space and Weight Limitations

Another consideration is how long you will be staying at your destination and how much clothing, personal items, and equipment you'll need. I travel with my portable office: laptop computer, printer, paper, printer cartridges, camera, tripod, etc. Admittedly, with each trip I've made, I've had too many things to fit into my room and have had to use my car trunk as a satellite closet.

If you will be visiting a major metropolitan area with shopping nearby, you can easily replace items you've used. For me, living and working in Stehekin, Washington, meant traveling two and a half hours by ferry to go shopping for basics like soap, sunscreen, and batteries.

Train

Trains can be an enjoyable way to travel and see the sights along the way. It's worth looking into, particularly if your destination has good public transportation and you don't need your own car once you arrive. It's usually possible to rent a car for a special outing. As with any public transportation, factor in extra time to compensate for unforeseeable changes in schedules.

Bus

The advantage to bus travel is that you leave the driving to someone else. And you can often disembark to visit places along the way to enjoy the sights as you go. There are commercial bus lines such as Peter Pan or Greyhound and escorted trips for groups.

Research the Sights

The minute you settle on your location, begin researching interesting sights in the area or along the way. If using travelers' services such as AAA to assist with maps and directions, ask for places of interest to be included. If you use Google, MapQuest, or Yahoo Map, there will be suggestions for side trips and sightseeing excursions, along with hotels and restaurants. Most importantly, give yourself sufficient time to enjoy what you plan to do and allow for interesting diversions. Set a goal to achieve each day. If you get to more than one activity, great, but if not, then you've at least accomplished one thing that you wanted to do.

An Added Bonus for Volunteers

It is possible that your volunteer immersion experience might be tax deductible. Whenever you combine travel with volunteering, it's worth checking with your accountant or the IRS. The deciding factors are the intent of the trip and the organization involved. If the trip is for the sole purpose of being a volunteer or serving as part of a volunteer delegation, it might very well qualify as a tax deduction.

A number of the trips described in Chapter 1, Helping, and Chapter 4, Caring, qualify for tax deductions. For example, you can volunteer with your family, on your own, or with a group of friends, through Global Volunteers, to spend a week working with communities in Minnesota or West Virginia. It's very rewarding to donate your time and use your talents to assist families much like your own, but living in different circumstances. Global Volunteers charges fees for housing, food, and materials, which could qualify your week as a tax-deductible vacation, an added benefit of doing good.

Or maybe you'd like to participate by joining a volunteer effort to help count the loggerhead turtle population. If that is the intent for the entire trip, chances are it will be tax deductible. However, if part of the trip is volunteering and part is for other activities, like visiting friends

Enjoy a unique adventure, cruising down the Rio Grande Gorge in motion with the wind, with Eske's Air Ventures/Paradise Balloons in Taos, New Mexico. *Adam Schallau/www.recapturephoto.com*

and sightseeing, new IRS guidelines might disallow it. But this is certainly worth considering.

If the whole trip isn't tax deductible, some contributions to specific charitable activities with legitimate registered organizations can be itemized as deductions. This might include some organizations, colleges, and universities, but not all charitable organizations qualify. It can be worthwhile to inquire about the possibility of tax deductions for the immersion travel experiences you are considering.

Working on a Budget

After deciding where to go and what to do, the next question will surely be, How much will all of this cost? Use the following cost assessment inventory to help you figure out how much money you will need and to track your costs:

Cost Assessment Inventory		
	Estimated Cost	**Actual Cost**
Travel costs		
Airfare		
Car preparations		
Gasoline & oil		
Personal supplies		
Special clothing		
Fees		
Room & board		
Sightseeing		
Entertainment		
Total		

Always ask about current fees. If you're encouraged to book ahead due to limited space or rising costs, inquire if booking ahead guarantees you the current fees. Prices and Web sites quoted in this book will vary with time.

The Accommodations Pricing Key		
	Lodging	Restaurants (per person)
$	Up to $50	Under $10
$$	$51–100	Up to $25
$$$	$101–150	Up to $50
$$$$	$151–250	Up to $75
$$$$$	Over $250	$100 or more

Job Listings Identification Key

 FREE: There are no fees to partake in this activity.

 STIPEND: A stipend is awarded for participation in this activity.

 WAGE: An hourly wage is paid for this position.

 TRADE: Services are exchanged for room and board.

Frequently Asked Questions about Immersion Travel

Do I need a big chunk of vacation time for immersion travel?

Immersion travel can add interesting dimensions to everything from an afternoon's excursion or a day trip to a weekend, weeklong, or extended adventure.

What qualifies a trip as immersion travel?

Immersion travel is any trip that gives you the opportunity to become involved in your surroundings through helping, learning, working, caring, and playing.

Are immersion travel trips only for the young?

These trips are for everyone. They can be personalized and streamlined to meet your needs, challenge your abilities, and expand your horizons at any age.

Do I need to be physically fit?

Whatever you choose to do, your health and capabilities need to be considered in the planning stages. Some immersion travel trips and activities are physically challenging and others are not.

Does immersion travel cost more than a standard vacation?

No, immersion travel enhances standard vacations by adding more activities and options without adding to the costs. In fact, many immersion travel experiences include a stipend, room, board, trade of services, or hourly pay.

Do I have to travel alone on immersion travel trips or can my spouse and children come with me?

Sometimes you might choose to take a trip on your own to refresh and rejuvenate. Other times you'll want to include your partner and children. Immersion travel trips can be planned for everyone, including those with special needs.

Can a travel agent help me plan my trip?

A travel agent might recommend vendors who specialize in immersion travel, such as Adventures in Good Company, Close-Up Expeditions, or Canyonlands Field

Institute. With immersion travel you have the option of not using a travel agent and planning your own excursion or consulting with professionals to see if they have suggestions or access to special discounts or details.

Things Change

Although every entry has been researched with personal interviews and visits where possible, things do change. People sell businesses or hire new staff. It is best to use this book as a guide and then ask questions and make the necessary calls to learn about any revisions. Also be aware that e-mail addresses and Web sites may be adjusted from day to day. The travel industry is a fluid business. Ask for references and speak with former clients. Do not make plans or reservations based on anything you find in this book or on the Internet without completely checking it out.

Share the Info

Please remember: After visiting any listing, log on to www.immersiontraveler.com to provide your feedback or updates for future readers and to share your favorite immersion travel trips. Immersion travelers have so much great information to share with each other.

Now go have a great time using this book to plan the most fantastic immersion excursions ever. Begin wherever you wish—allow one idea to lead you to the next as you plan the immersion excursion of a lifetime.

1

Helping

Volunteer in Great Locations with

Phenomenal People

Never doubt that a small group of thoughtful, committed citizens can change the world; indeed, it's the only thing that ever has.

—Margaret Mead, *anthropologist*

Giving of yourself is the greatest gift there is to give. Programs that need volunteers flourish all over the country, creating wonderful mini-immersion excursions that encourage participants to commit time, talent, and energy to a myriad of meaningful and worthy causes. Whether you choose to raise funds for a nonprofit organization, or lend your talents tutoring schoolchildren, or

Immersion Travel

Make new friends, help yourself and others along the way.

spend an afternoon raking and clearing a trail, volunteering has enormous benefits. Here you will find a wide array of ways to express yourself. Follow your passion across the country or just around the corner.

Select When, Where, Why, and For How Long

One Brick (www.onebrick.org). Headquartered in San Francisco, California, One Brick is an all-volunteer, nonprofit organization that doesn't even maintain an office. Its mission is to enable people to get involved by creating a social and flexible volunteer environment for those who want to make a contribution. There are currently chapters in San Francisco, New York City, Chicago, Washington, D.C., and Minneapolis–St. Paul.

Each volunteer event, which typically lasts three to four hours, is followed by a gathering at a local restaurant or café so participants can relax and get to know one another. Events are both indoors and outside and benefit children, the environment, food banks, schools, inner-city neighborhoods, and other worthy causes.

You choose when and where you want to volunteer, without making a longer-term commitment, and you can adjust your volunteer activities to your own schedule, whether you live nearby or are traveling to one of the participating cities. One Brick supports over 500 organizations, and last year brought over 50,0000 volunteer hours to the communities it serves. There is a long list of organizations that have benefited from One Brick's efforts, and more are added each month. The activities are creative and fun, from a fundraiser boutique day to cleaning up a park zoo pond, to spring planting with senior citizens.

Check the calendar of events on the One Brick Web site. When you click on the event that interests you, there will be a detailed description that includes the date and

Immersion Travel

Trips with benefits.

time commitment; what you will need and what will be provided for you; meeting, driving, and transit directions; and the e-mail address of the contact person for the event. You can also RSVP online, add the event to your personal calendar, or sign up for an e-mail reminder.

When you plan your next trip to any of the five cities currently served by One Brick, remember to check their Web site for volunteer opportunities and events during your stay. You will return from your travels with the satisfaction of having made a difference, and with new friends you'll want to visit again.

Assist Families in the Midwest

Global Volunteers (375 E. Little Canada Rd., St. Paul, MN 55117; 1-800-487-1074; 651-407-6100; fax 651-482-0915; www.globalvolunteers.org; email@globalvolunteers.org; 1-week program, $895, with discounts for Internet users, returning volunteers, and students). Connect with local people on a weeklong community project, and learn about a different culture as you help others to make a better life for themselves and their children. Teach children of new immigrants to speak English, in a rural Midwestern community. There are opportunities in Worthington and Austin, Minnesota, to help children and adults communicate effectively, fostering understanding and trust.

Renovate homes or tutor children in West Virginia and learn about the people in the coal-mining towns of Appalachia. You can also assist with labor and education projects, and learn construction skills while you help provide affordable housing for low-income families. You can mentor local youth and help students study for their GEDs, and assist with an after-school program.

You will have free time after your workday to enjoy cultural activities in your host community, participate in team sports, hike and explore your surroundings, and engage in other leisure activities. Lodging can be in cabins or dormitory style. Volunteer teams usually prepare their own breakfasts and lunches, with dinners in local restaurants or prepared by local cooks. You will have an experienced team leader and extensive preparation materials, with on-site orientation sessions and team-building exercises. Your contribution will make a difference, and you can have a satisfying and meaningful volunteer vacation.

Check the Web site for the complete schedule and dates of service projects, and fill out an online application or call a volunteer coordinator. You will need to send a deposit to receive a volunteer manual, and then complete information forms and send personal references before your application is processed. The service program fee is tax deductible.

Michael's Story: From San Francisco to Montana

My wife, three children (ages 11, 14, and 17), and I volunteered for a week on an Indian reservation in Montana. My kids have traveled the world and they agreed that volunteering together as a family, helping other families, was the best vacation we've ever had. We were all busy doing things we liked and did well. I painted and repaired houses, my wife sewed clothing and gardened, the kids worked with other kids doing odd jobs, helping with homework, and hanging out. There were fees to cover food, housing, and materials. We stayed together and lived and ate with people in the community. It changed our lives. Now we think differently about vacation and travel time.

Amizade Promotes Friendship

Amizade Global Service-Learning (P.O. Box 6894, Morgantown, WV 26506; 304-293-6049; fax 757-257-8358; www.globalservicelearning.org; volunteer@amizade.org; volunteer program in Washington, D.C., $697 for 7 days, $976 for 10 days, and $1,310 for 14 days; Navajo Nation program, $849 for 7 days, $1,137 for 10 days, and $1,546 for 14 days; Montana, $599 for 7 days, $805 for 10 days, and $1,035 for 14 days). Amizade offers volunteer and service-learning programs here in the U.S. and around the world.

Amizade volunteers feed the hungry and homeless in Washington, D.C. In partnership with the DC Central Kitchen (www.dccentralkitchen.org), surplus food from area restaurants, groceries, and food businesses is distributed to community agencies. There's also a culinary job training program for the unemployed who are either homeless or are receiving public assistance, and an extensive catering project that provides food to businesses, government, and local nonprofits, while offering training and employment to graduates of the culinary program. This program keeps on giving through outreach programs and a Campus Kitchen Project that brings colleges and universities together with student volunteers, campus dining professionals, and community partners, to open new community kitchens on campuses across the country.

Amizade volunteers of all ages and backgrounds visit the Navajo Nation in Tuba City, Arizona, and donate time and energy working in the schools. *Amizade Global Service-Learning*

Volunteers are placed in a variety of locations including the DC Central Kitchen, So Others Might Eat, McKenna's Wagon (food distribution service), Georgetown Shelter, National Coalition for Homeless, Capital Area Food Bank, and Street Sense (newspaper distributor).

At the Navajo Nation in Tuba City, Arizona, Amizade provides service opportunities in partnership with the Navajo Nation schools. Besides tutoring in the classrooms, volunteers develop and implement a weeklong art program and serve as aides in the library, reading rooms, and physical education classes. The Tuba City Boarding School encourages its students to grow into responsible adults, and offers a quality education enriched by the efforts of parents, community, and volunteer partners.

One-on-one assistance, when needed, can make a major difference in students' lives.
Amizade Global Service-Learning

Amizade works with the Tuba City Boarding School to promote classroom success and to mentor the youth of the Navajo Nation.

In Montana, Amizade and the Gallatin National Forest, Gardiner Ranger District, are working together to preserve and restore historical sites. Projects include restoring cabins, rebuilding fences, and maintaining the land.

Amizade sponsors 7-, 10-, and 14-day programs in both Washington, D.C., and the Navajo Nation as part of its comprehensive service and learning mission. Fees are based on groups of six or more and do not include transportation. Group fees include room and board, on-site staff, community placement, and cultural and recreational activities. Volunteer applications are available on the Web site. *Amizade* is Portuguese for "friendship."

Tracy Patterson Kee, Navajo Nation Site Director, Tuba City, Arizona

We live here in Tuba City, Arizona, about an hour and a half north of Flagstaff and in the heart of the Painted Desert. My husband is native Navajo. As the Amizade local site director, I meet arriving groups, provide a culture awareness orientation, and answer questions about what the volunteers can expect for the week. Typically their trip is from Saturday to Saturday, and they stay in a hogan built specifically for visiting groups, with meals provided. Monday through Friday from 8 AM to 3 PM, the volunteers tutor at our local school in grades kindergarten through eighth. I meet them every day after school and we do different activities to help them get a sense of our community and location. The first day they visit the Grand Canyon. After that almost all of their time is spent on the reservation. On Monday afternoon we visit the Navajo Cultural Museum, which is a really neat interactive museum, and on another day we go to a traditional sweat lodge only a mile from here and everyone loves that. We

Often not a word is needed, simply being present is sufficient. *Amizade Global Service-Learning*

meet a lot of the local people. A teacher who is also a silversmith demonstrates beautiful Navajo jewelry making. Another woman demonstrates how to make Navajo tacos with fry bread, beans, meat, cheese, and tomatoes. She also gives a cultural presentation to the group, modeling traditional Navajo dress and hair with her daughter. Some days we hike and visit a Navajo farm. Another day we visit with a Navajo singer who teaches us native songs and dances. A highlight of the week is on Saturday, when we go to the local

swap meet and the more adventurous enjoy the
chance to taste a mutton sandwich, a big local tradition. The week is packed with nonstop action
and beneficial experiences for the visitors and
the visited.

*"Life, like a mirror, never gives back more than we
put into it."*

—ANONYMOUS

A Commitment to Service

✉ **City Year** (287 Columbus Ave, Boston, MA 02116;
617-927-2500 or 617-927-2510; www.cityyear.org; joinus
@cityyear.org; applications accepted until Nov. 30, Feb.
15, Apr. 15, and May 31 for programs beginning with the
school year—late Aug. or early Sept. depending upon location). City Year is a member of AmeriCorps, a federally
funded network of national service programs in education, public safety, health, and the environment.

Young adults, ages 17 to 24, commit 1,700 hours of
service over a 10-month period working in 17 locations
around the United States, including Chicago, Cleveland,
Detroit, Los Angeles, New York, Seattle, and Washington,
D.C. Participants serve full-time as tutors or mentors in
schools, running after-school programs, leading and
developing youth leadership programs, and organizing
vacation camps for children and their communities. A living stipend is awarded; the amount is determined by the
location, with a $4,725 AmeriCorps education award upon
completion of a full term of service. More information
about the application process can be found online at
www.cityyear.org/faq.aspx.

Jessica's Story

I am the youngest of four siblings to graduate high
school and everyone in my family went to college.
I hadn't even thought about doing anything else
until I attended a college fair at my high school.
Two boys in line behind me were talking about
City Year. I listened to this excited voice talking
about his older brother who took a year off before
going to college to work with City Year. He was
assigned to an inner-city middle school in

As tutors and mentors, City Year corps makes a difference in children's lives by helping them
read. *Jennifer Cogswell*

City Year corps engage community members of all ages and show them the difference they can make by giving back. *Andrew Dean*

Philadelphia, tutoring students in Spanish and science, which were his best subjects. He was also running a basketball after-school clinic and starting a basketball team in a community center.

I'd never heard of City Year before but somehow I knew it was for me. I started researching it immediately and found a program that really spoke to me. I applied to colleges and City Year. I was accepted to three great schools and City Year and chose City Year. I think it will give me the time and experience I need to figure out what I really want to do when I go to college.

The hardest part of the whole process was telling my parents, three brothers, grandparents, and aunts and uncles that I wouldn't be going to college right now. Most people understood and my parents actually complimented me on my reasoning. I can hardly wait to get started with City Year. I know I have a lot to offer and a lot to learn.

City Year corps members extend the school day by engaging children in after-school programs. *Jennifer Cogswell*

Visit or Volunteer at the Opera House Where Lilly Langtry Sang

Pioneer Living History Village (3901 West Pioneer Rd., Phoenix, AZ 85086; 623-465-1052; fax 623-465-068; www.pioneer-arizona.com; pioneerarizona@earthlink.net; open mid-Sept.–May, 9 to 5, Wed. to Sun.; June–mid-Sept. 9 to 3, Wed. to Sun.). Volunteers are needed to staff every aspect of this living history attraction. The Pioneer Living History Village performs and operates historically correct programs about Arizona's history and pioneer life from 1863 to 1912. They are looking for reenactors for gunfighters and townsfolk and need volunteer archivists, curators, museum technicians, landscapers, contractors, electricians, laborers, and more. Call to help and they'll gladly use your services.

Divers of the Deep

Reef Check Foundation (P.O. Box 1057, Pacific Palisades, CA 90272-1057; 310-230-2371; fax 310-230-2376; www.reefcheck.org; rcinfo@reefcheck.org). An international organization with volunteer reef-monitoring teams around the world, Reef Check Foundation is based in the United States, with offices in Hawaii and California. Volunteer divers can participate in a training course over two weekends and become certified to do Reef Check California surveys, monitoring the rocky reefs following a specific research protocol.

Claudette's Underwater Story

We spent the first training dives alternating between being excited new volunteers and over-

Divers volunteer their training time and additional dives to collect important data for the California Reef Check Foundation in Pacific Palisades, California.

whelmed new research divers. Not everything looked like the flash card pictures. Giant kelp and sea palms? Easy. The rest? You've got to be kidding me! How can I count what I can't identify traveling at nine feet per minute over jungle-covered boulders with a frisky surge swinging us around? What's the difference between a warty sea cucumber and a California sea cuke? I'm terrible at this! What was

I thinking? I'm a nurse, not a scientist. I dive for
fun, not work. Oh my, three days of being an idiot!
I should not be here.

Back on deck, the instructors talked us down
off the ledge, showing us what part of our data
was good and what was not so good. We were
taught what we didn't know (red urchins can be
black) and given plenty of opportunities to practice. Our confidence grew as the instructors
poured on the teaching and encouragement. The
second day focused on teaching fish ID and
counts. Like a slow-motion shooting gallery (without the armaments), we cruised the transect line
identifying and estimating sizes and numbers, not-
ing everything on our survey data sheets and
thumping our heads over the vagaries of black
rockfish versus blue rockfish, pile perch versus rub-
berlip, sea perch versus female rock wrasses. I was
getting better at this. Wow. Who was I? And what
had they done with the idiot who had been wearing my dive gear yesterday? Proficiency testing
began to go very well.

Day three instructions: be ready to splash in by
nine to begin fish ID and count proficiency testing.
And then the big surprise was revealed. We were

about to do the first all-volunteer California Reef
Check site survey. Us. Not the scientists. Not the
Reef Check head honchos. Us. The calibrated, the
validated, the nervous, and the eager.

Under the Sea

The Hawaii Whale Research Foundation (HWRF,
P.O. Box 1296, Lahaina, HI 96767; www.hwrf.org;
dsalden@siue.edu). Staffed by skilled, committed, and

An accomplished, happy group of diving volunteers who just passed their reef-check training.

Making a Difference

"Young people don't have to wait until they grow up or have jobs or wait at all to make a difference in the world. They can make a difference now. There are 7 billion people in the world and 3 billion are under age 25. That's a force to be reckoned with. We are the first generation with the resources and power to end poverty and environmental problems. We are the generation that we've been waiting for."

—Erin Blanding, Director of Leadership Programming, Leaders Today

caring volunteers who are actively conducting field research on humpback whales through observation for data collection and photo documentation. They are looking for qualified research assistants. The best way to contact the organization is through e-mail or postal mail.

Moved to Action: Volunteering Across America

The Arizona Wind-Song Peace and Leadership Center (Leaders Today, 233 Carlton St., Toronto, Ontario, Canada M5A 2L2; 416-964-8942; fax 416-964-2199; www.leaders today.com; info@leaderstoday.com; $1,750). People ages 11 to 25 take part in a personal discovery and leadership development program held in Patagonia, Arizona. The bulk of the brainstorming and programming is initiated by the participants themselves, from their interests, concerns, and passions. They work with a Native American reservation and build strong bonds of solidarity and friendship with the host community. The two-week trip fee of $1,750 covers accommodations, food, and volunteer placements. Airfare is not included.

Rebuilding a turtle habitat at Treehouse Farm and Sanctuary through the Arizona Wind-Song Peace and Leadership Center.

Leadership at Every Age: Emma's Story

I was 12 years old when somehow I convinced my parents to drop me off at a college campus to attend my first Leaders Today camp. The first night away I called home and said, "Today I learned how to shake someone's hand and that I can have fun changing the world."

A student's T-shirt after a Wind-Song painting project.

Giving

"Some people give time, some money, some their skills and connections, some literally give their life's blood. But everyone has something to give."

—Barbara Bush

Last summer (at age 18) I attended The Arizona Wind-Song Leadership Center program in Patagonia, Arizona. Facilitators taught us that anything you are passionate about is important and to figure out a way do something related to what you are passionate about because that's what's going to make you happy and fulfilled.

I have a real tangible dream. I want to create a program for the year between high school graduation and college to explore borders around the world: the United States and Mexico, Palestine and Israel, India and Pakistan, everywhere. I believe there's a better way to address border issues and that each and every one of us can be an active agent of social change.

In Your Neighborhood or Coast to Coast

The Volunteer Family (161 Worcester Rd., Suite 300, Framingham, MA 01701; 508-405-2220; www.volunteer family.org; info@thevolunteerfamily.org). The Volunteer

Emma and her friend at Wind-Song.

Family was started by a mom looking for appropriate volunteer activities that would involve the entire family. The Web site is a cornucopia of information, including events that need volunteers and corporate sponsorships. Links connect potential volunteers with organizations and suggest interesting activities to do with children, helping you find the right opportunity in your neighborhood or in a place you'd like to visit.

Pedaling to End Poverty Housing

Bike & Build (20 Jay St., Suite M08, Brooklyn, NY 11201; 718-599-5925, fax 718-752-9806; www.bikeandbuild.org; info@bikeandbuild.org; donation $4,000). Bike & Build organizes cross-country bicycle trips for young adults (ages 18 to 25) to benefit affordable housing groups. Each participant is responsible for raising a $4,000 contribution. Some people solicit contributions from family, friends, and local organizations or businesses. Others hold car washes, gourmet dinners, or other creative

The paceline shadow of bikers cycling cross country with Bike & Build.

fundraising events. Following the initial $1,000, he or she receives a brand-new road bike to keep after successfully completing the trip. Housing is provided along the way in churches, synagogues, YMCAs, and campgrounds, with many donated potluck suppers. Bike & Build has contributed over one million dollars to affordable housing projects.

Lynn's Bike & Build Story

Originally I'd considered biking through Europe, but I really wanted to see and experience my own country first before going to someone else's. I'm really glad I did. I selected the central United States route from Virginia Beach, Virginia, to Canon Beach, Oregon, biking 3,682 miles across the beautiful U.S.A. while working for a great cause.

Whenever I wanted to explain to someone how rewarding the "build" part of Bike and Build could be, I told them this story. On our first day at the first building site in Norfolk, Virginia, we were just becoming comfortable with our tasks and falling into a rhythm of getting things done. Above the normal construction sound track of hammers, saws, and organized commotion, I heard someone chatting and laughing nearby. The woman's voice sounded out of place because of its elevated pitch and, as I watched her struggle to put a single nail

Reaching the ridge after a steep uphill climb is reason for jubilation.

into the sheathing on the side of the frame, I wondered if she had ever held a hammer in her life.

After several failed attempts, she finally succeeded and threw her hands above her head in celebration. She turned, grinning exuberantly, clutching the hammer to her chest as if it were something very dear to her. That's when I realized she was the homeowner. This woman's dream had become a reality and she had contributed to it. Being part of that moment felt pretty cool to me so I can't even begin to imagine how amazing it was for her.

Bike Iowa Border to Border

RAGBRAI®: The Register's Annual Great Bicycle Race Across Iowa (P.O. Box 622, Des Moines, IA 50303; 1-800-474-3342; www.ragbrai.org; info@ragbrai.org; entry fee weeklong rider, $125; entry fee for nonrider, $35; fee for daily wristband, $25, with maximum of three days). RAG-BRAI® is sponsored by the *Des Moines Register,* and is the longest, largest, and oldest touring bicycle ride in the world. It is a celebration of Iowa and a way to help all Iowans. The first ride, in 1973, was initiated by two columnists from the *Register,* who invited a few friends to ride with them. The annual, seven-day ride takes place the last week of July and averages 472 miles. Beginning along the western border of the Missouri River and ending along the eastern border of the Mississippi River, the exact route changes each year and the eight host overnight towns are announced in January.

The host towns open their campgrounds to riders at no charge, and you will need to pack a tent and camping equipment, which will be transported, with your clothing and personal items, by truck. You do not need to commit to riding all seven days, but if you apply for a one-day wristband, you may not apply for more than three wristbands. The fee includes daily luggage transportation, emergency medical services, a "sag wagon" to pick up or otherwise assist riders, camping areas, maps and route markers, wristband discounts, bike shops along the route to service your bike, a free entry for a bike raffle, and access to long-term parking and bike-shipping stations. Charter services are available to transport you from the end point back to your starting point. Check the Web site or call for a list of charter services.

RAGBRAI® is limited to 8,500 riders, and all entries are included in a random lottery selection. Check the registration deadline on the Web site. Vehicle passes are limited to 1,500, no more than three vehicles per group.

Participants in Bike & Build's cross-country cycling tour begin their adventure in Virginia Beach, Virginia.

Only groups of three or more may apply for a vehicle pass. After expenses, funds are given to nonprofit programs in Iowa, with the Register/Gannett Foundation focusing on families and children, literacy, community-enrichment programs, and supporting statewide programs. Contributions are also made to the communities that host the RAGBRAI® riders.

Happiness is successfully biking and building 3,682 miles across the beautiful USA.

You need not be an Iowan to participate in this annual event, which attracts participants from all 50 states. What a great way to help, and experience a state, its communities, and the people who live there.

Chicks with Picks and Social Awareness

Chicks with Picks (P.O. Box 486, Ridgeway, CO 81432; 970-626-4424; www.chickswithpicks.net; info@chicks withpicks.net; Jan. and Feb. 3- to 4-day clinics start at $1,100, which includes accommodations, meals, lessons, workshops, and other activities). Chicks with Picks offers

The thrill of climbing a frozen waterfall with Chicks with Picks in Ouray, Colorado, is an accomplishment you'll remember forever. *Dyana Marlett*

women's ice-climbing clinics in Ouray Ice Park in Ouray, Colorado. All levels are welcome and most of your time will be spent on the ice with world-class guides.

Clinics have a four-to-one participant/guide ratio, and teach self-reliance through the development of technical skills in a safe, noncompetitive environment. Chicks with Picks is about "women climbing with women, for women," and promotes women's empowerment and service. Chicks with Picks has raised $135,000 for local women's shelters, supporting women in need.

Anchored and secure; happy and triumphant. *Dyana Marlett*

You will learn the basics in Beginning Ice Climbing, which includes climbing knots, belay techniques, safely lowering your partner off the top of a hill, and ice-climbing techniques. In Intermediate Ice Climbing you will review knots and belaying, and focus on techniques: footwork, tool placement, how to conserve energy, and body positioning. You will also learn how to climb more difficult ice, practice taking out ice screws, and review and practice anchor systems. Chicks with Picks recommends climbing at this level for several years, but when you are ready to move up there are Vertical Ice Focus, Advanced Intermediate, and Advanced courses to challenge even the most experienced ice climber.

Now that women account for 70 percent of outdoor adventurers in the world, join the fun, meet new friends, and contribute to a worthy cause. This is an immersion adventure that will make a difference in your life and benefit others too. There is a printer-friendly questionnaire and registration form on the Web site, where you will also find a packing list, frequently asked questions, advice on training for ice climbing, detailed transportation information, and dates and pricing.

Kids Helping Kids

Kidz Online (Herndon CIT Studio, 2214 Rock Hill Rd., Suite P2, Herndon, VA 20170; 571-203-8990; LA Studio, Studio 120, 600 W Seventh St., Los Angeles, CA 90017; 213-624-3900; www.KidzOnline.org; Staff@KidzOnline .org). Kidz Online (KOL) is a nonprofit educational organization whose mission began with educating inner-city children in Washington, D.C. in advanced digital technologies, utilizing teen volunteers. Cofounded by Wes Cruver, with an idea he'd been working on since age 11, the organization pairs children who had never been exposed to sophisticated computer software or Webcasting tools with tech-savvy students from the suburbs with more access and exposure to digital cameras, graphic design, and television production. The benefits of kids helping kids last a lifetime for all participants.

Volunteer Projects Kids Can Do

IdeaList.org: Action without Borders (1220 S.W. Morrison, 10th Floor, Portland, OR 97205; fax 503-914-0344; www.idealist.org). The Internet is filled with interesting organizations, but occasionally you find one that makes you jump out of your seat to shout, Wow! IdeaList is such a find. If you are interested in discovering volunteer projects you can do as a kid, with other kids or with your family, check out this page: www.idealist.org/ kt/youthorgs.html#sec1. The number of available non-profit jobs, volunteer opportunities, internships, volunteers, speakers, and events is tracked on the IdeaList.org home page.

Annie Started Her Foundation at Age 11

Care Bags Foundation (Annie Wignall, 2713 N. 4th Ave. E., Newton, IA 50208; www.carebags4kids.org; helping kids@carebags4kids.org). Annie Wignall started the Care Bags Foundation when she was 11 years old, after she heard about children who had to leave their homes in crisis situations without most of their cherished belongings. "I love kids and wanted to do something to help make their lives better," says Annie. Her idea, to create and hand-deliver fabric Care Bags filled with essential and comforting items for needy children, has grown from a small home-based project helping a few Iowa kids into a nationally recognized nonprofit organization supported by businesses, agencies, and individuals that provides services to thousands of kids worldwide. The Care Bags Foundation is entirely run by volunteers. Contact the organization to start a similar project, or donate time, money, or needed items.

Select Your Conservation Interest

Earth Team National Headquarters (USDA–NRCS,5140 Park Ave., Suite C, Des Moines, IA 50321; 1-888-526-3227; 515-289-0325; fax 515-289-4561; www.nrcs.usda.gov). Earth Team began in 1981 when Congress passed legisla-

Annie Wignall, founder and director of the Care Bags Foundation, Newton, Iowa.

tion allowing the Natural Resources Conservation Service (NRCS) to use volunteers in all programs. In 2006, approximately 45,000 Earth Team Volunteers donated over one million hours to conservation projects protecting soil, water, and wildlife at an estimated value of $17 million. In Massachusetts, Earth Team volunteer engineering students from Smith College worked together with NRCS to design a culvert to help restore the Weir Creek Salt Marsh. Ongoing programs in California, Wisconsin, Tennessee, and Illinois all contribute to the future health of soil, water, and wildlife in these states. Find out more about programs in your own state through their Web site.

Volunteer as a Lighthouse Keeper

Pictured Rocks National Lakeshore (N8391 Sand Point Rd., P.O. Box 40, Munising, MI 49862; 906-387-2607; www.nps.gov/piro). Pictured Rocks National Lakeshore is located on the south shore of Lake Superior in Michigan's Upper Peninsula, between the communities of Munising (west) and Grand Marais (east). It was designated as America's first national lakeshore in 1966. The Au Sable Light Station, built in 1873–1874, is located in the Pictured Rocks Lakeshore. The tower's base diameter is 16 feet; the tower itself is 87 feet high. The National Park Service seeks live-in volunteers to staff the Light Station.

Advertised in the *Lighthouse News* (www.lighthouse-news.com/2008/01/17/volunteer-lighthouse-keeper-wanted; pamela_baker@nps.gov), the position of volunteer lighthouse keeper requires a one- or two-month commitment. Apartments in the lightkeeper's house will be provided for a volunteer Au Sable Light Station Museum Attendant and for an Au Sable Lighthouse Interpretive Guide.

Both openings run from July 1 through September 1 and include duties in the museum or leading tours. Volunteer attendants provide museum staffing, assist rangers, and facilitate tours of the residence and tower. Interpretive assistants provide interpretive programming with a park ranger during guided tours. Orientation is provided by park staff. Call or e-mail for more information.

40 Mile Point Lighthouse Society (P.O. Box 205, Rogers City, MI 49779; 989-785-2468; www.40milepointlight house.org; abyrnes@i2k.net). Located in Presque Isle County, along Lake Huron on the northeastern shore of Michigan's lower peninsula, the 40 Mile Point Lighthouse is 40 miles east of Old Mackinaw Point and 40 miles northwest of Thunder Bay. The 40 Mile Lighthouse

Everything You Need to Know about Lighthouses

Lighthouse News (P.O. Box 19, Bristol, ME 04539; 906-387-3700; www.light house-news.com). *The Lighthouse News* has the latest news, opinions, commentary, and feature articles on lighthouses worldwide. The Web site was created to collect and dispense information about lighthouses to promote the history, protection, and preservation of lighthouses everywhere. Sign up on the Web site for the newsletter to find news reports, job openings, and everything that's happening at and around lighthouses everywhere.

Society, dedicated to the restoration and preservation of the 40 Mile Point Lighthouse, has an Assistant Lighthouse Keepers program, also advertised in the *Lighthouse News* (www.lighthouse-news.com/2008/01/17/volunteer-light house-keeper-wanted; pamela_baker@nps.gov) with openings for volunteer lighthouse keepers.

You would be required to greet visitors and provide historical information about the Lighthouse Museum, work in the gift shop, museum, and pilothouse, and keep the buildings clean. Applicants need to be able to climb stairs, work the required hours, and be comfortable with public speaking. Fully equipped RV parking spaces are available nearby, but you provide your own self-contained RV—no tents permitted. For more information on position, requirements, fees, and to print an application, go to the Assistant Light Keepers Program Web site at www.40milepointlighthouse.org/assistinfo.htm.

Enjoy One-Week Service Trips

Wilderness Volunteers (P.O. Box 22292, Flagstaff, AZ; 928-556-0038; fax 928-222-1212; www.wilderness volunteers.org; info@wildernessvolunteers.org; all trips,

1 week, $259). Volunteer to help maintain national parks, forests, and wilderness areas. Wilderness Volunteers, a nonprofit organization, works with the National Park Service, the Forest Service, the Bureau of Land Management, and the U.S. Fish & Wildlife Service, and offers one-week trips with a variety of service projects. All food, including snacks, is provided; participants supply their own camping gear and enthusiasm. The benefiting agencies supply tools and supervision for the projects. Wilderness Volunteers embraces Leave No Trace outdoor living skills and ethics.

Help with restoration and maintenance projects, trail work, planting native trees and shrubs, building protective fencing, invasive plant eradication, wilderness first-aid instruction, removing barbed-wire fencing, greenhouse work, campsite restoration, construction of new bridges, erosion control, archaeological surveys, and a variety of other projects. In your free time enjoy hiking, fishing, bird-watching, swimming, photography, wildlife viewing, canoeing, snorkeling, and other activities, depending on your location.

The Web site has an extensive list of ongoing projects, with trip dates and a detailed description of the park or other natural area, as well as a map. Trips are rated for difficulty—active, strenuous, or challenging—and accommodations are specified, usually tent or backpack camping, sometimes a nearby hostel or dormitory. There is also a list of equipment and personal items needed. Check the project list and choose your destination. The slots fill quickly, but there are usually waiting lists if your first choice is full.

"Wilderness is not a luxury but a necessity of the human spirit."

—EDWARD ABBEY, *American writer and environmentalist*

Make a Difference

Earthwatch (Earthwatch Institute National Headquarters, 3 Clock Tower Place, Suite 100, Box 75, Maynard, MA 01754; 1-800-776-0188; fax: 617-461-2332; www.earth watch.org; U.S. tax-deductible contribution varies for 1- to 20-day expeditions). Here you will find some amazing short-term volunteer opportunities to assist scientific researchers in a variety of locations. For example, there is an incredible nine-day backpacking trip through the remote Isle Royale National Park in Michigan to collect data for the longest-running predator-prey study. Participants should be comfortable backpacking and able to cover up to 10 miles a day. This expedition is offered from May to August with accommodations for singles or couples with a tax-deductible contribution of $1,046.

Earthwatch New Orleans Opportunity

Help collect caterpillars in ecosystems damaged by Hurricane Katrina to measure parasitism rates, do chemical analysis, update the forest caterpillar database, and help a scientist rebuild his insect collection by restoring a damaged greenhouse. This is a five-day trip to New Orleans; contribution fee $746. Participants provide their own accommodations, with some meals included.

Earthwatch Barnegat Bay, New Jersey, Research Project

Immerse yourself in a nine-day program at the Lighthouse Center for Natural Resource Education on 180 acres at Barnegat Bay, New Jersey, to actively contribute to the study and research of diamondback terrapins, balanced by recreational time in the salt marsh birding, hiking, kayaking, and canoeing. A contribution of $1,846 is requested, which covers housing and meals.

Hiking to Heal the Land

American Hiking Society (1422 Fenwick Ln., Silver Spring, MD 20910; 301-565-6704; www.americanhiking .org; Andrea Ketchmark volunteer coordinator, 301-565-6704, ext. 206 or volunteer@AmericanHiking.org; fees are $245 for a first trip; $220 for registration before the end of February and for Hiking Society members; $275 for a first trip, $250 if registering before the end of February for nonmembers, includes a one-year membership; added

An American Hiking volunteer crew is hard at work in the Mt. Baker–Snoqualmie National Forest in Washington State. *Mark Going, Columbia*

Teenagers, Take Note

Do you know that you want to share your time and talents with nonprofit organizations in some special way but are not sure how, what, where or when to make that happen? There is a reason why www.dosomething.org is dubbed one-stop shopping for teens wanting to change the world for the good. Check it out.

trips in the same calendar year are $175). Volunteer Vacations through American Hiking provides the opportunity to enjoy the great outdoors, preserve and protect the environment, and to give back by providing essential services that benefit all of us. American Hiking protects the country's hiking trails. The Society works with lawmakers to shape policy and secure funding and is committed to education and outreach programs. There are over 280 member trail clubs that represent half a million people who enjoy hiking and want to make certain that hiking trails are preserved for future generations. Through its Volunteer Vacations program, as well as other innovative initiatives, American Hiking seeks to establish and support trail development and promote the hiking experience.

Join the American Hiking Society for a weeklong immersion excursion building and maintaining trails across the country. Choose from magnificent locations and meet interesting like-minded people from all over. This is a great family experience and an opportunity to introduce people of all ages to hiking or for more advanced hikers who want to add another dimension to your adventures.

Challenge yourself and experience hiking in a whole new way. Check out American Hiking's Web site, select

American Hiking's Volunteer Programs Manager, Andrea Ketchmark, volunteers out in the field building the Donner Lake Rim Trail in California. *Allison Waterbury*

Volunteer Vacations from its Work menu, and choose the state you are interested in visiting, the difficulty level of the hike, and your preference for accommodations from tents to bunkhouses and cabins. You may view a multitude of possibilities on a chart that includes locations, hosting organizations, the beginning and ending dates of hikes, and photographs of destinations. There is also a complete schedule of 75 stewardship projects in 25 states, with new locations and shorter projects highlighted.

No hiking or trailblazing experience is necessary, but participants need to be in good physical condition. Trips are scheduled from February through November, with alternative breaks for college groups throughout the month of March. The American Hiking Society partners with the Leave No Trace Center for Outdoor Ethics, an organization that promotes responsible outdoor skills and ethics. There is a registration form available on the Web site.

Go on a Volunteer Vacation, renew your spirit, enjoy nature, contribute by preserving hiking trails, and have an amazing outdoor immersion excursion.

Special Needs Travel Assistance

Diversity World Traveler (10404 Santa Cresta Ave., Las Vegas, NV 89129; 702-245-8286; fax 702-233-9605; www.diversityworldtraveler.com; jcohen@diversityworld traveler.com). Diversity World Traveler (DWT) takes the guesswork out of special needs travel. Plan the trip of your dreams or book a trip with any provider and Diversity World Traveler and Enhancement Services handles the special considerations needed for the trip, including identifying handicapped-accessible accommodations, providing itineraries printed in Braille or audio recorded, transportation with wheelchair lifts, rental cars equipped with hand brakes, or whatever is needed. Their job is to think through what needs may arise on a trip before problems occur.

Matchmaker, Matchmaker, Make a Great Match

Volunteer Match: Where Volunteering Begins (717 California St., 2nd Fl., San Francisco, CA 94108; 415-241-6868; www.VolunteerMatch.org; support@volunteer match.org). Volunteer Match provides a strong network of volunteers that match hundreds of nonprofit programs that need help with thousands of people looking to help. It's wonderful what great software can do. With a few clicks of your mouse and shared information, you can end up with a personalized perfect volunteer match. What an appropriately named organization!

Be a Leader and See the Sights

✉ **Sprout Vacation Programs** (893 Amsterdam Ave., New York, NY 10025; 1-888-222-9575; 212-222-9575; fax 212-222-9768; www.gosprout.org; Vacations@gosprout .org). Have fun seeing the sights as a volunteer coleader for small groups of adults with mild to moderate mental retardation on three- to seven-day vacations in groups with three leaders and 11 participants. What a great way to tour and volunteer all at the same time. This is a wonderful opportunity to travel and enjoy what you see through your own and others' eyes. Sprout Vacation Programs offer custom-designed trips, a weekend Sproutstock music festival, an annual Sprout film festival, and trips to New York City, Niagara Falls, Lake George, the Catskills, Cape Cod, Virginia Beach, Washington, D.C., and many more locations. The time commitment is for a weekend or longer. Group leaders must be 21 and proficient in English.

Everyone on the Slopes

The Adaptive Sports Foundation (P.O. Box 266, 100 Silverman Way, Windham, NY 12496; 518-734-5070; fax 518-734-6740; www.adaptivesportsfoundation.org; asfwindham@mhcable.com). You don't need to be a skier to help out at the Adaptive Sports Foundation (ASF). Volunteers come from all walks of life and range in age from 15 to senior citizens. Contact your local adaptive ski program via the Internet or at your local ski area and ask what you can do. People are needed at events to direct traffic, distribute snacks, supervise participants, and for many other positions. If you are a skier, contact the foundation to find out how to become a guide to disabled skiers.

Wounded Warrior Disabled Sports Project and Wounded Warrior Project (7020 A. C. Skinner Pkwy., Jacksonville, FL 32256; 1-877-TEAM-WWP; 904-296-7350; fax 904-296-7347; www.woundedwarriorproject.org). The Wounded Warrior Project (WWP) is a nonprofit organization that assists severely wounded men and women of the U.S. Armed Forces and eases their transition back into civilian life. WWP provides competitive sporting events in addition to many other services. Volunteers are needed at events and throughout the year for advocacy programs and fundraising.

Disabled Sports USA (451 Hungerford Dr., Suite 100, Rockville, MD 20850; 301-217-0960; fax 301-217-0968; www.dsusa.org; information@dsusa.org). **The Hartford Ski Spectacular** is one of the largest winter sports festivals for people with physical disabilities. All ages are welcome and encouraged to enjoy snow sports made accessible by adaptive equipment and instruction from seasoned professionals and skilled volunteers. Kids and adults alike share fantastic fun on the slopes, regardless of the nature of a disability.

The Hartford Ski Spectacular (Beaver Run Resort & Conference Center, 620 Village Rd., Breckenridge, CO 80424; 1-800-265-3560; 970-453-6000; fax 970-453-4284; www.beaverrun.com; stay@beaverrun.com). The Hartford Ski Spectacular is part of a cooperative effort to provide year-round sports programs for severely wounded veterans of the conflicts in Iraq and Afghanistan. With the help of adaptive equipment and trained instructors, warrior athletes compete in challenging sports events. The equipment, instruction, transportation, and lodging are provided free of charge for veterans and their families.

The Beaver Run Resort & Conference Center offers something for everyone, including a day spa and ski-in, ski-out access to the chairlift. Allow time to visit and enjoy Breckenridge, originally settled as a mining town over 150 years ago. The quaint Victorian setting is a constant reminder of the way life used to be when people swarmed in to find gold and silver. When making your reservations, be sure to mention attending the Hartford Ski Spectacular to receive a special rate of $89 per night.

Volunteers Personified: The Sarubbi Family Story

The Sarubbi family of Brooklyn, New York, attends the **Hartford Ski Spectacular** every year and the whole family volunteers. "It's expensive flying all of us to Colorado," says Cathy, referring to their five children—Caitie, 17; Jamie, 14; Breanna, 11; John, 8; and baby Casey. "My husband and I cook for hundreds of people. Caitie is a volunteer ski instructor. She also works at the fund-raisers—live and silent auctions. There are about three hundred volunteers who transport, cook, socialize, cheer everyone on, and attend the awards dinners. We all work and it's really great to see people with all kinds of disabilities achieving great personal triumphs."

Abundant Choices and the Flexibility to Help

U.S. Department of Agriculture, Forest Service (USDA Forest Service, 1400 Independence Ave., SW, Washington, D.C. 20250; 202-205-8333; www.fs.fed.us/fsjobs/jobs_

volunteers.shtml; fsjobs@fs.fed.us). Volunteer with the Forest Service and work full- or part-time on ongoing or onetime projects or throughout the season. Your skills and preferences will be matched with the needs and goals of the Forest Service to provide a safe and satisfying experience. It's a great way to try out different opportunities with a career in mind, or to live in a national forest while working as a volunteer. Helping to care for one of the country's most valuable resources will enable you to give back as you benefit from your experience.

Whether you prefer outdoor work or working in an office, there are many ways to help and many opportunities to explore. You can work in fields as diverse as Archaeology, Back Country/Wilderness, Botany, Fish and Wildlife, Mineral and Geology, Natural Resources Planning, Computers, Campground Hosts, Construction and Maintenance, Historical Preservation, Conservation Education, Range and Livestock, Timber and Fire Prevention, Tour Guide and Interpretation, Trail Maintenance, and Visitor Information, among many others.

Go to Volunteer Opportunities on the Forest Service Web site or directly to www.volunteer.gov/Gov and search featured positions. When you choose a position, you will find information including location, start and end dates, contacts, activities, project details, suitability (ages, family, etc.), a direct link to the program, and a choice of either adding the opportunity to your volunteer folder or applying for open positions. You may also search by state or by field of interest. Additionally, there is a list of national events in which you may participate, and current featured programs.

Build, Educate, and Beautify

The Corps Network (666 Eleventh St., NW, Suite 1000, Washington, D.C. 20001; 202-737-6272; fax

202-737-6277; www.corpsnetwork.org; sdavison@corps network.org). The Corps Network represents 115 corps nationwide, with individual conservation programs run by local nonprofits or state or federal government. There are chapters in 41 states and Washington, D.C., with 23,000 participants contributing 17 million hours of service yearly. Activities include improving inner-city housing, educating the public on conservation and fire prevention, beautification projects, and staffing after-school programs.

Maintain the Continental Divide

Montana Conservation Corps (206 North Grand Ave., Bozeman, MT 59715; 406-587-4475; fax 406-587-2606; www.mtcorps.org; mcc@mtcorps.org). The Montana Conservation Corps posts job openings on www.cool

works.com for conservation crew members with work in Billings, Bozeman, Helena, Missoula, and Kalispell. The tasks include planting trees and rebuilding the Continental Divide Trail and other trails. A living stipend and monetary educational award are offered. Similar and additional positions are available in other parts of the country as well.

Montana Conservation Corps volunteers build a trail in the Beartooth Mountain Range. *Montana Conservation Corps*

Career Experience That Pays

Student Conservation Association, Inc. (P.O. Box 550, 689 River Road, Charlestown, NH 03603-0550; 603-543-1828; fax 603-543-1700; www.thesca.org). The Student Conservation Association (SCA) is the nation's largest and oldest provider of conservation service opportunities through a tuition-free summer volunteer program for high school students and a 3- to 12-month, expenses-paid internship program for students over 18. SCA's mission is clear: "To build the next generation of conservation leaders and inspire lifelong stewardship of our environment and communities by engaging young people in hands-on service to the land."

This access-to-service crew surveyed the recreational facilities around Tony Grove Lake. *Front row, left to right:* Kenneth, Andrew, Kate. *Back row, left to right:* Blake, Chris, Russell, Brigitta, Craig, and Brett. *Utah Conservation Corps*

Hillary's Story

My job here today, as a biological technician in exotic plant control in the Everglades, started with my internship with the Student Conservation Association. SCA is geared toward helping young professionals get a foot in the door in national resources and conservation through internships and volunteering with the Park Service. Right after completing my Bachelor of Arts in biology, I volunteered in Michigan doing seasonal biological data collection. Then I came to the Everglades National Park (Florida) for six months as an SCA intern. I was told about a new position starting in the Everglades and encouraged to apply for it, so I did, online through USA Jobs. Then for six months I worked at Sequoia National Park (California) before returning to the Everglades as a full-time biological technician.

The SCA enables people just starting out to see different places in the country while making it affordable by awarding stipends and sponsorships. Upon completing my internship, I received an AmeriCorps scholarship to be used toward education. These organizations, the SCA and AmeriCorps, are nonprofits dependant upon donations. Every

Hillary's internship with the Student Conservation Association (SCA) helped her secure a job as a biological technician in exotic plant control in the Everglades National Park, Florida.

SCA participant has a benefactor and at the end of the internship writes a letter thanking the benefactor for the sponsorship. If you can't be a student conservator you can sponsor one. Many professionals working in the park started out through SCA.

Grandparents Are Wonderful

Senior Corps (1201 New York Ave., NW, Washington, D.C. 20525; 202-606-5000; www.seniorcorps.gov; help@join seniorservice.org). Michigan has over 11,000 seniors volunteering in Foster Grandparents, Senior Companions,

Train as a Docent or Oral Interpreter

If you're considering volunteering somewhat regularly at an accessible location near your home, consider becoming a docent: a highly trained volunteer who interprets cultural, natural, and recreational resources. It's not unusual to find docents involved in living history programs, conservation, wildlife management, archaeology, anthropology, school group programs, and conducting nature hikes. Extensive training and periodic refresher courses usually come with the "job." Tourists ask a lot of questions and the docent needs to know the right answers, but there's also room for individual creativity and personal experience.

and Retired and Senior Volunteer Programs through the National Senior Service Corps. The Web site has detailed information on what's happening all over these United States.

VIPs Unlimited

Volunteers-in-Parks (VIP) Program (www.nps.gov/gettinginvolved/volunteer/index.htm). Over 137,000 VIPs donate over 5.2 million hours to national parks annually at an estimated value of $91.2 million. Volunteer options are available all over the country in national, state, county, and city parks.

All VIPs: Everglades National Park Volunteers' Voices

Melanie's Story

I went to the National Park Service's Web site, www.nps.gov, to explore volunteering in the national parks. On the left side of the home page there were a lot of different options. I clicked Getting Involved, Volunteers and Opportunities. It was insane how many volunteer jobs appeared, and I applied right there on the Web to three parks and heard back from two with offers I just couldn't refuse.

I'm volunteering in the Everglades National Park, assisting the director of the volunteer program from December 25 through the end of March. Housing is provided and I supply my own food and travel costs. Then I'll return home to my spring and summer job, lecturing on botany at the University of Michigan.

December 1 through February of the following year I'll be living and volunteering at the Hawaii Volcanoes National Park on the Big Island, doing interpretive work and helping out however I'm needed. I'm totally psyched.

Louie's Story

In my other life, I worked as an IBM service computer tech, but I kept volunteering in any capacity the Everglades National Park could use me, including maintenance. I work with the research center botanist in exotic plant control. Landscapers brought Brazilian pepper in from South America. It's an aggressively invasive plant that releases a toxin into the soil. We do a basal bark treatment spraying an herbicide around the base trunk of the plant. When I go home to Illinois for the summer I hire someone to mow my lawn and weed the garden.

Dick and Kathleen's Contributions

I'm a wildlife biologist working on the python project. We have a freezer full of dead pythons. We want to know what they are eating and their reproductive status and how they affect the environment. There have been estimations that the python population in the Everglades National Park numbers between 50,000 and 500,000. There are four kinds of pythons living here, the result of an unauthorized and unfortunate pet release. My wife is a botanist working on a project drawing the trees along the walking paths to create a tree identification guide for tourists.

Dick and Joyce

I just went online to NPS volunteers and found this position. This is the third year my wife, Joyce, and I are camp caretakers for Hidden Lake Camp, which

is part of the environmental education program in
the Everglades for fifth-grade students. The students come in for two nights, and this year we are
running 19 camps and are booked for the year.
We're here from October through April and have
lived in our motor home full time since 2000.

Artist-in-Residence Programs

National Park Service's (NPS) Volunteers-in-Parks
(VIP), www.nps.gov/archive/volunteer/air.htm. The artist-
in-residence programs bring together professionals in the
arts to publicize, share, and preserve resources in our
national parks and to educate and communicate with the
public. Visual artists, photographers, sculptors, performers, writers, composers, craftspeople, and other artists
are invited to apply to live and work in the parks. Twenty-
nine national parks currently offer artist-in-residence programs, including Acadia National Park, Maine; Buffalo
National River, Arkansas; Cuyahoga Valley National Park,
Ohio; Devils Tower National Monument, Wyoming; Herbert
Hoover National Historical Site, Iowa; Isle Royale National
Park, Michigan; and North Cascades National Park,
Washington; among others.

It's exciting to visit a national park, but it's a life-
changing experience to live inside one for an extended
period of time. Each participating park must be applied to
individually and each has its own eligibility requirements,
application guidelines, time line, and expectations.

Artist-in-residence programs usually host one artist at
a time. They provide housing, accessibility, and education
about the park with the hope that the artist's experience
will be expressed in future work. The artist is expected to
interact with the public by offering a workshop or presen-

tation and donating a piece of work, representative of the artist's style and reflecting his or her stay, to the park's permanent collection. The artist bears expenses for professional supplies and personal needs such as transportation and food.

The application process involves submitting a one- or two-page résumé, a one-page statement of what the applicant hopes to accomplish as an artist-in-residence, a description of the proposed presentation, references from people familiar with the artist's professional work, and samples of recent work. Applications are available online by contacting the individual parks (search "Artist-in-Residence" at www.nps.gov). A few programs charge a nominal nonrefundable application fee.

Poet Anne Sullivan's Story

I arrived for my month as the Artist-in-Residence in the Everglades National Park (AIRIE) in Homestead, Florida, and something magical happened. I connected with the place and everything in it. I became passionate about learning the names of plants and animals and their stories, and about figuring out my own obsession.

I did fieldwork every day, made observation notes, followed the oral interpreters around and recorded their programs. Each night I returned to my room to transcribe every word, and as I transcribed, I began to see connections I hadn't seen during the day and poems would emerge. I ended

up with a book-length manuscript with the working title *Ecology II: Poems from the Everglades*
(WordTech Communications).

I moved an hour south of where I used to live
to get easier access to the park. I now serve on the
AIRIE board of directors and work in the park as a
volunteer interpreter whenever I can.

Self-Appointed Volunteers

In Stehekin, Washington, visitors carrying plastic
bags walk around the dock and along the one
9-mile road, pulling out spotted knapweed, a
prolific and aggressive weed that grows all over
Stehekin. Each plant produces one thousand or
more seeds, stays in the soil for over five years,
and releases a toxin that kills other plants.
Livestock eat knapweed only if nothing else is
available. The only remedy is to remove the
knapweed and reseed the area.

It's a great way to see, help, and get to know
the community because it is truly a one-of-a-kind
place. Stehekin is only accessible by foot on the
Pacific Crest Trail or by pontoon plane or ferry.
Once you arrive there is only one road. It is in the
Lake Chelan National Recreation Area, which is a
part of the North Cascades National Park

Complex. Every garbage bag filled with knapweed delivered to the transfer station can be traded for a one-dollar coupon to the Stehekin Pastry Company. It is the only bakery there, 2 miles from the dock and known for its extremely rich and delicious cinnamon buns. The National Park Service promotes the project and reimburses the bakery.

Huge infestations of spotted knapweed have also been found in North Dakota, Montana, and Minnesota. Perhaps they need great pastry shops to encourage weeding.

Expanding the Wilderness

John's Story

For 27 summers in a row, John could be seen running through Denali National Park, Alaska, carrying a plastic Wal-Mart bag. Officially he worked as a tour bus driver. His wife worked in administration, and together they earned enough money to cover their traveling expenses for the rest of the year to fulfill his personal mission. He's visited every state and 67 nations, jogging as he picks up trash. "My goal is to visit every place on earth and leave it cleaner than when I arrived," says John. "Each piece of trash I remove expands the wilderness."

Amateur Archaeology Certification

(www.nps.gov/archaeology/PUBLIC/certify.htm). Check out which state archaeological societies offer vocational certification programs. This is a great experience for families or a one-on-one opportunity for a parent and child fascinated with archaeology. You never know. It is hands-on experiences like these that lead to career choices or a lifelong avocation.

Diggin' Deep

The National Park Service Passport in Time (P.O. Box 15728, Rio Rancho, NM 87174-5728; 1-800-281-9176; 505-896-0734; fax 505-896-1136; www.passportintime.com). The U.S. Forest Service (USFS) Passport in Time program provides information about archaeology projects through a variety of federal agencies and oversees archaeological sites. Rules and regulations might differ from site to site since management can be under local, state, tribal, or federal jurisdiction.

To find out about archaeological digs, contact the state archaeologist in your state or in other states you'd like to visit. Many of the programs are regional and often work in collaboration with other organizations. When inquiring about archaeology sites on the Web or over the phone, always ask about events in your state, volunteer opportunities, and sites open to the public.

Link into the Past

Alexandria Archaeology (105 North Union St., #327, Alexandria, VA 22314; 703-838-4399; fax 703-838-6491; www.alexandriaarchaeology.org; archaeology@alexandria va.gov). It's awesome how much there is to experience: a hands-on museum, archaeological sites, family activities,

In 2007, Alexandria Archaeology field-school students worked at Freedmen's Cemetery, an abandoned 19th-century African-American burial site that was recently rediscovered. Archaeologists identified grave locations but were careful not to disturb the burials. Alexandria plans to use the archaeological findings in the design of a memorial on the site. *Alexandria Archaeology*

dig days, summer camp, walking and biking tours and much more. The Friends of Alexandria Archaeology (FOAA) is a non-profit organization whose mission is to expand the volunteer opportunities and increase public awareness of archaeology. FOAA's organization has grown to over 300 members. FOAA programming includes tours of local archaeology-related sites; lectures by leading archaeologists, and a yearly scholarship for the Alexandria Archaeology Summer Camp.

The Story from Amy Bertsch, Public Relations

Alexandria Archaeology has a very active volunteer program with volunteers working one or two days a week. Some volunteers work in the museum, greeting and assisting visitors, answering phone calls, and performing routine office duties. Other volunteers do traditional archaeology lab work, cleaning and cataloging artifacts. There are occasions when trained, experienced volunteers work in the field, under the supervision of staff archaeologists, digging at a site and screening soil for artifacts.

Alexandria Archaeology also runs a two-week field school late each spring through George Washington University. Recently field school students worked at the Freedmen's Cemetery site. Unpaid internships are available on a limited basis

Archaeology Links

Don't miss these great links for getting involved with archaeology projects with the National Park Service:
   www.nps.gov/gettinginvolved/index.htm
   www.nps.gov/archeology/sites.nationwide.htm
   www.nps.gov/archeology/sites/parks.htm

year-round to college students. Most of the students are pursuing degrees in anthropology, historic preservation, history, or museum-related studies, and they receive college credit. There's an application online as well as descriptions of projects potential interns may wish to pursue."

Around the Campfire

Volunteer Campground Hosts. Campground hosts are needed in both state and national parks around the country to welcome campers, educate them about the park facilities and regulations, answer questions, and assist visitors in planning their activities. The season depends on the location, often from mid-May through mid-September. Hosts are asked to volunteer 30 to 40 hours weekly for a few weeks or the season. Google "state park campground hosts" and links are available to individual states like these for Texas, Oregon, and California:

Cedar Hill State Park (1570 F.M. 1382, Cedar Hill TX 75104; 972-291-3900), www.tpwd.state.tx.us/spdest/findadest/parks/cedar_hill

Oregon State Parks, www.oregonstateparks.org/park_146.php

California State Parks, www,parks.ca.gov

Alaska State Parks (Volunteer Coordinator, Alaska State Parks, 550 W. 7th St., #1380, Anchorage, AK 99501-3561; 907-269-8708; fax 907-269-8907; www.alaskastateparks .org; volunteer@dnr.state.ak.us). There are about 60 campsite host openings yearly. Hosts receive a free campsite, stipend, and training. The season is from May to September with a minimum commitment of four weeks.

2

Learning

Education, Self-Help, and Alternative Lifestyles

Learn as if you were going to live forever. Live as if you were going to die tomorrow.

—MAHATMA GANDHI, *political leader, activist, and philosopher*

Whatever it is you've longed to do, or learn, or try, or become, here are the trips and the know-how to spark your creativity and imagination—give it a whirl, and have the time of your life while you're at it. Let go of the inner critic and learn how to paint, write, dance, or speak a foreign language. The only one who knows what you yearn to try is you, and here are the opportunities for you to accomplish your heart's desire.

Immersion Travel

Live it to learn it.

Speak Fluent Spanish in Five Days

Berlitz Services (5825 Callaghan Rd., Suite 200, San Antonio, TX 78228; 210-681-7050; www.berlitz.us/web/html/locations.aspx?idLanguageCenter=57). Berlitz is the leading provider of language instruction, with over 130 years of success and programs in locations across the country. In San Antonio, Texas, they offer an Immerse and Converse[SM] course that will boost your confidence and Spanish skills in just five days. With intense private instruction requiring you to speak, listen, and think in Spanish, and personalized coaching, you will learn quickly and experience an immense sense of accomplishment along with your new language skills. An immersion course in Spanish is the perfect way to fully appreciate your visit to San Antonio, Texas; Taos, New Mexico; New York, New York; and other cities where Spanish is spoken.

If you have a little more time to dedicate to your studies, there is also a Berlitz Total Immersion® language and cultural experience that takes place over a one- to three-week time span. This course comes with a special guarantee, so be sure to inquire when you contact Berlitz for more information and prices, or you can set up an appointment by filling out a form on the Berlitz Web site.

Fly Away

The British School of Falconry (Equinox Hotel, 3567 Main St., Rt. 7A, Manchester Village, VT 05254; 802-362-4780; www.equinoxresort.com/amenities_and_activities/falconry.cfm; falconry@equinoxresort.com; 12 years of age or older, introductory lesson, $89 per person for 45 minutes; one-hour hawk walk, $149 per person; one-hour lesson with 45-minute hawk walk, $225 per person; falconry for groups, from 1½ hours, from $75 per person.

A British School of Falconry instructor teaches the ancient art of falconry using a trained Harris's hawk. *Steve Woods*

Imagine the thrill of having a Harris's hawk glide onto your leather-gloved hand. The ancient sport of falconry is alive and thriving at The British School of Falconry, located at the Equinox Hotel in Manchester Village, Vermont. There are a variety of packages offered, including a three-day beginners' course that covers three days and three nights, with a falconry lesson, a hawk walk, and time to relax at the hotel and explore Manchester.

You will learn how to handle and fly a hawk, and explore the role of falconers in the conservation of raptors or birds of prey. A hawk walk involves free flying the hawks along the Equinox's walking trails. This training could lead to a great hobby or variety of positions volunteering your time or working with nature centers, bird rehabilitation programs, or educational programs, just to name a few options.

To extend your stay in the Manchester area, contact the Manchester and the Mountains Chamber of Commerce (www.manchestervermont.net, 1-800-362-4144 or 802-362-6313) for restaurants, events, and other attractions.

Howard's Advice: Wear a Hat

The first time I went was during the winter for my birthday. My wife had heard about the British School of Falconry, and knows I love animals and birds and that I really love raptors. It was the perfect birthday gift. Our lesson was held in the barn. The time was used to get used to the birds, how they flew and landed on your arm. We were so blown away by the experience that we decided to return in nicer weather.

On our next visit we were taken out into fields with two sister Harris's hawks. They followed us in the trees as we were walking. I'd put up my arm and one would land on my gloved hand. It was fantastic how they would launch into flight and then swoop down in a burst of air and feathers. It was amazing to watch since they are so fast. The sisters were really taking a liking to me. I put my arm up and they both came at once. One landed on my

Students at the British School of Falconry learn how to become comfortable with the falcons.
Steve Woods

arm and one on my head. I have really curly hair.
My wife tried to get a photo of the hawk unhap-
pily tangled on top of my head, but she was laughing too hard.

Accelerated Learning

Cornell's Adult University (CAU, 626 Thurston Ave., Ithaca NY 14850-2490; 607-255-6260; fax 607-254-4482; www.sce.cornell.edu/cau/off_campus/index.php; www.sce.cornell.edu/cau/on_campus/index.php; cauinfo@cornell.edu; $1,195 for Assateague Island, Virginia, trip includes lodging, meals, and programming). The School of Continuing Education and Cornell's Adult University offer seminars, study tours, and on-campus summer programs. The Web site and catalogs present the diverse range of course offerings and interesting trips led by University personnel and experts in their fields.

A fall study tour, led by two Cornell naturalists, is offered to Assateague Island, Virginia. This trip takes participants far beyond the heartwarming story *Misty of Chincoteague,* written by Marguerite Henry and Wesley Dennis, to a field study of the islands during the peak of the fall migration season. Explore the 9,000-acre Chincoteague National Wildlife Refuge on Assateague Island, with over 260 species of birds, sika deer, the Delmarva Peninsula fox squirrel, and, of course, the famous ponies.

Ashokan Field Campus (477 Beaverkill Rd., Olivebridge, NY 12461; 845-657-8333; fax 845-657-8489; www.newpaltz.edu/ashokan/index.html; ashokan@newpaltz.edu; one-day field trips, $12 per person for two activities, $14 per person for three activities). Ashokan Field Campus is an outdoor and environmental center owned and operated by the Campus Auxiliary Services of the State University of New York at New Paltz.

There are one-day field trips for school groups, scout groups, staff training groups, senior citizens, and other adult groups. Programs include Natural History, Colonial Crafts, Adventure Education, Living History, and Seasonal

The Wild Horses of Assateague Island

There are several wonderful stories about the origins of the ponies that inhabit Assateague. The most popular is that the ponies swam ashore from a Spanish ship that had run aground, and another claims that pirates brought them to Assateague. They are called wild because they are feral, meaning they've descended from domestic animals that have reverted to the wild. Legends aside, they were most likely brought to barrier islands like Assateague by their owners to avoid fencing laws and taxation. They are called ponies because they are small, probably because of their poor diet and the harsh environment. Although they are small, they may appear bloated because of their diet of coarse salt marsh cord grass and American beach grass, which causes them to drink large amounts of freshwater. The National Park Service manages the Maryland herd, and the Chincoteague Volunteer Fire Department oversees the Virginia herd, which grazes on Chincoteague National Wildlife Preserve by special permit issued by the U.S. Fish & Wildlife Service. The cooperating agencies try to balance the needs of the horses with the need to protect their coastal bay habitat. You can help support this effort through a Foster Parent program. Visit the Assateague National Seashore Park Foster Horse program at www.assateaguewildhorses.org/index.cfm?fuseaction=foster, and choose a horse from the online photo album. For your donation you will receive a photo of your horse, a certificate that recognizes your contribution, a biography of your horse with a map of the island showing you where your horse can be found, and a copy of their "Horsin' Around" newsletter.

Activities. A typical day usually includes two or three activity periods, and the fee covers one instructor for 10–15 students, and one chaperone, facility use, 90-minute activities, and a 30-minute lunch break.

Adult retreats are offered throughout the year, and they include Winter Weekend, Environment Weekend, and

Outdoor Weekends. You may also bring your own retreats or conferences to Ashokan. Food service, accommodations, and meeting spaces are available.

Ashokan programs include a Solar Energy International program, Earth Day Celebration, a Fiddle and Dance program, Summer Songs, the Wayfinder program for children six and older, and a Weekend Sustainability Workshop event. Contact the reservation secretary for dates, fees, and program details.

Time Off for Art

Vermont Studio Center (P.O. Box 613, Johnson, VT 05656; 802-635-2727; fax 802-635-2730; www.vermont studiocenter.org; info@vermontstudiocenter.org; $25 application fee; $3,500 per month; work-study scholarships available). Vermont Studio Center (VSC), founded by artists in 1984, is an international artists' and writers' residency program that hosts 50 emerging and mid-career painters, sculptors, installation artists, printmakers, photographers, poets, and writers per month, in 4- to 12-week programs. Participants are assigned studios and private bedrooms. This is a great opportunity for people with families and demanding jobs to take a break from their responsibilities and focus on their art.

Arrowmont School of Arts and Crafts (556 Pkwy., P.O. Box 567, Gatlinburg, TN 37738; 865-436-5860; www.arrowmont.org; info@arrowmont.org; average cost of a one-week workshop $1,190, including application fee, tuition, housing, materials, lab, and technology). Arrowmont offers one- and two-week contemporary arts and crafts workshops throughout the spring and summer, and one-week and weekend workshops in the fall. Located in the Great Smoky Mountains, Arrowmont is open year-round, and has five galleries, a resource center, and a book and supply store. Arrowmont's mission is to enrich lives through art, and in addition to the workshops there are artist residencies, assistantships, work-study programs, scholarships, community outreach services, conferences, and music programs.

Most courses are for all levels, and offerings include workshops in clay, fiber, metal, glass, painting, drawing, photography, printmaking, book and paper arts, sculpture, woodturning, and woodworking. A complete class schedule, including course descriptions, dates, and current costs, is available on the Web site. Download a registration form and mail or fax it to Arrowmont.

On-campus housing includes meals (costs vary depending on room type, shared or private bath, single, double, or triple occupancy) and if you choose to live off-campus there is a meal plan available. For information on off-campus housing, contact the Gatlinburg Chamber of Commerce (1-800-822-1998 or www.gatlinburg.com). Information about scholarships, work-study programs, and studio assistantships is also available on the Web site.

Five artists are chosen annually to participate in Arrowmont's one-month Artist-in-Residence program, which provides emerging artists with time and space to produce a body of work within a creative environment. Artists work with faculty and other residents, and become involved with community outreach, conferences, classes, and other programs. Complete descriptions of residency can be found on the Web site, including accommodations, requirements, and benefits, as well as an application.

Arrowmont hosts Elderhostel opportunities for people over age 55, and select workshops have a limited number of places for Elderhostel applicants. Find Elderhostel course offerings listed under Applied Arts and Crafts in the Tennessee section in the Elderhostel listings. For course descriptions, tuition, and to register through Elderhostel, visit www.elderhostel.org and type Arrowmont in the search box.

Bringing History into the Future

Gettysburg Convention and Visitors Bureau (102 Carlisle St., Gettysburg, PA 17325; 1-800-337-5015; 717-334-6274; fax 717-334-1166; www.gettysburg.travel; info@gettysburg.travel; varied tour fees). Gettysburg is best known for the three-day Battle of Gettysburg, in July 1863, as the largest battlefield site in the country, and as the site of Lincoln's Gettysburg address. The Union victory that ended General Robert E. Lee's invasion of the North was a turning point in the Civil War. It was also the war's bloodiest battle, with 51,000 casualties.

There are historic tours to suit all tastes: in your own car with an audiotape tour, on a bus with a guide, on a National Park Service self-guided or ranger-led walking tour, or on bicycle or horseback. There are 10 Civil War museums, Civil War house tours, and even a haunted ghost tour at night. A living history theater performance enables visitors to see President Lincoln and speak with the soldiers in encampments and reenactments as history comes alive.

Gettysburg National Military Park has a variety of summer programs, battlefield walks, evening campfire programs, living history groups, and band concerts. There is a new museum and visitor center adjacent to the battlefield, which includes a film presentation and interactive exhibits throughout the museum. The Gettysburg Foundation and the National Park Service at Gettysburg work together to restore and protect the battlefield, preserve Civil War artifacts and archives, and enhance the experience of those who visit.

Check the Visitors Bureau Web site for an events calendar, and for travel information, accommodations, dining, tours, and other area attractions. Request a free visitor guide, view maps, or use the trip-builder feature. Log onto the National Park Web site (www.nps.gov/gett) for a schedule of park events.

Can You Dig It?

Crow Canyon Archaeological Center (23390 Rd. K, Cortez, CO 81321; 1-800-422-8975; 970-565-8975; fax 970-565-4859; www.crowcanyon.org; day tour, every Wed. and Thurs. in June, July, and Aug., over 18 years, $50, children, $25, lunch included; family week sessions, Jun./July, and Aug./Sept., adult $1,175, child $1,050). Participate in an archaeological dig in southwestern Colorado, and add to your understanding of the ancestral Pueblo Indians who once inhabited the area.

Choose a one-day archaeological adventure for adults and children over 10 years of age to add to your trip to Mesa Verde National Park and other area attractions. Or sign up for a family archaeology week program that will teach you about the history and culture of the Pueblo Indians. There is also an adult research week, a fall lab week, a three-week high school field program, and a course for educators. View details on the Crow Canyon Web site or call for more information.

Crow Canyon also offers travel programs, led by scholars and cultural consultants, to remote areas of the Southwest. Past programs have included learning about the archaeology and oral histories of Chaco Canyon, a Hopi silver workshop, backcountry archaeology and hiking in northeastern Arizona, and a study of northern New Mexico's Dinetah and Jemez Pueblo. Check the Web site for current adventures, call, or e-mail travel@crow canyon.org for more information.

Immersion in Yellowstone

Yellowstone Association (P.O. Box 117, Yellowstone National Park, WY 82190; 307-344-2293; fax 307-344-2486; www.yellowstoneassociation.org; registrar@yellow stoneassociation.org; tuition rates vary by class). This is a nonprofit association educating Yellowstone National

Park visitors through field seminars taught by experts. Select from guided wildlife-watching, a combination of naturalist-guided excursions and recreation activities, and adventures featuring a wide variety of very short educational immersion programs and backpacking courses. This is a great way to enhance your visit to Yellowstone and balance an instructional, guided tour with time to explore at your own pace.

An Amazing Ancient Culture

Mesa Verde National Park (P.O. Box 8, Mesa Verde, CO 81330; 970-529-4465; fax 970-529-4637; www.nps.gov/meve; open daily, year-round; annual pass, $30; entrance fee for private vehicles, $10–$15 depending on season; ranger guided tours, seasonal, $3 per person; campsites, $20 per site per night, plus tax). *Mesa Verde* means "green table" in Spanish. Mesa Verde National Park is located in southwestern Colorado. It was established in 1906, by President Theodore Roosevelt, to "preserve the works of man." The Park preserves the ancient culture of the Puebloans, who made Mesa Verde their home from about A.D. 550 to 1300. There are over 4,000 known archaeological sites, including the famous cliff dwellings (the stone communities built into the alcoves of the canyon walls). Sites can be located on maps on the Park's Web site, along with amazing photographs.

With 150 rooms and 75 open areas, Cliff Palace is the largest cliff dwelling in the Park. There are 23 kivas, or subterranean community pit houses. It is thought that the number of ancestral Puebloans living in Cliff Palace was 100 to 120. The Cliff Palace tour descends 100 feet into the canyon, and visitors need to be able to climb five 8-foot ladders. Like all cliff dwellings, it is located at approximately 7,000 feet elevation. Tickets must be purchased for the one-hour tour. Top sites include Cedar Tree

Tower, Badger House Community, Sun Temple, and Far View Sites.

Children ages 4 to 12 can become Junior Park Rangers. Pick up an activity sheet at the Far View Visitor Center or Chapin Mesa Museum, complete the activities, and take it to a ranger at either site for review, and your child will be awarded a Mesa Verde Junior Ranger badge. There's an online program for kids that assists parents in beginning the learning process about what will be seen upon arrival and also helps build excitement about the trip.

Park activities include hiking, bird-watching, observing wildlife, stargazing, plant walks, cross-country skiing, and evening campground programs. From May to September enjoy a free, 45-minute presentation on the history of the Park, given by park rangers at 9 PM. Campsites are available in Morefield Campground, 4 miles inside Mesa Verde, open from May to October. Check dates and current prices on the Web site or call 1-800-449-2288. Camping is open to tents, trailers, and RVs, with 15 full-hookup RV sites. Base camping includes a carpeted tent, two cots, and a lantern. Morefield also has a village with café, gas station, laundry, and grocery store.

Comments from Brothers Bradie (Age 11) and Levi (Age 10)

We've been lots of different places. Mesa Verde was the best and most interesting. Learning all about the Cliff Dwellers was fun and very different from anything we've learned in school. Climbing up on the ladders was like climbing up a mountain; that's what made it very exciting.

Another great place we stopped was Bishop's Castle (Beulah, Colorado). The man there, Mr.

Bishop, is building a real castle all by himself. Now that's cool. It's really big, with towers and every-thing just like pictures of castles we've seen in books and movies, but he's doing it all by himself.

A Covered Wagon Tour Along the Oregon Trail

Oregon Trail Wagon Train (Rt. 2, Box 502, Bayard, NE 69334; 308-586-1850; fax 308-586-1848; www.oregontrail wagontrain.com; three-hour tour of Chimney Rock, $15 per person; canoe rentals, $8 per hour, per canoe; 10 RV/ camping sites, $18 per night for full service [electricity, water, and sewer] and $10 for your tents, with laundry and showers available; 24-hour wagon train treks, $200 adults, $175 children under 12). Travel back in time on a covered wagon tour of the Oregon Trail. See historic Chimney Rock the same way the pioneers did, and tour the scenic North Platte River by canoe. Oregon Trail Wagon Train offers historic tours, tent camping, evening cookouts, and wagon train treks.

Experience life as it was in the mid-1800s. There are scheduled trips in June, July, and August, with trail rides available upon request. Spend a full day out on the Nebraska prairies on a wagon train tour from noon to noon, with tents, sleeping bags, and three meals included. The evening meal is cooked over a campfire and accompa-nied by stories about the history of the area.

The Oregon Trail Wagon Train is located south of Bayard across from Chimney Rock, along the North Platte River and the historic Oregon Trail. The Chimney Rock the pioneers saw was about 100 feet taller than the rock for-mation that stands today, but it is the same landmark that is mentioned in more pioneer diaries than any other along the trail. Pioneers made side trips to climb Chimney Rock and placed their names as high up on its walls as possible, but because it is made of soft sandstone, the names soon eroded.

The Oregon Trail in Nebraska was blazed, in 1813, by a small band of fur traders who made the route known, and then used by other traders on horseback and on foot. In 1830, small wagons driven by fur traders used the trail, and the pioneers soon followed, carrying all their possessions in wagons that were only about 10 feet long and 4 feet wide. Called "prairie schooners" because their canvas coverings resembled sails, they were pulled by oxen. The pioneers traveled in groups called trains, and it took those trains about a month to cross Nebraska. Many of Nebraska's highways today are on or near routes used over 100 years ago.

Plan your trip to coincide with the Oregon Trail Wagon Train Bluegrass Festival held annually in late August with performances by eight bands. In addition to the music, a festival highlight is the nightly chuckwagon cookout with traditional western-style fare: ribeye steaks cooked over an open wood fire, creamed green beans, roasted potatoes, warm sourdough bread, and homemade ice cream. Check the Web site for dates and performers at the festival. There's also on-site camping for tents or RVs.

And as long as you're in the neighborhood, stop in nearby Bridgeport, Nebraska, to visit the Pioneer Trails Museum (south end of Main Street, east on US 385; 308-262-0108; free, open Memorial Day weekend–Labor Day, 10 AM–6 PM. This is a great stop before or after the Oregon Trail Train Wagon. It's helpful to understand the history of the trail and rewarding to have a culminating learning experience.

The Way Things Used to Be

School of Homesteading (Center for Essential Education, P.O. Box 869, Elm Mott, TX 76640;

Students at the School of Homesteading make a variety of breads and learn about traditional and modern methods of baking. *School of Homesteading*

254-799-1480; www.cfeeschool.com/index.html; info@ cfeeschool.com; 1-, 2-, 3-, and 6-day courses ranging from $65 to $890). The School of Homesteading, located in the Homestead Traditional Crafts Village on the banks of the Brazos River in central Texas, offers gardening, home-steading, crafts, and other essential self-sustaining skills. There are hands-on workshops and seminars taught by experienced craftspeople, farmers, and gardeners, and programs are open to everyone 17 years and older.

Agricultural offerings include Beekeeping, Family Goat, Family Cow, Growing Culinary Herbs, Home-steading, Orchards and Vineyards, Raising Poultry, Horse Farming, and the Homestead Garden. Crafts classes include Sewing, Spinning, Weaving, Baking Breads, Canning and Preserving, Cheese Making, Soap Making, Basketry, Blacksmithing, Woodworking, and Homestead Carpentry. You will find detailed descriptions of seminars and workshops on the Web site, along with a current schedule, dates, and costs. Tools are provided and the cost of materials is included in the class fee.

There are walking tours of Homestead Heritage Village and Heritage Farm from Monday through Saturday, with demonstrations of homesteading skills and crafts, as well as exhibits about organic farming, vegetable gardening, and culinary herbs. Heritage Farm is a teaching and research facility on four acres, and it includes a log cabin, barn, greenhouse, orchard, vineyard, berry patch, animal enclosures, pastures, and a field that is farmed with draft animals.

Students can find accommodations in the many nearby hotels and motels listed on the Web site. Workshops begin at 9 AM and end in the late afternoon with a lunch break in the middle of the day. A continental breakfast and an afternoon snack are provided, and lunch is available at the Homestead Farms Deli. Enrollment is limited, so personal attention can be provided. Register for courses online or by telephone.

Paul's Story of Stepping Back

The School of Homesteading is part of the de-industrial revolution. Visitors come to realize that they can step back from the industrialization of their lives and connect with more things that matter. There are a variety of experiential workshops for people who want to fill their leisure time constructively. You become immersed in a very progressive movement by stepping back into a time when people made and did things on

People fly in from all over the world to take woodworking workshops at the School of Homesteading with master craftsmen like Paul Sellers and Frank Strazza.

their own. The most practical skills can make you feel the most valued, useful, and confident in your own ability to create and lead a self-sustaining lifestyle.

Spud City

Idaho Potato Museum (130 NW Main St., Blackfoot, ID 83221; 208-785-2517; www.potatoexpo.com). Bingham County, Idaho, grows the most potatoes of anywhere in the world—producing 100 million hundredweight sacks per year. Appropriately, it's also where the Idaho Potato Museum celebrates the *Solanum tuberosum,* also known as the potato. This is not a typical museum. The expo sprouted to life in 1990, when the Citizens for a Positive Image of Blackfoot, Idaho, decided to let it be known that the town is the epicenter of the potato industry. Although the seed stock for potatoes originated in the Andes

Mountains of Peru around 200 B.C., the modern potato, as both a cash crop and a concept, is indisputably an Idaho invention. The museum's collection of potato-related paraphernalia, stories, potatoes, and recipes makes all the propaganda digestible.

Though on the surface the subject of potatoes might seem rather starchy, the museum puts a spin on spuds that's whimsical and wacky. For instance, a newspaper columnist once remarked that Marilyn Monroe would look good in a potato sack. She responded by posing in one. There are photos for sale that attest to Monroe's sumptuous exploration of the limits of burlap. If you prefer something a little more formal, check out the burlap tuxedo hanging in all its coarse-stitched splendor or the intricately and flamboyantly decorated potato sack gown worn in 1994 by rodeo queen Carol Young.

Potatoes are synonymous with Idaho. Be sure to buy at least a 20-pound bag on your way out of town. Present all of your friends and family with a gift that represents the true wealth of Idaho—a giant-sized, nutritious, and delicious tater. Every adult paying admission to the museum receives a box of hash browns as a yummy souvenir.

Ohm

⑤ Dhamma Dharā Vipassana Meditation Center (386 Colrain-Shelburne Rd., Shelburne Falls, MA 01370; 413-625-2160; fax 413-625-2170; www.dhara.dhamma .org; no fees). Vipassana Meditation is an advanced, rather extreme, and controversial approach to meditation recommended by its ardent followers but not appropriate for everyone. The 10-day silent meditations offered are serious classes with the expectation of "noble silence" and dedicated personal work without interaction with anyone else. Shelburne Falls is one of a hundred centers offering Vipassana Meditation taught by S. N. Goenka and his fol-

Pizza for Dessert

After indulging in everything potato at the Idaho Potato Museum, be sure to stop at Mr. Pizza (125 NW Main St., Blackfoot, ID 83221; 208-785-3785) directly across the street before moving your car. Their pizzas are very good and their dessert pizzas are sensational. Created by the owner to compete with all of the pizza chains moving into town, the dessert pizza crust has a fruit filling and is covered with a sweet, thick cheese which melts perfectly. The blueberry dessert pizza is the very berry best.

lowers in the tradition of Sayagyi U Ba Khin. There are no fees for the classes, housing, or meals; however, there is an extensive application and reservation process. Returning students who have completed at least one 10-day program are permitted to make donations and volunteer their services in the kitchen, on the grounds, and running courses at any of their centers, silently of course.

Meditation's Medicinal Effects: Lisa's Story

I was 33 years old when my doctor called me a walking time bomb. Type A personality, blood pressure in the danger zone, my stress level was astronomical and my nerves were shot. He recommended meditation.

I became a meditation junkie, trying every program I could find, but none of them seemed to work for me. I couldn't fathom how to direct and clear my mind no matter how hard I tried, yet it was something I really wanted to achieve. My favorite aunt had great success using meditation for pain management and I was unwilling to live my life on medications with side effects I didn't want.

I canceled my vacation to Cancún and signed up for a 10-day silent retreat to totally immerse myself in the experience. Participants were encouraged to embrace the meditative lifestyle in every way. I borrowed a friend's tent and sleeping bag to camp out by myself for the first time in my life.

The days started at 4 AM with a wake-up bell a half hour before the first meditation. There were two basic vegetarian meals a day and early evening tea. I learned to eat mindfully without looking at others since no talking was allowed. That was very tough the first few days.

The course work was studying your own breath, coming in and going out, all day long every day, to build awareness of the present moment or mindfulness. Hours upon hours of directed meditation slowed down my entire body and taught me the mental discipline I needed. Within three months of twice daily practice my blood pressure reached the normal range and I weaned myself from the medications, restructured my life, and lost weight. That was quite a productive vacation with long-lasting benefits, and I return when needed for a tune-up.

Yoga and Meditation Training for All

Kripalu Center (P.O. Box 309, 57 Interlaken Rd., Stockbridge, MA 01262; 1-866-200-5203; 413-448-3152; www.kripalu.org; registration@kripalu.org; program fees vary). The Kripalu Center offers over 60 programs a month and also has certification training programs for professional yoga instructors and massage therapists. The beautiful buildings and property were once the site of a Jesuit seminary. There is a wide range of accommodations, from a dormitory to private rooms with baths. Families are encouraged to participate, and the surroundings are particularly conducive to family get-togethers and/or girlfriend getaways.

Pat's Story

Occasionally I'll just pick up and go to Kripalu for a long weekend mini-vacation or what Kripalu calls R&R (rest and relaxation). A few times I have attended a week of workshops, but I like R&R the best. I can go at my own pace and do everything or nothing. It's a tranquil and affordable treat.

The grounds are beautiful. I love looking out, from the fourth-floor solarium, at the lake with the blue/gray mountains in the background. Walking the labyrinth is another favorite activity. It's located in a field off the front entrance with more great views of the lake and mountains. I enjoy participating in the early and late afternoon yoga classes and yoga nidra, a form of relaxation, meditation, and chanting.

The last time I visited I stayed in the six-person dorm room and there was only one other person, so it was private and quiet. The whole visit, including meals, yoga, workshops, and the great sauna and spa, is about $144 per day. Often they have some musicians in the evening for *kirtan* (chanting) or other types of entertainment. I live in Watertown, Connecticut, so I can just travel up old Route 8 to Lee and then over to Lenox. It takes about an hour and the ride is scenic along parts of a river and many wooded areas.

Low-Key Community Meditation

Des Moines Meditation Group (4100 Grand Ave., Des Moines, IA 50312; 515-255-8398; charlesday1@mchsi .com). The Des Moines Meditation Group is a community for mindful living. Contact Charlie Day to discuss meditation, sitting groups, retreats, or meditation experiences. Here are some other recommendations from Charlie:

- Any book by Bhante Gunaratana or Thich Nhat Hanh.

- **Mid-America Dharma** (455 E. 80th Terrace, Kansas City, MO 64131; 573-874-0881; www.midamerica dharma.org; info at midamericadharma.org). Mid-America Dharma is a nonprofit organization listing retreats, meditation, and sitting groups in the Midwest.
- **Ryumonji Zen Monastery** (2452 Ryumon Rd., Dorchester, IA 52140; 563-546-1309; www.ryumonji .org; shoken@ryumonji.org). This is a Soto Zen Buddhist Monastery near Decorah, Iowa. *Ryu-mon-ji* means "Dragon Gate Temple" in Japanese.

A School Without Walls

National Outdoor Leadership School (284 Lincoln St., Lander, WY 82520; 1-800-710-NOLS; 1-800-710-5300; 307-332-5300; fax 307-332-1220; www.nols.edu; admissions@ nols.edu). The National Outdoor Leadership School (NOLS) offers 10-day to full-semester courses in wilderness settings. NOLS teaches leadership and outdoor skills to students 14 years and older, and to adults, in spectacular settings around the world. In the United States, there are semester programs in the Rockies, the Yukon, the Teton Valley, the Pacific Northwest, the Southwest, and Alaska.

By choosing a location, you will be able to view the different courses offered, the age group, dates and duration, as well as the costs and optional college credit. For example, select school locations on the Web site menu, and choose the Teton Valley. Then select Backcountry Skiing and you will find two programs, one for ages 17 and over, and one for ages 23 and over. For ages 17 and over there is a 14-day course for $1,680, with optional college credit of two semester hours. The course begins and ends in Driggs, Idaho, and the nearest airport is in Idaho Falls. There is a $250 equipment fee. A complete course description and equipment list can be downloaded from the Web site.

You can also view a complete course catalog online or request a print version be sent to you. You may apply online or download an application and mail or fax it to NOLS with a $65 application fee. For questions or to apply by phone, call 1-800-NOLS and press 1 to speak to an admissions officer. When filling out application forms, be sure to provide several choices in order of preference. Once accepted, an enrollment packet with all necessary information about your course and travel information will be sent to you.

NOLS also has an adult education program for students ages 23 and over. Most courses are two weeks long to minimize time away from work. These include Wilderness Horsepacking, Light and Fast Backpacking, Backcountry Skiing, North Cascades Mountaineering, Alaska Sea Kayaking, and others. There are also courses specifically designed for ages 40 and over. Learn more about NOLS adult education at www.nols.edu/courses /find/byage/adult_education.

How Tom Found His Calling

The three months that I spent taking a National Outdoor Leadership School (NOLS) course, living completely outdoors in the southwestern United States with only what I and 14 other people carried on our backs, changed the course of my life. Upon arrival, we were required to take a three-day wilderness medical training course. This was my first experience with any sort of medical training or practice and it was love at first sight. After only three days learning everything from simple bandaging of cuts and burns to full-body immobilization I knew that I wanted to dedicate my life to medicine and helping people. The first three days changed my life and were very easy compared with the next 87.

The only people there for me were 14 strangers and at first living with them was very tough. Nobody really cared what I was doing or how I was doing, and that was the idea. When you are trying to become a leader, you have to learn to lead yourself before you can attempt to lead anyone else. Camping in the wild I learned to take care of myself physically like I never had to do growing up in the suburbs, and emotionally, which was even more challenging, without my friends and family around me.

NOLS taught me to look past the differences in others and learn to live first with myself by communicating honestly, which sounds pretty easy, but it's a lot harder to do. By the end of the three months I was better friends with everyone on that course than almost all of my friends back home because we learned how to communicate and say what we needed and what we felt and what we knew to be true. I went to NOLS because after graduating high school and not applying myself in my first year of college, I had no direction or understanding of what I wanted to do. Now I am enrolled in my first semester of nursing school, confident with my life's choice and clear direction.

Learn How to Make Authentic Windsor Chairs

The Windsor Institute (44 Timber Swamp Rd., Hampton, NH 03842; 603-929-9801; fax 603-926-1097; www.the windsorinstitute.com; info@thewindsorinstitute.com; 5-day classes, $700). Students begin by taking the introductory sack back class before proceeding to any of seven advanced classes. Class size is limited to 18 students, with an age range (so far) from 12 to 84 in many combinations of fathers and sons, brothers and sisters, husbands and wives, friends, and individuals from every state except South Dakota and Hawaii.

"Windsors are perfection," says Mike Dunbar, founder of the school, "comfortable, strong, good looking, and made to last about 250 years."

Roberta and Don's Story

Don, an avid reader of woodworking magazines, ran across an ad for the Windsor Institute in Hampton, New Hampshire. This ad played on his mind for a few years until, nearing retirement age, he finally decided he had to go and learn how to make authentic Windsor chairs as they were made in the 18th century," says his wife Roberta. Upon registering for the sack back chair class, he began accumulating the hand tools needed to construct the chair. Tools with names like scorp, adze, and spokeshave were soon arriving in the mail. He

A Windsor Institute chair-building graduation class.

chose an October class, which pleased me and
allowed us to be in New England during the height
of the fall colors.

"It is daunting at first to know that when you
walk into the Windsor Institute workshop on
Monday that somehow you will walk out with a
completed chair by Friday, all done by hand.
Everyone is new to the process and class members
come from all walks of life and all over the world.
Don and I made our base a nearby motel, com-

plete with cooking facilities. I came by the workshop each evening to pick him up and check on the progress of the chair. It all looked very complicated and overwhelming to me, but for Don, taking it step by step, all went well.

"The chair bug really bit. Don was eager to return to New Hampshire to learn more styles of chairs. I was happy to return as I loved the area and found the folks living there to be just the nicest, most polite folks I have ever been around. We eventually returned six more times and Don learned nine more styles of Windsor chairs. We are in contact with chair makers in Maine, Texas, and Utah concerning chairs and chair-making materials. Don continues to make chairs in his workshop in Stehekin, Washington. Each year folks come to visit his shop and several have left with a wonderful Windsor chair to enjoy in their homes. To date Don has made 50 chairs. Each is a work of art and brings great satisfaction to him as well as to those who are lucky enough to own one."

Stay Nearby

Windsor Institute students need to arrange their own room and board. Hampton is a resort area with dozens of inns, motels, and B&Bs. Contact the Chamber of Commerce for more information.

The Old Salt Restaurant in Lamie's Inn is a local, award-winning favorite in Hampton, New Hampshire.

Hampton Area Chamber of Commerce (1 Lafayette Rd., P.O. Box 790, Hampton, NH 03842; 603-926-8717; fax 603-926-9977; www.hamptonchamber.com; info@ hamptonchamber.com).

$-$$ **Lamie's Inn** (490 Lafayette Rd., Hampton, NH 03842; 603-926-8322; www.lamiesinn.com). Lamie's Inn is a 32-room restored colonial New England inn with modern conveniences. Its Old Salt Restaurant is a local, award-winning favorite. Windsor Institute attendees receive a discount.

$-$$ **Best Western, the Inn of Hampton and Conference Center** (815 Lafayette Rd.; 603-926-6771; www.theinnofhampton.com; Info@TheInnatHampton.com).

This is an upscale motel with restaurant and indoor pool. Rates are highest May to October, continental breakfast included. Children under 12 stay for free.

Lifelong Learning

Elderhostel (11 Ave. de Lafayette, Boston, MA 02111-1746; 1-800-454-5768; Mon.–Fri., 9 AM to 6 PM; www.elder hostel.org; registration@eldershostel.org). Elderhostel is a nonprofit organization that specializes in lifelong learning and educational travel for people over age 55. Select from more than 8,000 learning adventures, from history and music to outdoor activities to crime-scene forensics. Hostelers immerse themselves in a wide range of activities such as studying food and wine in the Napa Valley, California, or social science and culture in Branson, Missouri, or jazz in New Orleans. There's also the Intergenerational Program, which offers trips for grandparents and grandchildren (ages are dependent upon the destination and activity).

For Grandparents and Grandchildren: Brian's Story (Age 9)

Grandma Bea's favorite Elderhostel trip was learning about the history of Florida because she lives in Florida. She was really surprised how much there was to see and learn about in her own state that she'd never heard of before. But now that she's here with me at the Denali Foundation, this is her favorite trip because it's intergenerational; that means that grandparents come with their grandchildren. No one else can come. This is the first time she's traveled with one of her grandchildren, probably because I'm the oldest. She loves it. We're sharing a bedroom and we talk all night. It stays light here really late, so last night we played basketball and Grandma Bea surprised everybody. She's really good at it. Now we're getting ready to go on a helicopter tour and glacier landing. I am so excited and a little nervous. I don't want Grandma Bea to know I'm nervous because then she might not want to go, but she really wants to go because she's never been on a helicopter before. I'll tell you all about it when we get back. I'm sure we'll love it.

A Spinning 'Round Adventure

The New England Carousel Museum (95 Riverside Ave., Rt. 72, Bristol, CT 06010; 860-585-5411; fax 860-314-0483; www.thecarouselmuseum.org; info@thecarousel museum.org). Dedicated to the acquisition, restoration, and preservation of operating carousels, preserving antique memorabilia, and creating new carousel materials, the collection is a unique immersion in art, music, and engineering. The museum houses one of the largest collections of antique carousel pieces in the country and manages the historic Park Carousel in Hartford.

Park Carousel (Bushnell Park, Hartford, CT; open Apr.–Oct., 11 AM to 5 PM Tues. through Sun., closed rainy days; 850-585-5411; $1 a ride). There are less than two hundred remaining antique carousels, and this is one of three surviving carousels hand carved in 1914 by two Russian immigrants, Solomon Stein and Harry Goldstein, that is still in operation. The carousel has 36 jumper

What Do Harriet Beecher Stowe and Mark Twain Have in Common?

Mark Twain (1835–1910) and Harriet Beecher Stowe (1811–1896) are both famous American writers and they were next-door neighbors in Hartford, Connecticut. Visit their homes to see how and where they lived.

The Mark Twain House (351 Farmington Ave., Hartford, CT 06105; 860-247-0998; www.marktwainhouse.org). The house itself was custom built for the Twain family. Its opulence, luxury, and detail are startling, even by today's standards. The biggest thrills are seeing the desk where he wrote and listening to recordings of his work. Lack of funding made future uncertain at time of publication.

Harriet Beecher Stowe Center (77 Forest St., Hartford, CT 06105; 860-522-9258; www.harrietbeecherstowecenter.org). Harriet Beecher Stowe was committed to social justice and effected positive change through her writings and actions. With excerpts and readings from *Uncle Tom's Cabin,* the exhibit is a powerful message that needs to be heard by each generation. These are two very important American writers. The museums can be viewed on one ticket, open to the public Monday through Saturday, 9:30 to 4:30, and on Sundays, noon to 4:30.

horses that go up and down, 12 stationary horses, and two chariots.

Diana, John, and Darla's Story

"I have an important message to share with parents everywhere: Don't assume that children can handle only children's museums. We visited the Bushnell Park Carousel and the New England

Experience a Connecticut Favorite Treat

Middletown, Connecticut, is about a 20-minute drive from Hartford. After a busy day of sightseeing and carousel riding, you'll surely be hungry. It's worth the drive to O'Rourke's Diner (728 Main Street, Middletown) for a central Connecticut culinary treat, a steamed cheeseburger. It sounds odd but tastes terrific.

Carousel Museum in Hartford, Connecticut, because friends with older children took us there. Darla is only five. We knew she'd do fine at the carousel but were very hesitant about taking her into a real museum. She proved us wrong. She had the greatest time and asked terrific questions of the docent."

"It's probably best to visit the museum first and then the ride," added her husband John.

"Right," laughed Diana. "We went to the park first and rode the carousel over and over for about an hour. When we walked into the museum Darla yelled very loudly, 'Oh this is where the horses go when they get off work.'"

Learn How to Milk a Cow

Shatto Milk Company (9406 N. Hwy. 33, Osborn, MO 64474; 816-930-3862; www.shattomilk.com; leroy@shatto milk.com). This local family dairy offers visitors an opportunity to tour their farm, pet the baby calves, milk a cow, sample their products, and watch how they bottle their milk right there on the farm. It is the best family attraction in the Kansas City area, and it was just awarded the Missouri Tourism of the Year award by the State Tourism Department. No growth hormones are used on their farm, and there's a lot to learn about the animals residing there. Educational tours are conducted daily, with special arrangements for groups. Themed events occur around the holidays, with family days and seasonal activities posted on their Web site. This is a relaxing, easy-to-see attraction that people age 1 to 100 will enjoy.

Thirty-Five Centuries of Glass

Corning Museum of Glass (One Museum Way, Corning, NY; 1-800-732-6845; 607-937-5371; www.cmog.org; info@ cmog.org; open Sun.–Fri., 11 AM–4:20 PM; Sat., 9:20 AM–5:20 PM; entrance fee $12.50 adults, children free; additional costs for classes). The Corning Museum offers a wide selection of residencies, classes, activities, and scholarship programs. It is the world's largest glass museum, featuring 35 centuries of examples and styles. Instructors from all over the globe teach participants ranging from beginner to more advanced students, with internships also available throughout the year. Some classes meet weekly while others are offered for a few weeks, a weekend, or one day. It is an opportunity to learn a highly skilled art from the most skilled craftsmen. There are daily workshops where all ages can experience some form of glassmaking on the most basic level. It's a great family learning and doing activity.

Third Choice Became the Best Choice: Aviva's Story

When my husband Mark and I visited the Corning

Glass Museum, an Italian master craftsman was in

residence. It was fascinating to watch him because he spoke absolutely no English besides yes, no, and good, but it didn't seem to matter. He and the many students around him spoke the language of glass. He pointed and gestured, they asked and responded, all working together in a very fluid and fluent way.

Call before you go to the museum to reserve glassmaking activities of interest. Each activity was charged separately and ranged between $9 and $25. I wanted to make glass flowers or a picture frame, but the classes were filled, so I created glass beads, which were then shipped to my home after they hardened.

Build Your Own Home from the Ground

Cob Cottage Company (P.O. Box 942, Coquille, OR 97423; 541-396-1825; www.cobcottage.com; fees $240–$1,800 depending on the course, includes meals and campsite accommodations). Since 1993, Cob Cottage has taught workshops, conducted in cob buildings, on all

A Helpful Tool

The Hand Sculpted House, by Ianto Evans, Linda Smiley, and Michael G. Smith, is available through Cob Cottage Company.

aspects of building cob and natural homes. Earth mixed with straw makes cob, which has been widely used for building homes in harsh climates. Cob is inexpensive, natural, nonpolluting, cool in the summer, and warm in the winter. Families are encouraged to attend, and ages have ranged from 8 to over 80.

Ianto's Story

Cob Cottage Company is a private service serving the public. It's more like a theater company than a corporation. We're a group of friends who really like one another who put on public acts. We're basically here to help people review their lives and how they live, teaching them how to get off the treadmill. All of our workshops have that as the backdrop, to learn how to build their own houses with the overall aim to reduce consumerism and help people have more satisfying lives. In recent years we've had an increased number of middle-aged women attending workshops and actively building their own homes. It's very empowering and practical. We have about 3,000 alumni and know there are substantial numbers of people who not only learned technical tricks from us, they have also adjusted their way of life to align their lifestyle to their conscience.

Bill's Off-Grid Story

I'm a professional with a master's degree who
chooses to be a full-time property caretaker specializing in all-around maintenance and off-grid
homesteading experiences. I wanted to learn how
to build with cob and attended a workshop that
blew my mind. It's amazing how many resources
there are. Go to alternative building Web sites for
links to other such workshops. Google "natural
building workshops" or "traditional skills workshops," that sort of thing, if that's what you're
interested in learning about. There are entire
schools devoted to off-grid living that are informative, doable, and the future.

Learn, Work, and Study

White Oak Farm and Education Center (P.O. Box 450,
Williams, OR 97544; 828-524-9133; www.whiteoakfarm
csa.org; info@whiteoakfarmcsa.org). Work-study positions
and volunteer days are available for those who want to
learn organic farming and natural building.

Sustainable Lifestyles Workshops

**Build Here Now: Natural Building, Permaculture, and
Sustainable Lifestyles Convergence** (Lama Foundation,
P.O. Box 240, San Cristobal, NM 87564; 505-586-1269;
fax 206-984-0916; www.lamafoundation.org; info@lama
foundation.org; $525, includes vegetarian meals and tent

sites). This is an annual event for one week of hands-on workshops, classroom theory, discussion, slide presentations, and networking dedicated to natural building, permaculture, and sustainable lifestyles.

Learn How to Fly a Seaplane

Ryan Aviation Seaplane Base (Flagler County Airport, 201 Airport Rd., Suite 4, Palm Coast, FL 32164; 1-800-338-3044; local or fax 386-437-0620; www.ryansea planes.com; info@ryanseaplanes.com; Private and Commercial Single-Engine Sea training programs, $1,500 each; ATP Land and Sea combined training, $2,350). Learn to handle a single-engine seaplane in the air and on the water. A seaplane is always in motion on the water, and learning to assess wind speed and direction; find a suitable landing area, dock, or beach; and secure the plane are all essential and the most challenging parts of the training program. Takeoffs and landings depend on water conditions and crosswinds, with different requirements for glassy (calm) water, which inhibits depth perception, and rough water, which may require rapid deceleration upon landing and quicker takeoffs.

At Ryan Aviation, a private seaplane rating can be completed in two days in a Cessna 180 Amphibian. The course includes ground training, flight training, examiner's fee, and aircraft for a check ride. If you hold a commercial certificate you can add on to it with Ryan's commercial airplane single-engine sea training program. Pilots may also train for their seaplane rating while completing a 10-hour course for a commercial license. There is also an ATP (Airline Transport Pilot) single-engine sea course that adds instrument approaches and an opportunity to fly the Dehavilland Beaver, one of the most famous, rugged, and versatile bush planes in the world.

Flagler County Airport is 15 miles north of Daytona Beach International Airport in Florida. There is a map and a list of nearby lodging on the Ryan Aviation Web site. With Orlando (and Disney theme parks) and other attractions nearby, this lends itself to planning an extended or family vacation.

Sedona, Arizona, Named America's #1 Most Beautiful Spot by *USA Today*

Visit Sedona (Visitor Information Services, 331 Forest Rd., Sedona, AZ; 1-800-288-7336; 928-282-7722; fax 928-282-3916; www.visitsedona.com; info@sedonachamber

Airport Mesa in Sedona, Arizona. *S. Wolf and E. Lamadrid*

.com). This is a comprehensive resource for everything Sedona—resorts, time-shares, cabins, B&Bs, you name it, you can find it in Sedona. Vortex tours, medicine wheel tours, healing ceremonies, horseback riding, hiking, and shopping are just a very few of the hundreds of possible activities in the area. Allow enough time to fully enjoy and appreciate your surroundings.

Visits to the Vortexes

Ed visits Bell Rock in Sedona as often as he can.
S. Wolf and E. Lamadrid

"When I first started going to Sedona about 15 years ago," said Ed Lamadrid, DAOM (Doctor of Acupuncture and Oriental Medicine), "there were no signs or maps marking where to go. I read about the vortexes in books by Dick Sutphen and Tom Dongo. The directions were to turn at this rock onto this dirt road and when you reach the old cattle gate you're there. Today everything is clearly marked and all of the hotels have vortex maps. The red-rock natural landscape is beautiful. Driving in from Phoenix the landscape is flat and beige until a half hour from Sedona. Suddenly you feel like you must be on Mars with the red dirt and 5,000-foot elevation.

"I visit whenever I can to recharge my batteries. It's a healing experience for me. The vortexes are like acupuncture points for the planet. Similarly, there are specific energy points on the body where the body's energy is very close to the surface. When I put a needle in or apply pressure I

can affect the energy very easily. The energy just releases like through meditating but more profound. A lot of spontaneous healing transpires at the vortexes."

Hiking up to the rock formation called Kachina Woman. The rock is shaped like a woman looking down at the canyon below, with her head facing left and with a shawl over her. *S. Wolf and E. Lamadrid*

Cook for Your Health

The Conscious Gourmet: Culinary Retreats for the Body, Mind, and Soul (203-622-1189; www.theconscious gourmet.com; dcarlsonsspirit@aol.com; prices vary with destination and length of retreat). Combine your love of good food with your desire to eat more healthfully, and immerse yourself in a hands-on cooking adventure that nourishes mind, body, spirit, and soul. You will learn new ways of eating along with new recipes that use whole,

The Conscious Gourmet offers immersion in hands-on cooking adventures that nourish the mind, body, and soul.

Immersion Travel

> "Food is our common ground, a universal experience."
>
> —James Beard

fresh, natural, and mostly organic foods at retreats that emphasize vegan, vegetarian, or mostly vegetarian with some fish or grass-fed animal protein choices. All ages and levels of cooking skills are welcome.

Culinary retreats are of varying lengths, which affects costs and locations as well. Some recent retreats have included cooking adventures in Sedona, Arizona; Santa Fe, New Mexico; and Jupiter, Florida, near West Palm Beach. The retreats are all based on a core program that includes morning yoga and movement classes followed by a whole foods breakfast buffet and daily four-hour cooking classes with a full-course organic meal. Instruction in technique and healthy food choices are part of each cooking class, and lectures and workshops will teach you to think about food in different ways to ensure that you take home and use what you've learned. By the end of your culinary retreat you'll be refreshed, revitalized, and equipped with what you need to know to become a conscious gourmet.

Free afternoons in Sedona allow time to explore the amazing red-rock formations, hike, visit vortex sites, enjoy spa services, or simply relax. The Santa Fe retreat includes an excursion to Bandelier National Monument to visit ancestral Pueblo sites, with afternoons free for sight-seeing, hiking, shopping, visiting art galleries and museums, spas, or a drive to Taos.

In Florida, spend free afternoons at the beach, sight-seeing, visiting galleries and museums, or relaxing at a spa or on your own.

There have also been recent intensive weekend retreats in Greenwich, Connecticut, and Phoenicia, New York. Check the Conscious Gourmet Web site or call for information about current programs and destinations, and prices of retreats and accommodations. Some program fees include shared accommodations. At others, lodging reservations can be made for you at an additional cost. Travel expenses are not included.

Great Southwest Fare Is More Than Chiles

Jane Butel Southwest Cooking School (2655 Pan American NE, Suite. F, Albuquerque, NM 87107; 1-800-473-8226; 505-243-2622; www.janebutel.com/cookingschool .html; info@janebutelcooking.com; weekend classes, $1,050; weeklong classes, $1,995; team-building classes, 3 to 4 hours, $2,500 for 9 people or less, $250 each for 9 people or more). Jane Butel offers weekend and weeklong classes, as well as team-building. Plan a trip to Albuquerque or Santa Fe and treat yourself to an immersion experience into southwestern cooking in Corrales, a Spanish Colonial village along the Rio Grande, on the outskirts of Albuquerque. Classes are held in Jane Butel's kitchen, and your weekend culinary adventure starts with a get-together on Friday evening, with your first class beginning at 6 PM as you cook and then enjoy a delicious dinner.

Mexican cuisine expert Jane Butel, of Santa Fe, is the author of more than 20 cookbooks on southwestern cooking, including *Real Women Eat Chiles, Jane Butel's Tex-Mex Cookbook,* and *Jane Butel's Quick and Easy Southwestern Cookbook,* among many others. Jane Butel's *Southwestern Kitchen* TV series was developed from her series of cookbooks, which incorporate history, technique, and tradition into her recipes.

Saturday and Sunday classes begin with a southwestern continental breakfast, and continue with a lesson on the history of the cuisine. You will cook in groups of two or three, after an explanation of menu items and a demonstration of techniques, with Jane and her staff guiding your efforts. Each class ends with a wonderful meal accompanied by the appropriate beverages. Saturday and Sunday sessions conclude at about 2 PM, leaving you time to explore the area, visit art galleries and spas, go horseback riding, hiking, play golf, or indulge in other leisure activities. The fee for your weekend getaway includes a reception, three classes, dinner Friday, breakfast and lunch on Saturday and Sunday, a cookbook, apron, and diploma.

The weeklong class also has a reception Friday night, but dinner is at a local restaurant with New Mexican specialties. There are southwestern continental breakfasts each morning, followed by a history of the cuisine, a review of menu items, and demonstrations, before you cook the midday meal. Each session ends after lunch, so you can explore and enjoy your surroundings. Class fee includes five individual classes, breakfast and lunch each day, two dinners, a get-acquainted reception, plus a cookbook, apron, and a diploma to take home.

There are also cooking demonstrations and full-participation team-building classes for groups. Classes can be scheduled in the morning, afternoon, or evening, and choices include Traditional New Mexican, Southwestern Lite, Fajita Party, Southwestern Sampler, A Tale of Two Tortillas, New Mexican Favorites, Southwestern Grilling and Smoking, Finger Lickin' Barbeque, and other topics.

Contact the school for more information or to make reservations. For touring information and lodging suggestions, contact the Albuquerque Convention and Visitor's Department (1-800-733-9918, www.itsatrip.org), the Santa Fe Convention and Visitor's Bureau (1-800-777-CITY, www.santafe.org), or the New Mexico Department of Tourism (1-800-545-2040, www.newmexico.org).

Immersion Travel

"I am learning all the time. The tombstone will be my diploma."
—Eartha Kitt, American singer and actress

The world premiere of the 1941 film *Santa Fe Trail*, starring Errol Flynn, was held at the Lensic Theater, built in 1931. Today, it is the leading downtown venue for Santa Fe's performing arts, including the prestigious Readings and Conversations author series presented by the Lannan Foundation. *Barbara Harrelson*

The Best Way to See Santa Fe Is on Foot

Santa Fe Literary Walking Tour (924 Old Taos Hwy., Santa Fe, NM 87501; 505-989-4561; www.sfaol.com/books/littour.html; barbarah@newmexico.com; $20 per person; $40 minimum per tour). Santa Fe resident and author of *Walks in Literary Santa Fe: A Guide to Landmarks, Legends, and Lore,* Barbara Harrelson offers a two-hour walking tour of downtown Santa Fe and the opportunity to learn all about the literary greats who were there at one time or another. Santa Fe has many bookstores, and an extensive, exciting, and active literary community. Writers and artists have long thrived in the natural beauty of the area and are still drawn to the spectacular landscape, rich culture, and creative environment. Explore the history and traditions of the Southwest through stories and literary landmarks and by visiting bookstores and former homes of Santa's Fe's most prominent writers. The history of storytelling includes the contributions of the Anasazi culture, the Spanish colonists, and the settlers who migrated west across the Santa Fe Trail.

The tour also includes contemporary authors whose work is representative of the culture of the Southwest. You will also find out about the many readings and other literary events that take place in Santa Fe each week.

The Most Popular Art Museum in New Mexico

Georgia O'Keeffe Museum (217 Johnson St., Santa Fe, NM 87501; 505-995-0785; www.okeeffemuseum.org; 505-946-1000; info@okeeffemuseum.org; open daily except Wed. from May–Nov., 10 AM–5 PM, Fri. to 8 PM; general admission $8, NM residents and students 18+ $4, seniors $7, under 18 free, Fri. 5–8 PM, free; docent tours, 10:30 AM, daily). The Georgia O'Keeffe Museum is the most visited museum in New Mexico, and the first museum in the country dedicated to a single female artist. Georgia O'Keeffe said her art expressed "the wideness and wonder of the world as I live in it." Her instantly recognizable work includes large-scale flowers, animal bones, and the deserts and cliffs of New Mexico. There are paintings, drawings, and sculptures, with special exhibitions as well as the permanent collection. Some of the special showings also include works by O'Keeffe's contemporaries.

O'Keeffe spent many summers painting in New Mexico, and moved there full-time in 1946, three years after her husband, the photographer Alfred Stieglitz, died. She lived and worked at her house in Abiquiu until she moved to Santa Fe, two years before her death at age 98. There are tours of the house and studio, which are located 48 miles northwest of Santa Fe, and now managed by the Georgia O'Keeffe Museum. To make a reservation to visit, call 505-685-4539.

Prepare the Finest Foods

Erna's Elderberry House (P.O. Box 577, Oakhurst, CA 93644; 559-683-6800; www.elderberryhouse.com/eeh CookingClassLink4.html; cooking classes are $1,250 per three-day session). Erna's Elderberry House, a top-rated northern California restaurant, is on the grounds of the Relais & Chateaux Hotel, Chateau du Sureau, located in the foothills close to the southern entrance of Yosemite National Park. Erna's offers three-day food and wine cooking classes, limited to 12 students per session. Enjoy a culinary adventure in a spectacular setting, taught by expert chefs.

Begin your first day of classes by putting on your chef's "whites" and enjoying your morning coffee as you meet for a review of the day's menu. You can work at your own pace on soups, salads, entrees, and desserts. Each eight-hour day of classes ends with a full-course dinner, at which students may be joined by spouses or friends for the cost of their dinners. Two wine seminars, Learning the Secrets of Wine and Pairing Food and Wine, taught by the restaurant's sommelier, are included in the program.

Your cooking experience will conclude with an awards dinner and a diploma. The fee includes tuition, recipes, three lunches, and three six-course dinners, with gratuities additional. Special student rates at Chateau du Sureau are available. Inquire by calling the hotel at 559-683-6800 or e-mailing to chateau@chateausureau.com.

Erna's Elderberry House also offers half- and full-day cooking classes. Check the Web site for current class schedule, descriptions, and costs.

The restaurant and hotel are a 45-minute drive from Fresno, three hours from San Francisco, and about four hours north of Los Angeles. There are daily commuter flights to Fresno from San Francisco and Los Angeles. Call Erna's Elderberry House for directions, more information, and to book your class.

The Best of Cajun and Zydeco

Chef Patrick Mould: Louisiana Regional Cooking

(520 Cedar Crest Ct., Lafayette, LA 70501; 337-983-0892; www.louisianaschoolofcooking.com/html/tours.html; 337-983-0892; kjnchef@cox.net; Cajun Country Culinary Tour, three nights' accommodations included for $1,595 per person, $310 single supplement). Named by *Forbes Traveler* as one of the world's best cooking vacations, and featured on the Food Network's *The Best of Culinary Vacations,* Chef Patrick Mould's Cajun four-day tour is a delicious immersion excursion into the heart of Cajun country.

Just west of New Orleans, you will hear the sounds of Cajun French and Cajun Zydeco music and delight in the aromas and taste the flavors of Cajun cooking. You will stay in a historic bed & breakfast in Lafayette and experience hands-on cooking lessons taught by an award-winning chef. You will learn about the food, the people, and the culture of a unique region of the United States.

Arrive on a Thursday and enjoy a welcome dinner at a local Cajun restaurant. Your first cooking lesson the next morning with Chef Patrick will cover the basics of Cajun cooking, with lunch following the lesson. There will be an afternoon excursion to Vermilionville, where you will step back in time as you tour a Cajun/Creole folklife park that recreates life in Acadiana (named for the Acadians who had migrated from French Canada in the 18th century) between 1765 and 1890. The historic village contains 18 structures, and there are costumed interpreters who demonstrate crafts, music, cooking, and other activities. Afterward there will be dinner out and then an evening of dinner and dancing to Cajun music.

On Saturday there will be another cooking lesson, and you will prepare such dishes as shrimp remoulade, shrimp Creole, seafood okra gumbo, and bananas Foster, with lunch following. Then enjoy an excursion to Avery Island, a salt dome island and the home of Tabasco sauce. You will tour the pepper factory and the island gardens. On Saturday night there will be a graduation dinner with six courses and complementary wines. Checkout and departure are on Sunday morning.

Included in the price are accommodations, cooking classes, all meals and excursions, taxes, and gratuities. No transportation is included; participants use their own vehicles. It is possible to extend your trip with additional days in New Orleans with prices available upon request. Call or e-mail for tour dates and details.

Visit California Wine County

Epiculinary: Distinctive Cooking Journeys (321 E. Washington Ave., Lake Bluff, IL 60044; 1-888-380-9010;

847-295-5363; fax 847-295-5371; www.epiculinary.com; www.epiculinary.com; Wine Country Weekend, $995 per person, $360 single supplement). Epiculinary is the leading provider of culinary vacations throughout the world, and some of the best are right here in the United States One of the three cooking adventures offered in California is a Wine Country Weekend. Visit beautiful Sonoma County, California, fewer than 30 miles north of San Francisco, with its scenic coastline and beaches, towering redwoods, 21 golf courses, fabulous restaurants, museums, festivals, spas, galleries, boutiques, and over 200 wineries.

Accommodations for the Wine Country Weekend are at McArthur Place, located 0.5 mile from Sonoma Center, a 15-minute drive from Napa Valley, and a 45-minute drive from San Francisco. McArthur Place is a 19th-century inn and spa that was originally a 300-acre vineyard and working ranch. The Manor House was built in the 1850s. Enjoy the seven acres of gardens filled with sculpture, and the full-service spa.

Your getaway weekend will include two cooking lessons at Ramekins Culinary School (www.ramekins.com/cookingabout.html) in Sonoma. The classes last about three hours and include recipes and a sampling of the dishes prepared. Arrival is on Friday, with check-in at McArthur Place, followed by an evening cooking class. Topics differ according to the season and session and may include pasta making, Mexican grilling, and global seafood. After a continental breakfast at the inn Saturday morning, there will be another cooking class, an afternoon massage, and a wine and cheese tasting at the inn followed by dinner on your own. After continental breakfast on Sunday, you may schedule a private food and wine tour of Sonoma County at an additional cost.

The price of the Country Wine Weekend includes two nights' accommodations, daily continental breakfast, two cooking classes, and one massage. Other spa services are available at an additional charge. For more information, log on to the Epiculinary Web site. For more information about Sonoma County, contact the Sonoma County Tourism Bureau: www.sonomacounty.com/contact/index, 1-800-576-6662, or info@sonomacounty.com.

Summertime Learning

Chautauqua Institution (1 Ames Ave., P.O. Box 28; Chautauqua, NY 14722; 1-800-836-2787; 716-357-6200; fax 716-357-9014; www.ciweb.org; boxoffice@ciweb.org; ticket prices vary widely from half-day and weekend rates to season passes). Chautauqua is a renowned summertime feast in the arts, philosophy, education, and recreation. Started in 1874 as a training center for Sunday school teachers, it grew into a center to explore both the spiritual and secular. There's something for everyone of every age with over 1,200 lectures, ballet, symphony, golf, and more.

A Classic Hotel

⑤⑤⑤⑤ **Athenaeum Hotel** (P.O. Box 33, 4 South Lake Dr., Chautauqua, NY 14722; 716-357-4444; 1-800-821-1881; www.ciweb.org; athenaeum1881@hotmail.com). This historic 1881 hotel on the Chautauqua grounds, listed on the National Historic Register, was renovated in 1984. The brick walkways and huge shade trees will make you want to sing "In the Good Old Summertime," sip lemonade, and read a great book.

Chautauqua County Visitors Bureau (P.O. Box 1441, Chautauqua Main Gate, NY 394, Chautauqua, NY 14722; 1-866-908-4569; www.tourchautauqua.com; info@tour chautauqua.com). Here you'll find lodging information on rented rooms (B&Bs to resorts), where to eat, and everything Chautauqua.

When Ann Met a Future President

> I'd heard about Chautauqua but never attended
> when, 20 years ago, friends who went there every
> summer called to ask if I wanted to take over their
> rental because they were unable to finish the sea-
> son. I said sure and that was it. The first time I
> walked into the philosophy hall I was totally
> hooked and keep going back for more. Last sum-
> mer, Dr. Ruth gave a fascinating lecture, but the
> most incredible event was when Bill Clinton was
> running for the presidency. He stopped by
> Chautauqua with his whole entourage, Al and
> Tipper Gore, the whole group. That was really
> very exciting.

Trailblazing

Kit Carson Home & Museum (113 Kit Carson Rd., Taos, NM
87571; 505-758-4741; www.newmexico.org/western/
learn/kit_carson_museum.php). Visit the former home of
Christopher Houston "Kit" Carson—rancher, guide, trap-
per, trailblazer, and army scout—listed on the State and
National Registers of Historic Buildings and Places and a
National Historic Landmark. See antique firearms, historic
artifacts, pioneer memorabilia, and books about the history of New Mexico. Born in Kentucky in 1809, Kit Carson
spent his childhood in Missouri before joining a wagon
train and traveling to Santa Fe, then settling in Taos,
which he used as his base for trapping expeditions
throughout the West.

Carson was employed as a hunter, then as a guide for John Fremont, who was a military officer, explorer, senator, and the first Republican candidate to run for the Presidency. Fremont's reports of crossing the mountains and deserts of the American West were read by many, contributing to Carson's fame. Fremont and Carson joined the Bear-Flag Rebellion just before the Mexican-American War, and led U.S. forces from New Mexico to California. Carson also carried dispatches to President Polk in Washington, D.C. before returning to Taos to ranch. He was appointed an Indian agent, and later became a colonel, then brigadier general, recognized for his bravery and service. He died in 1868, and was buried near his home in Taos.

Kit Carson's Love of Taos Lives On

Taos Solar Music Festival (P.O. Box 2110, Taos, NM 87571; 505-758-9191; www.solarmusicfest.com; taosfest@ solarmusicfest.com; three-day pass, $95). Time your trip to Taos to attend the Solar Music Festival, which celebrates great music, solar energy, and sustainable living. With an average of nearly three hundred days of sunshine a year, Taos is known as the Solar Capital of the World, so proclaimed by the governor of New Mexico in 1997. The festival takes place in June, in Kit Carson Park in downtown Taos.

Taos has a long history of sustainable living, from the earliest cliff dwellings with their southern exposure to the use of adobe bricks and passive solar design. Local green builders and a community dedicated to raise environmental awareness come together to offer interactive alternative energy displays and talented performers. Vendors, volunteers, and sponsors are welcome. Applications and information are available on the Web site.

For a taste of the preceding year's festivities, live downloads are available at FestivaLink.net. Call, e-mail, or

When visiting Taos, be sure to plan a day at Taos Pueblo, speaking with the people and learning all you can about this rich, vibrant culture. Good reading before or after your visit is *Taos Pueblo,* by Nancy Wood. Visit the beautiful native shops with all hand-made products; this drum shop has every size and sound available.

check the Web site for dates and scheduled events, lodging, and camping information. Additional information is available through the Taos Chamber of Commerce (1-800-732-TAOS, www.taoschamber.org).

Taos Pueblo (P.O. Box 1846, Taos, NM 87571; 505-758-1028; www.taospueblo.com; open to visitors daily from 8 AM to 4:30 PM, except when tribal rituals require closing, and 10 weeks late winter to early spring; adult, $10; students 13 and older, including college age with ID, $5; groups with 6 or more adults, $8 per person; children under age 13, free; camera and video fees; professional and commercial photographers and artists must apply for preapproval.) Taos Pueblo is an ancient community designated as a National Historic Landmark, and as a World

Taos Pueblo is a series of multistoried adobe buildings that have been continuously inhabited for over 1,000 years.

Heritage Site by the United Nations Educational, Scientific, and Cultural Organization (UNESCO). The all-adobe (earth mixed with straw and water) structures, Hlauuma (north house) and Hlaukwima (south house), have been continuously inhabited for over 1,000 years. The community holds an annual Powwow in July, Mother's and Father's Day Powwows in May and June, and Feast Days in the summer and fall. Visiting the Taos Pueblo will provide an

Tina and Susan prepare homemade fry bread and Indian tacos—absolutely delicious!

opportunity to learn about the history, art, and culture of the community. A map and walking tour can be found on the Web site.

A Native American Powwow

The Rappahannock Tribe's Annual American Indian Powwow (Rappahannock Tribe Cultural Center, 5036 Indian Neck Rd., Indian Neck, VA 23148; 804-769-0260;

www.rappahannocktribe.org/pow_wow.html; info@
rappahannocktribe.org; adults $5, children $3). The
Rappahannock tribe hosts their traditional Harvest
Festival and Powwow annually on the second Saturday in
October. They have a traditional dance group called the
Rappahannock Native American Dancers and a drum
group called the Maskapow Drum Group, which means
"Little Beaver" in the Powhatan language. Both of these
troupes perform locally and abroad in their efforts to edu-
cate the public on Rappahannock history and tradition.
Powwows have native dancing, drums, history, a native
village scene, crafts, and food.

The Powwow

Powwow is from the Algonquin *Pau Wau,* used to describe
medicine men and spiritual leaders. Native Americans
express their cultural heritage with sacred powwows all
over North America, which serve as meeting places for old
friends and new. Experiencing a powwow is a great way to
introduce children to Native American traditions. The Web
site www.powwow.com will help you find powwows in
your own community, nearby, or in a different location to
add a new dimension to your next vacation.

History Relived

Plimoth Plantation (137 Warren Ave., Plymouth, MA
02360; 508-746-1622; www.plimoth.org; www.plimoth
.org/dining-functions/thanksgiving-dining; program
services@plimoth.org; third Sat., Mar.–Nov. 30, 9 AM–5:30
PM, 7 days a week; $15–$90 for all-inclusive, two-day
pass). The museum has two locations: the Plimoth
Plantation, a 1627 English village, Wampanoag Homesite;
and the *Mayflower II,* on the Plymouth waterfront. The
1627 Harvest Dinners and Thanksgiving Day Dinners sell
out every year. The Annual Patuxet Strawberry

Thanksgiving is held in June. Native people celebrate thanksgivings throughout the year. The Strawberry Thanksgiving celebrated in the 17th century for the first fruit of the new growing season is reenacted through ceremony, singing, dancing, feasting, and games.

Myth vs. Reality

Donna Morganstern, Ph.D. (environment/social psychology) discusses myth vs. reality: "People visit places like Plimoth Plantation, Sturbridge Village, and Williamsburg, Virginia, looking for an idealized past. Living history museums, tied to public funds and historical societies, present the past as accurately as possible whereas an amusement park can make up its own version and doesn't have to be authentic. People go to Plymouth because of the myth that the Pilgrims settled on Plymouth Rock, worked cooperatively with the Native American Indians and, after a year, sat down and had a big dinner together. Too often when people go there they expect to go back in time to that myth, but it is only a myth. Because Plimoth Foundation is a museum, it doesn't reinforce that myth; it portrays people as they really were. It's worthwhile to instruct parents that they and their families will get more out of a living history experience if they educate themselves beforehand."

Joan and Dana's Experience

"I remember carefully watching my daughter's face as her mind worked through the information she was seeing and hearing," said Joan. "A woman dressed and speaking in character, preparing dinner for her family, asked us how we had gotten there."

"We drove," said Dana.

"Drove?" the woman asked. "What's that?"

"In a car," said Dana.

"I've never heard of a car," said the woman. "It brought you on your voyage?"

"Dana was quiet for a moment and then suddenly she caught on. "We came by boat."

"Ah, so did we," said the woman. "And how long did it take you?"

"A long time," said Dana. "We were in the boat for months and months."

"It was amazing. We were immersed in the time and place and a five-year-old shifted her perspective and understanding to experience differences between then and now."

To Remain True to Your Heritage

Amana Colonies (Amana Colonies Visitor Center and Convention and Visitor Bureau, 622 46th Ave., P.O. Box 310, Amana, IA 52203; 1-800-579-2294; 319-622-7622; www.AmanaColonies.org; info@amanacolonies.com). The Amana Colonies were established by settlers who had fled Germany looking for religious freedom. After first settling in Buffalo, New York, they traveled west in the 1850s, looking for farmland. The word *Amana* means "to remain true" and the settlers did, building their Community of True Inspiration in Iowa's River Valley. An example of successful communal living, on over 20,000 acres of land, the Colonies thrived until 1932, when the residents formed the Amana Society to manage their farmlands and businesses.

The seven villages of the Colonies were named a National Historic Landmark in 1965, and the Amana Heritage Society maintains the historic sites, which include four museums, a Communal Kitchen and Cooper Shop, the High Amana General Store, and Homestead Blacksmith Shop. You can walk through Amana, the largest of the villages, and see the site of the Amana Woolen Mill and the Amana Furniture Shop, two important industries for the community. You will see barns and agricultural buildings, communal kitchens, bakeries, schools, and churches. There are several historic communal buildings that offer hotel and bed & breakfast lodging to guests today, as well as restaurants that serve family-style German fare.

The Amana Society continues to manage the farm, pasture, and forests, and over 450 buildings remain today. The best-known business begun by an Amana native is Amana Refrigeration, Inc., now a modern, private plant at the site of the 19th-century Amana Woolen Mill. The Amana churches, however, look much the same as when the colonists first built them, and except for the addition of English, services have changed very little. There is a thriving arts community, and furniture and clock making are still prized industries, with workshops and galleries open to the public. For weekend and weeklong workshops, go to the Amana Arts Guild Web site at www.amanaartsguild.com.

Plan your visit to coincide with one of the many year-round festivals and events that include walking tours, craft demonstrations, arts and crafts exhibits, workshops, gallery tours, musical offerings, bike tours, GPS tours, a Renaissance Festival, and much more. For a complete schedule check the calendar on the Amana Colonies Web site. Complete your visit by driving the Amana Colonies Trail, which links the seven villages, walking or biking the

Practical Iowans

Iowans are practical-minded people. In addition to Amana appliances, the Maytag washer also had its roots in Iowa. Frederick Maytag arrived in Newton, Iowa, in 1893 via covered wagon and in 1907 produced the first washing machine.

Kolonieweg Recreational Trail, and hiking the Amana Colonies Nature Trail.

An Ongoing Teaching Memorial

Challenger Space Center (21170 N 83rd Ave., Peoria AZ 85382; 623-322-2001; www.azchallenger.org/index.htm; open 9 AM–4 PM Mon.–Fri. and 10 AM–4 PM Sat.; public programs 10:30–12:30 and 1–3). Educational programs for school-age children include a simulated space station, floating balcony, tour of the universe, and stargazing. Special programming includes camps, exploration of careers in aviation, online activities, and guest speakers.

Attend a Space Shuttle Launch

Kennedy Space Center (Cape Canaveral, FL 32899; 321-449-4444; www.kennedyspacecenter.com; daily 9 AM to 5:30 PM except Dec. 25 and certain launch days). Located 45 minutes from Orlando and Disney World, the Kennedy Space Center offers an entirely different world of possibilities: lunch with an astronaut, experiencing zero gravity, and astronaut training for a day. Space Center bus tours run from 10 AM until 2:15 PM daily for 2.5-hour rides. Check the Web site for upcoming launch dates and to order tickets to attend. Always review security information links on a Web site before visiting.

Bill's Dream

> My life's dream has been to see a space shuttle
> liftoff. It's one thing seeing it on television, but I
> can just imagine how powerful it would be to wit-
> ness it live. That's something I'd really like to do.

Space Adventures for Every Age

Cosmosphere (Kansas Cosmosphere and Space Center, 1100 North Plum, Hutchinson, KS 67501; 1-800-397-0330; 620-662-2305; www.cosmo.org/camps; laurieg@cosmo .org; Adult Astronaut Adventure two-day training pro- gram, $275, with two nights at local hotel, $400; Future Astronaut Training for grades 7–10, $650 for five days, including room and board; Mars Academy, a three-day res- idential camp for grades 5–6, $195; Overnight Space Adventures, a two-day program for grades 4–6, $50; Elderhostel Astronaut Training weeklong program, $300, commuter; $587, residential, double occupancy; $650, residential, single occupancy). The Cosmosphere offers astronaut and aviation camps for all ages.

The adult Astronaut Adventure is a two-day program for ages 18 and older and includes briefings by the Cosmosphere's staff, a tour of the Hall of Space Museum, and training on the Cosmosphere's flight simulators. Participants experience the Centrifuge, a G-force trainer, and fly the T-38 Advanced Flight Simulator. Not only that, you will direct a lunar mission, participate in a Robotic Challenge, and end your adventure with a space shuttle mission aboard the motion-based shuttle simulator, the Falcon. If you need accommodations, there is a package available that includes two nights' lodging in a local hotel.

The Future Astronaut Training Program, in its 23rd year, is a five-day, hands-on, fun-packed learning

Elderhostel Astronaut Training at the Kansas Cosmosphere and Space Center in the F-101 trainer.
Kansas Cosmosphere and Space Center

The Apollo 13 space capsule's third lunar attempt in April 1970 was aborted after the service module oxygen tank ruptured. Crew members James A. Lovell, John L. Swigert, and Fred W. Haise were successfully rescued. The capsule is located at the Kansas Cosmosphere and Space Center in Hutchinson, Kansas. *Kansas Cosmosphere and Space Center*

experience. Students entering grades 7 through 10 will train in spaceflight simulators, engage in shuttle crew exercises, take virtual spacewalks, have G-force training, and participate in rocket building and many other activities. There is a maximum of 30 campers per session, so check the Web site for availability, session dates, and detailed information.

The Kansas Cosmosphere and Space Center offers briefings, rocket building, and training on flight simulators, the Centrifuge, and the multiaxis trainer. *Kansas Cosmosphere and Space Center*

At the Mars Academy, students entering grades 5 and 6 will participate in a three-day program packed with space-related activities such as building robots, performing science experiments, watching IMAX movies and visiting the planetarium, and planning a simulated mission to Mars. Students will stay in Hutchinson Community College dorms and eat in the cafeteria, supervised by staff and counselors.

Overnight Space Adventures, for students entering grades 4 though 6, includes activities scheduled in the Cosmosphere until midnight. Students arrive at 5 PM, bring a sleeping bag, and sleep in the Cosmosphere. The fee includes supplies, evening meal, and breakfast, with children picked up at 10 AM

Elderhostel Astronaut Training, for adults 55 years and older, has been featured on NBC, CNN, NPR, and in the *New York Times.* The program includes educational briefings, rocket building, a tour of the Hall of Space Museum, and training on flight simulators, the Centrifuge, and the multiaxis trainer. Fly the T-38 Advanced Flight Simulator, plan a lunar rover mission, and fly a space shuttle mission aboard the shuttle simulator, *Falcon III.* Register through the Elderhostel program, www.elderhostel.org, or call the national office in Boston, 1-877-426-8056, and add your name to the catalog list.

Mary Catherine's Space Story

I've always been a big Apollo fan. I knew I'd never be an astronaut, but I wanted an experience to let me know a little bit about what it was like. Cosmosphere enabled me to do something I've always wanted to do and it is truly one of the best things I have ever done in my life. It was so much fun and it was the first class ever where there were more women registered than men. My team was four women and it was so neat getting to do a simulated space shuttle mission and seeing what it's like. It's pretty darn close to the real thing. Some astronauts have even done simulations there and said it's pretty darn close, too.

I liked the great teamwork and team-building exercises that were involved. You go into the centrifuge pull at about 4 Gs and it's quite an experience. I would think anybody who is a space buff or space nut would enjoy Cosmosphere for immersion space travel.

The instructors are incredible. They put the frosting on the cake, explaining things and bringing everything alive. I wish it had lasted a little longer. My program was two full days, Friday and Saturday. It was all so exciting it was over way too fast.

Salt of the Earth

Kansas Underground Salt Museum (3504 East Ave. G, P.O. Box 1864, Hutchinson, KS 67504; 620-662-1425; fax 620-662-0236; www.undergroundmuseum.org; info@ undergroundmuseum.org; open Tues.–Fri. 9 AM to 5 PM, Sat. 9 AM to 6 PM, and Sun. 1 to 6 PM; adults $13.50, children 4–12 years $8:50; discount for visitors who bring a Cosmosphere ticket stub). Travel 650 feet belowground to visit a museum in a working salt mine. The museum is built in a mined-out area and hard hats are required. The interior spaces are large and are rented out for events and weddings. The temperature remains at a constant 68 degrees, with low humidity, all year. In fact, because of the ideal climate conditions and depth, without risk of flood, tornadoes, and other natural disasters, there is a vault company that shares the mine space and many clients ship valuables to be stored there.

Your tour group will descend the equivalent of 65 stories into the earth, in a very dark, double-decker elevator, which takes only one minute and 15 seconds. After an electric-powered tram tour, dubbed "The Dark Ride," you can explore the exhibits on your own. The museum has developed the mine, with one huge room supported by columns of unmined salt. You will see old dynamite cases, a sinkhole formed by water that melts the salt, photographs and videos, and vintage mining equipment. The working part of the mine is located several miles from the museum, and there is no daytime blasting. The Hutchinson Salt Company excavates 500,000 tons of rock salt each year.

The city of Hutchinson, nicknamed Salt City, is also home to the Kansas Cosmosphere and Space Center (www .cosmo.org), the Dillon Nature Center (www.hutchrec .com/dnc), the Hutchinson Zoo (hutchgov.com/department /index.asp?fDD=18-0), and many other attractions. If you plan your trip in September, try to visit during the Kansas State Fair, the largest event in Kansas (www.kansasstatefair.com). For more information, visit the Hutchinson Convention and Visitors Bureau (www .visithutch.com/attractions.htm).

Lyle's Salty Story

They don't mine that far but the salt deposits extend under many states, from Missouri to New Mexico. I didn't realize we had that much salt under the ground, and it's thicker in some places than others. When we think of salt on the table, that's a very small part of where salt goes.

Another neat thing is the archives. The humidity and temperature are so constant in the salt mine, they store lots of documents and papers that they don't want to erode. Hollywood has costumes there for safekeeping, like the original Batman costume. There are X-rays and medical records that don't decay and an original newspaper from the time of Lincoln's presidency that hasn't yellowed at all.

Life as a Lighthouse Keeper

Chesapeake Bay Maritime Museum (213 North Talbot St., St. Michaels, MD 21663; 410-745-2916; www.cbmm .org; info@cbmm.org; for information on lighthouse program, contact the Education Department, 410-745-2916). This museum is geared toward learning, immersion, and interaction. They offer an array of activities, including learning to bait a crab pot, build wooden boats, and carve decoys. An immersion-travel delight is the restored Hooper Strait Lighthouse, one of only three screwpile lighthouses remaining in the country. Families can make reservations to stay overnight in the lighthouse to experience life as lighthouse keepers during the summer months. In the fall the overnight program is available to scout groups and organizations. For information on the overnight program for groups, call the Education Department at 410-745-2916. An Apprentice-for-a-Day program is offered every Saturday and Sunday from 10 AM to 4 PM; $15 for members, $25 for nonmembers. Make reservations with the boatyard manager: 410-745-2916, ext. 186, or e-mail afad@cbmm.org.

Protecting the Waterways

Hudson River Sloop *Clearwater* (112 Little Market St., Poughkeepsie, NY 12601; 1-800-67-SLOOP; 854-454-7953; www.clearwater.org/index.html; office@clearwater.org). Clearwater supports environmental education and advocacy programs, and believes people can make a difference in bringing about a safer and cleaner world. Its main mission is to protect the Hudson River and to educate people about the importance of the river's relationship with the coastal zone.

The *Clearwater* is a 106-foot wooden sailing sloop, launched in 1969, that accommodates nearly 13,000 children and adults each year for educational sails. Come aboard and learn about the Hudson River, New York Harbor, and Long Island Sound. You will help hoist the sails and then visit different learning stations, which may include: fish, plankton, invertebrates, sediments, water chemistry, sailing, and navigation.

There are public sails scheduled in conjunction with waterfront events, and members of the organization are offered regularly scheduled sails. Group sails may be chartered, and *Clearwater's* programs are also used by schools, education centers, and youth groups. Adult groups from nonprofit environmental centers and outing clubs also use the sloop, and the education staff will provide the right program for your needs. The *Clearwater* sails from April through November, and scheduling is usually done five months in advance. For information on scheduling and fees, call *Clearwater* or e-mail ClassWaves@Clearwater.org. Applications are easily downloaded from the Web site.

Where the Sea Lions Play

Monterey Bay Aquarium: Sailing Adventures (886 Cannery Row, Monterey, CA 93940; 831-648-4800;

www.montereybayaquarium.org/efc/efc_programs/
adventures_sailing.asp;aquariumadventures@mbayaq.org;
three-hour day sails, adults $69, youth ages 10–17 $59,
$10 discount for aquarium members; sunset sails, 90 min-
utes, $55 per person general public, $45 per person
aquarium members). Join aquarium staff aboard a 65-foot
sailboat and gather plankton, test water samples, and
learn about the Monterey Marine Sanctuary.

Take a turn at the helm and learn about navigation and
sailing. Most probably there will be whales, dolphins, and
sea otters, all common visitors to the bay. The three-hour
day sails are for ages 10 to adult, on Saturdays and
Sundays, May 11 to June 15; Wednesday through Sunday,
June 18 to August 31; Friday through Sunday, September
5 to 28. On Saturdays there are sails at both 10 AM and
2 PM, on Sundays at 10 AM, and other days at 2 PM.

The Aquarium also offers sunset sails for ages 10 to
adult on Fridays and Saturdays, May 16 to June 14;
Wednesday through Sunday, June 18 to August 30; and
Fridays and Saturdays, September 5 to 27. These are 90-
minute sails at 6 PM, May 16–31, and at 5:30 PM, June 6 to
September 27. Wine and refreshments are served.

Explore the Aquarium too, view films, and come early
for the Morning Rounds: Behind-the-Scenes Tour, ages 8 to
adult, and see what goes into the start of each day at the
Aquarium. Interact with exhibit animals and even feed
some of them before the Aquarium is open to the public.

There are two wonderful adventures offered for children. They can be underwater explorers (ages 8–18) and
surface scuba dive with Aquarium staff in the Great Tide
Pool, or join the Youth Group Seashore Sleepover program
(ages 6–14) and spend a night at the Aquarium, exploring
after hours, with a variety of staff-led activities all
evening. Check the Aquarium Web site for dates, times
and fees, and for information on other programs and
guided tours.

Mark's Story

The Aquarium and the sailing are terrific, but don't forget to simply look at the water on your way in and way out. The day my wife and I were there, between the buildings on Cannery Row and in Monterey Bay, there were so many sea lions just doing their thing it was awesome. I had to remind myself that I wasn't in Disneyland and that the animals were there because they wanted to be; they lived there and I was privileged to see them enjoying their natural habitat, eating, playing, and sunning themselves. It was a highlight of my trip and made me want to learn more about sea lions and seek out other places that I could observe them. They are truly fascinating creatures.

Build a Boat and Take It Home

The Antique Boat Museum (750 Mary St., Clayton, NY 13624; 315-686-4104; fax 315-686-2775; abm.org; lnadolski@abm.org; open May–Oct., 9 AM to 5 PM daily; Family Boatbuilding, 5 days, $1,250 per boat; Double Paddle Canoe Building, 2½ days, $250; Traditional Paddle-Making, 1 day, $135; Junior Sailing for ages 8–15, 42 hours of classes, $240, scholarships available). The museum has a waterfront campus on the St. Lawrence River shoreline that includes exhibit space, facilities for public programs, boat collection storage, archives, and a library. Programs include something for every boating enthusiast. Learn to sail or build a boat with your family.

The annual Family Boatbuilding Program is when families and friends work together at the Antique Boat Museum to learn how to build their very own cottage skiff. *Antique Boat Museum*

Family Boatbuilding is a five-day course, using a kit for the "Cottage Skiff," a flat-bottomed design, to build a boat you will be able to take home with you. No experience is necessary, as you will learn the basics of boatbuilding, and the museum provides all materials and hands-on help. At the end of the course you and your family will launch and row your finished skiff.

In Double Paddle Canoe Building you will learn how to build a skin-on-frame boat in a 2½-day course. You and your classmates will work on a canoe that will be raffled

This shellback dinghy was built at the Antique Boat Museum by a group from the Crescent Yacht Club of Chaumont, New York. It now serves as part of the museum's sailing fleet. *Antique Boat Museum*

off at the end of the course. There are additional charges to cover the materials. This course is for all levels, and you will return home with the knowledge and skills to build your own skin-on-frame boat. Choose a one-day course in Traditional Paddle-Making and starting with a cherry plank, using only hand tools, you will craft a finished paddle to take home with you.

The museum offers a Junior Sailing program for beginner and advanced students. It is a two-week course that includes classroom instruction and hands-on boat handling and is limited to six students. There is also a popular Wednesday Night Sailing program, which has recently been expanded into an Oar, Paddle & Sail Night. Museum gates open, free to the public, at 5 PM, and participants are able to try all different kinds of small craft. No experience is necessary, as there will be experienced staff and volunteers to help you. Check the museum Web site for dates during July and August. No reservations accepted.

The museum also offers boater safety courses, a class in GPS navigating, and an opportunity to get your captain's license, towing endorsement, or marine radio operator permit. Check the Web site for a complete schedule, dates, and prices, and a calendar of events. And don't forget to visit the museum's many exhibits, including a tour of a 1903 houseboat.

In the Appalachian Mountains

John C. Campbell Folk School (One Folk School Rd., Brasstown, NC 28902; 1-800-365-5724; fax 828-837-8637; www.folkschool.org; info@folkschool.org; rates vary with accommodations, meals, and length of stay). Name any handcraft and you can learn how to make it at this school, which began in 1925. Blacksmithing, beading, basketry, broom making, banjo picking, arbor sculpture, cooking,

In the blacksmith shop, students learn how to shape hot metal into useful and ornamental objects such as hooks, fireplace tools, candleholders, and bells. *John C. Campbell Folk School*

cabinetry, doll making, enameling, quilting, furniture, and woodworking are a few of the 800 classes offered. Housing and meals are provided for an easy weekend escape or longer getaways for travel groups, couples, singles, friends, and intergenerational family reunions.

Rand McNally Atlas named Brasstown as a "Best of the Road" destination in the westernmost corner of North Carolina in the Appalachian Mountains.

Exploring the infinite possibilities of kaleidoscope making. *John C. Campbell Folk School*

Anne's Story

Brasstown is a tiny mountain town in North
Carolina that's not too far from Georgia or
Tennessee. I wanted to learn quilting and realized I
wasn't going to do it unless I separated myself
from my daily life to focus on learning the skills I
needed. I had read about the John C. Campbell
School of Folk Art in a magazine, called them, and
signed up. They have cabins, campground, and a
lodge. The price includes all of the classes,

Learning the traditional craft of weaving colorful rag rugs from strips of cotton. *John C. Campbell Folk School*

housing, and delicious meals with wonderful homemade breads.

Every day for two weeks I went to the quilting shed. I had to bring my own sewing machine. We pieced by machine and then quilted by hand. We worked solidly all morning and broke for a wonderful communal meal, and then worked through the afternoon and broke for dinner. The experience took on a very satisfying rhythm, and I learned in the most relaxed way, in a beautiful mountain landscape surrounded by lovely people and nice conversation. I made a wall hanging with three large squares in an intricate pattern that hangs on my wall and brings me great pleasure.

Vision Quest

Animas Valley Institute (P.O. Box 1020, Durango, CO 81302; 1-800-451-6327; 970-259-0585; fax 970-259-1225; www.animas.org; soulcraft@animas.org). Bill Plotkin, Ph.D. began the Animas Valley Institute, which centers on soul encounters, in 1980. The 10-day Vision Quest is a contemporary interpretation of a Native American coming-of-age ritual that involves staying alone and fasting for three days in the wilderness. The program has five phases: preparation, severance, initiation, reincorporation, and implementation. Preparation involves preparing your gear and creating ceremonies that will be used to begin the process. Severance includes purification rites, walking out into the wilderness to find your spot in nature, and a review of wilderness and camping skills. Initiation is three days of staying in the desert wilderness alone. Then there is the reincorporation phase of rejoining civilization. Finally, there is implementation, the socialization transformation occurring after returning home and applying what has been learned. Fees: $1,395 for 10 days; does not include transportation. Financial aid is available.

Venita's 40th Birthday Present to Herself

I have three wonderful children ages 10, 8, and 6. In the last 10 years I never stopped to come up for air. Now here I am, turning 40, and my kids are old enough for me to step back and breathe a little bit and assess what now and where to go. I can do what I want to do, but I have no awareness of what that is, nor do I have the time to even think what it might be.

One night when I couldn't sleep I started searching the Internet for some answers. When I found Vision Quest, I knew the 10-day journey was what I needed to do. Now that I'm preparing to go, I can see all of the pieces fitting together.

Today I ventured off, fasting for the day on my first sunrise-to-sunset walk. I was very nervous and kept telling myself I'm going to get to the hiking path and just go for it. I'll have a ceremony at the

Venita's personal vision quest began with a day's solo hiking and fasting in the Everglades National Park, Florida.

beginning of the day for strength and wisdom. I said to the universe, Wherever you want me to go, whatever you want me to do, I'm just going for it. I followed a sketchy map through a pinelands forest, not knowing where I was going, and I ended up

6 miles later at a lake, burning hot, exhausted, and spent. At that moment the rains came to cool me off. The walk symbolized my life in many ways, my not knowing exactly where I'm going but having what I need to get there.

3

Working

Explore Internships and Short- and Longer-Term Job Opportunities

Work is either fun or drudgery. It depends on your attitude. I like fun.

—COLLEEN C. BARRETT, *President, Southwest Airlines*

Working a real job, albeit temporarily for a short or longer period of time, is a great way to step into other people's lives. The job provides a structure to fit into the population and earn respect. It helps the outsider appreciate the local culture and ways of life, contribute in a positive way, and get to know the community and vice versa.

In this chapter you'll also find information about paid and unpaid internships. With these come the possibility of expanding new interests, studies, and careers. Seasonal tourism locations need people to work all kinds of jobs that often do not require previous experience. It's a great opportunity to live in a new place, with the income paying for the experience. Activity listings include a wide range

Immersion Travel

Work it out.

of sales, food services, housekeeping, hotel management, and tourist guide positions.

How to Find a Job in a National Park

In looking for employment within national parks it might surprise you that working for a national park doesn't necessarily mean that you'll actually be employed by the park. Glacier, Yellowstone, and Denali National Parks, among others, are run by hired concessionaires. Each park has its own system for hiring, which includes online applications. Some are managed by outside companies that do the hiring, such as Xanterra or Aramark. Tips for evaluating jobs found over the Internet, handling telephone interviews, references, and tweaking your résumé can be found in the introduction of this book. National Parks employ people of all ages. It is very common to meet retirees who travel from park to park during the summer in a motor home or live in employee housing for the season. Couples and singles are encouraged to apply and enjoy an extended vacation that can pay for itself.

Jack's Take-Action Story

Sitting in the Metropolitan Opera House in New York City, waiting for the curtain to rise on the second act of *La Traviata,* the man seated next to me leaned over and said, "Can you believe this is

Ryah and a coworker staff the front desk in the McKinley Village Lodge, Denali, Alaska.

the first opera I've ever attended and my first trip into New York City?"

"Where are you from?" I asked.

"Whitefish, Montana, surrounded by Glacier National Park."

"I've always wanted to go there."

"You'd best start planning your trip right now or down the road you'll be doing what I'm doing, sitting here kicking myself, wondering what I was so busy with that I didn't do all of the things I wanted to do. Go to Glacier before the glaciers are gone, be sure to take a tour in a red bus and, better yet, get yourself a job in the park and have the time of your life."

Be a naturalist who shows tourists the sights along nature trails or in the wilderness.

Park Transportation

In the 1930s, the White Motor Company built about five hundred touring sedans for use in Bryce Canyon, Glacier, Grand Canyon, Mt. Rainier, Yellowstone, Yosemite, and Zion National Parks. Glacier National Park has a fleet of historic red buses that are driven by seasonally hired drivers who give oral histories of the park for visiting tourists.

Ryah's Career Plan

I was finding it difficult breaking into hotel management positions in California, and a friend suggested that large tourist areas, like Denali National Park and others, desperately need bodies to fill all of the positions. I applied for the front desk with Aramark Corporation's McKinley Village Lodge. My second year I had top seniority, and my third year I worked as an assistant manager, giving me the experience and credentials I needed to continue in the field wherever I want.

How to Find a Job at Glacier National Park

Glacier National Park Service (P.O. Box 128, West Glacier, MT 59936-0128; 406-888-7800; www.glacier. national-park.com/jobs.htm; www.usajobs.opm.gov; www.gpihr.com; www.gpihr.com/positions.asp?CO=USA &tJobsPage). Temporary, seasonal, and full-time positions are available through the National Park Service as well as

Dave manages hotel restaurants in a seasonal position.

Glacier Park, Inc. (GPI), a concessionaire of Glacier National Park. Summer intern positions are filled locally through the Park Service. Applications and information are available by e-mailing the Park Service Information Office at Glacier: glac_information@nps.gov.

GPI operates seven hotels and restaurants, five gift shops, a pro golf shop, four camp stores, and the Red Bus Tours. The season is mid-May through September. Applications can be made directly online at www.gpihr .com/hronline/application.asp?season=2008?CO=USA%3Ft JobsPage%3D3. Summer employee positions include main-

Work as a massage therapist in a hotel.

tenance workers, personnel manager, guest service agent, dining room host, night auditor, restaurant chef, tour guides, shuttle bus drivers, employee recreation coordinator, bell porters, security guards, hospitality, sales, and more.

Employment housing and dining halls are provided (often for a fee that is deducted from the employee's salary), along with employment. Securing a temporary seasonal job is like applying for any other job in that you need to be your own advocate. Ask to negotiate the room and board fees. If you need a block of time off during the summer, let the employer know up front and be honest regarding your availability to work.

"We often run short on staff mid to late season," says Cindy Bjorklund, interpretive specialist, North Cascades National Park, Sedro Woolley, Washington. "If you didn't get a position you wanted preseason it could be very wise to check back in with the employer later in the season."

Retail Sales in the Parks

Arlene's Story

I'm 57, single, and like to travel in the summer to interesting places. I'm a bookkeeper and find that my work can travel with me for the few months I'm away. Seasonal jobs in retail sales are simple to get all over the country because of the influx of tourists. It's as simple as that.

I found my first job through www.cool works.com, in the gift shop at Yellowstone National Park. I loved the work itself, talking to the guests, and keeping the merchandise in good shape. The housing left a lot to be desired. I was given a top bunk and three drawers to hold all of my stuff. Luckily I'd driven, so I used my car as my closet.

The hardest adjustment was sharing the bunkhouse with 19 college kids playing loud music and staying up all night. I now know that I could

Sales positions in gift shops are fun and will leave you time off to tour.

have applied for certain management positions that came with private housing instead of the bunkhouse. I've learned that I don't want to room with workers my children's ages and now only take on adventures with a private room included or arrange my own housing. Another adventure I'm considering is investing in a motor home. Then, as they say on the road, I'd always be home wherever I go.

Living and Working in the Grand Canyon

Greg's Story

I used to live in Phoenix and visit national and state parks on the weekends. Now I live in Grand Canyon Village, work for Xanterra on the South Rim, and visit Phoenix occasionally. Fifteen years before I moved here, a park ranger at Painted Desert (Arizona) planted the seed by saying that living in a national park is the ultimate life experi-

A Must Stop on the Way to the Everglades National Park

Robert Is Here (19200 SW 344th St., Homestead, FL 33034; 305-246-1592; fax 305-242-4122; www.robertishere.com; fresh@robertishere.com; open daily 8 AM–7 PM; closed Sept. and Oct.). Make sure you stop here on the way to Everglades National Park. The story goes that Robert was six years old when his father sat him in a chair, on the corner of their property, with a bushel of cucumbers and said, "Sell these." At the end of the day Robert hadn't sold any, so the next day Robert was again assigned to the corner, but this time he was seated under a huge sign that read Robert is Here, with a huge arrow pointing down. People stopped to find Robert. Before noon he'd sold out and walked home. Robert is still farming that corner and selling the produce in an extensive fruit stand with live music on the weekends and fresh fruit milkshakes to die for, especially the cherry key lime and papaya passion fruit.

Tamara worked her way up through housekeeping to manage entire hotel properties.

ence. It took me a while, but eventually I took the
plunge and found a park job. Every day here is full
of unexpected pleasures, with deer casually walking by my front door, elk scraping their antlers
along the outside of my office, and my hiking up
Bright Angel Trail with bighorn sheep.

The lifestyle is even better than what I imag-
ined it could be. The Grand Canyon is my work
and playground. I wake up every morning and walk

five minutes out of my front door to watch the sunrise over the Grand Canyon. It's unbelievable.

Finding a Career

Andrew's Story

I applied for park ranger positions through www.USAjobs.com. Five years ago, I worked in the Everglades at Shark Valley for the winter as a seasonal employee, and then went to Mesa Verde for their four-month winter season, and while I was

Drive a bus.

working in Colorado, I was applying to return to
the Everglades. There were few positions and I had
to stay on top of it.

My undergraduate degree is in natural
resources land management and outdoor recreation. I wanted law enforcement, so I decided to
gamble on myself and my future by investing
$3,000 of my own money (which included room
and board but not transportation) to attend the
Seasonal Law Enforcement Academy, a 7 1/2-week
course in California. There was no guarantee of a
job after completing the course, but it worked out
okay. I have a full-time year-round position as a
United States Park Ranger in law enforcement,
vehicle and vessel coordinator, Flamingo District,
Everglades National Park.

How to Apply for a Park Ranger Position

National Park Service (NPS) job offerings
(www.nps.gov/personnel; www.usajobs.com). The federal
government's official job site is USA Jobs. Research available positions in locations where you are interested in living. Full-time and seasonal jobs are listed according to
the park and include the dates during which applications
are accepted. For the summer season, jobs are posted in
the winter and most applications are due in December.
For the winter season, applications tend to be due in July.
Once you are registered, keep checking the job page to

Become an oral interpreter, entertaining and educating tourists on the history, culture, and background of the locale.

see what additional positions of interest are posted and to update your résumé.

There will be positions for park rangers, program managers, superintendents, law enforcement personnel, environmentalists, lab technicians, biologists, botanists, interpreters, and possibly even bear counters. Each job description has a rating system used to evaluate experience, education, and qualifications. When applying for the first time you will not know your rating. Apply for every position you feel qualified for.

Seasonal Employees with a Full-Time Gig

Dale and Kirk's Story

"Lots of people thought we were nuts when we sold our home and business to buy a motor home and go to work for the National Park Service. At 68½, I've finally got the job I always wanted. It's like being a camp counselor for adults. I'm a park ranger doing oral interpretation. It's great. We live in the Everglades in the winter and Yellowstone in the summer.

"Since Kirk is applying for seasonal positions, he gets the job first and then I find one," says Dale. "He applies each season and lets his boss know he plans to come back and that his application is in the system. In Yellowstone, I was able to get a job through Xanterra selling retail in the gift shop. In the Everglades, I worked in the visitor center, at

the boat dock, and with the hotel. Now I'm fortu-
nate that a job was created for me. I rotate
between a number of departments that need
office, computer, and managerial help."

Park Your Camper in a Beautiful Spot

Workamping (www.work-camping.com) is the popu-
larly used shortened form of Work Camping, which refers
to people who own their own RVs and trade services for
free camping sites plus stipends or wages. The job usually involves overseeing and maintaining a recreational
outdoor facility in remote, beautiful surroundings, similar
to being a campground host in a state or national park,
usually with a salary.

Outgoing and Personable Are Valued Traits

Averill's Flathead Lake Lodge (P.O. Box 248, 150
Flathead Lake Lodge Rd., Bigfork, MT 59911; 406-837-
4391; fax 406-837-6977; www.flatheadlakelodge.com;
info@flatheadlakelodge.com). Flathead Lake Lodge is a
2,000-acre, family-operated dude ranch located on the
shores of Flathead Lake, in the Rocky Mountains of northwest Montana, just 35 miles south of Glacier National
Park. The ranch combines a western atmosphere and complete horse program with water sports, fishing, and tennis. Yearly, the lodge hires 40 to 50 individuals to work
various positions, including general ranch hands, fishing
guides, children's programming staff, receptionists and
front desk staff, wait staff, kitchen staff, wranglers, and
housekeepers. Requirements include good communication skills, excellent work ethic, gregarious personality,
and physical stamina.

Special training is needed to become a whitewater raft tour guide.

Joyce's Story

I was in my 40s and divorced when my executive job with IBM disappeared. I moved in with my father, who lived alone and needed a lot of medical support. That was fine for awhile until the rigors of being a full-time caregiver wore me down. I desperately needed an adventure. I'd always dreamed about going to Alaska, but money was tight. In the middle of the night, I searched the

Consider working in the kitchen as a cook, server, or dishwasher. *Rene Courtney*

Internet for summer employment and within one week landed a job as a food server at the Gold Rush Restaurant in Denali Park, Alaska. I hadn't worked as a waitress since my college days, but it came back even more quickly than riding a bike, and the income and tips more than paid for my adventure.

Hot Springs Are an Added Perk

The Sleeping Buffalo Hot Springs Resort (659 Buffalo Trl., Saco, MT 59261; 406-527-3370; www.sleeping buffalo.blogspot.com; mthotspring@gmail.com). This resort is looking for couples who would like to trade 20 hours of work in hotel management, maintenance, and housekeeping for a modern heated cabin. They have an ongoing need for helpers skilled in electric and plumbing and daily operations of the hotel and housekeeping. The area has significant Native American history. There's ice fishing, seasonal hunting, and bird-watching. The resort is rustic and in the process of restoration. There are four new hotel rooms and other vintage rooms on the property. There is also a café and for additional hours worked,

Be a wrangler, a ranch hand, or lead trail rides. *Rene Courtney* a discount of 50 percent on food purchases will be arranged with the owner. This could be an immersion swap to visit the area, work, and learn what goes into operating a hot springs resort. An added perk is full access to the hot spring pools.

Summer Jobs on the Water

San Juan Safaris (P.O. Box 2749, Friday Harbor, WA 98250; 1-800-450-6858; 360-378-1323; fax 360-378-6546; www.sanjuansafaris.com; fun@sanjuansafaris.com). Applicants should read the detailed Web site to understand the company's business philosophy before submitting a cover letter and résumé via e-mail, post, or fax in November or December. San Juan Safaris employs a staff of 30 in ecotourism, adventure travel, commercial outfitting, guide services, whale-watching/wildlife-viewing, and sea-kayaking tours. Positions include whale-watch naturalist, first mate, kayak manager, sea-kayak guide, desk manager for sales and appointment desks, dock hand, apprentice guide, vessel captain, and operations manager. Work commitment is five days per week in June, July, and August. The staff return rate is 75 percent. Staff often rent summer housing to share expenses, living on San Juan Island for about $300 per month rent, plus food and personal expenses. Employees are paid an hourly wage with an additional $2 per hour bonus upon completion of the contract agreement.

It Pays to Cruise

Carnival Cruise Lines (1-888-CARNIVAL; www .carnival.com). A cruise ship is like a self-contained traveling city with an estimated three hundred different kinds of jobs, including audio/visual media, casino, entertainment, gift shop, golf, information systems, medical, spa,

It would be nice to work with kayaks, leading tours and teaching others how to paddle.
Rene Courtney

beauty, fitness, and a destination shopping specialist whose job is to promote port sales in docking locations. Employees are of all ages, pay scales are comparable to land jobs, and room and board are included as part of the deal. An upbeat personality, being well-spoken, and having people skills all go far in this line of work. Jobs range from a few hours to years, depending on the position, and you can apply according to your needs and availability.

Erin's Entertaining Story

Carnival Cruise Lines say they are "Fun Ships" and that's exactly what they are. I went on a cruise my senior year in college, and thought it would be a great place to work after graduating as a theater major. I collected information on how to apply for a job, met people, and asked who to speak to and what the best job would be. I didn't want to be a singer or dancer. I wanted to be a production manager, organizing and executing the shows on the ship with the actors, dancers, and singers. As soon as I got home I applied and left for work the first day of August. I took a six-month position and stayed a year, running everything for three huge main stage shows a week, every other night another show. I worked six nights a week. It was too difficult a job to hand it over to someone else to fill in. There was constant movement and change with short-term musicians arriving for a

Erin and the Carnival Cruise Line mascot, Fun Ship Freddie.

week or two and comedians flying into one port and leaving at the next. People do that for years and years.

The hard part is that you have to be fully committed to the life on sea and not have much of a life on land. The traveling was the best and I loved meeting people. There was a crew of 1,000 people on the ship. I have friends from all over the world with places to stay wherever I want to travel.

🕐 ⇄ On-Board Lecturers

Cruise lines hire a wide variety of guest seminar speakers, workshop facilitators, and lecturers for seminars aboard cruise ships. Baby boomers are excellent candidates for these jobs, building on their expertise and know-how. Different cruise lines cater to different clientele and interests. It's best to plan a few program possibilities and begin doing your research of the ships and the curricula offered. Although the possible workshop topics are endless, many fall into two categories: destination lectures inform and educate guests about where they are going and what they will be seeing, and special interest lectures depend upon the speakers' expertise and credentials in everything from the stock market to wildlife to astrology. Speakers' contracts and salaries vary depending on the cruise line.

For Professional Emerging Artists Building Careers

Skowhegan School of Painting & Sculpture (year-round, 200 Park Ave. S., Suite 1116, New York, NY 10003-1503; 212-529-0505; fax 212-473-1342; www.skowhegan art.org; mail@skowheganart.org; summer, P.O. Box 449, Skowhegan, ME 04976, 207-474-9345). Skowhegan offers a nine-week summer residency program for emerging visual artists. Tuition, room, and board fees are $5,500, with an activities fee of $50 and an application fee of $40. Partial and full fellowships toward tuition, room, and board are available, and financial status is not a consideration in the admissions process. Financial assistance forms for each session will be available in November when the application is posted on the Web site. Admission is primarily based on work samples (10 images or a 5-minute video), and applicants must be at least 21 years old. Skowhegan

Elanit throws buckets the size of half a thumb at the Skowhegan School of Painting and Sculpture. The buckets evolved from drawings of the vascular vessels of the heart.

strives to admit a diverse group of artists each summer in order to provide a stimulating and rigorous environment for personal growth and artistic creation.

Participants live on campus with room and board and individual studio space. Accommodations are in cottages set on a large lake, with meals in a separate dining hall. There is a quiet rule in living quarters after 11 PM, and a 24-hour common house for social activity a short walk from the cottages. Artists' studios are open 24 hours a day. There are 300 acres of forest, pastures, and lakefront participants are encouraged to use for their work. Facilities include a wood and metal shop, a darkroom, a multimedia lab, and a library.

Faculty artists live on campus, lecture on their work, and meet individually with participants. Visiting artists also lecture and provide critiques. Participants get together weekly for an open critique. Performances, discussion, and reading groups, as well as community and off-campus projects, are also encouraged. Founded by artists and still run by artists for artists, a Skowhegan residency is an immersion experience of a lifetime.

Elanit's Artistic Points

Skowhegan is a highly competitive program. It is a very selective artists' residence summer colony. Some people apply three, four, or more times before being accepted, and others apply forever and never get in. When I attended, the majority of participants were new graduates from Master of Fine Arts programs with an age range from 21 to about 45 or 50. The selection committee is comprised of artists in the field who have shown their work at highly elite competitive venues such as the Venice Bienniale. It's a very rewarding experience surrounded by other professionals devoted to their art, viewing and reviewing yours, in tranquil and beautiful Maine.

Aye Aye, Captain

The Nautical School (178 West Hoffman Ave., Lindenhurst, NY 11757; 1-800-992-9951; fax 516-681-5589; www.nauticalschool.com; fees vary according to course).

Classes are offered in New York, New Jersey, Massachusetts, Maryland, and Connecticut, and they also create classrooms for groups to earn licenses to drive a boat with passengers. The faculty is composed of professional licensed captains working in the field. Students are from every walk of life, including boat owners who want to stay up-to-date and anyone interested in pursuing employment as a boat captain.

Working with Dolphins

Dolphin Quest Hawaii: (Hilton Waikoloa Village, 425 Waikoloa Beach Dr., Waikoala, HI 96738; 808-886-2875; fax 808-886-7030; dolphinquest.org; dqhawaii@dolphin quest.org; **Dolphin Quest Oahu:** The Kahala Hotel & Resort, 5000 Kahala Ave., Honolulu, HI 96826; 808-739-

Interns at Dolphin Quest in Oahu gain hands-on experience with a playful dolphin.
Dolphin Quest

Visitors and a dolphin interact with smiles all around in Hawaii. *Dolphin Quest*

8918; fax 808-737-8311; dqoahu@dolphinquest.org; internship coordinator, c/o Dolphin Quest, 1880 Harbor Island Dr., San Diego, CA 92101; interns@dolphinquest .org). Since 1988, Dolphin Quest has provided a place where people and dolphins can interact. It is an international organization dedicated to education and the preservation of marine wildlife. You can literally be immersed in the world of the dolphin, and share a connection few people ever experience. The Dolphin Quest mission is to touch hearts and minds through fun, innovative experiences that create a connection to nature and a passion to learn more.

Explore the marine mammal field as a full-time Dolphin Quest intern, and gain hands-on experience working with trainers, educators, and other crew members. Applicants are required to complete an online application as well as send a cover letter, résumé, three letters of rec-

A magnificent dolphin jumps for joy. *Dolphin Quest*

ommendation, and college transcripts. You must be at least 18 years of age and be able to maintain a high energy level throughout the day. You need to be a strong swimmer and be able to work, unpaid, for three to four months. Past experience with animals is not required but is favorable, as is scuba certification. You will be responsible for your own food, transportation, and lodging costs.

Interns will experience all facets of the training and care of Atlantic bottlenose dolphins, with emphasis on food preparation for the dolphin, interaction between dolphins and guests, public-speaking programs, children's education, daily swimming, and record keeping. A lecture series covering animal training, behavioral enrichment, veterinary practices, education, conservation efforts, natural history, and other topics will be given during the course of the internship. A part-time Conservation

Education Internship is available as well, with the opportunity to perform a variety of tasks relating to marine and environmental education with the goal of learning to conduct all aspects of Dolphin Quest's public education programs.

Check the Web site for program dates and application deadlines, as well as job opportunities, careers working with marine mammals, and animal welfare information.

Drive a Bus or Ride the Trains

Princess Tours (Seattle Port Operations, Seattle Port Operations Recruiting Manager; 206-336-5877; www.princessjobs.com). Princess Tours hires personnel to staff cruises, lodges, motor coaches, ports, and rails. The Web site is filled with many summer job opportunities in Alaska with motor coach and passenger services. Princess Tours conducts training programs to help new employees obtain their commercial drivers' licenses, most running from February through April. Training includes about six hours each week of individual and classroom work. Instruction programs are offered in Rexburg, Idaho; Provo, Utah; and Bellingham, Washington; among other locations. Course work is also available for tour guides.

Sarah's Road Gig

I've been driving for Holland America for six years in Alaska. The scenery is beautiful and the guests are very happy to be here. I enjoy collecting stories to share with my riders. It's a big responsibility and can get tense with mechanical failures, but all in all I've learned to be very self-reliant and confidant about my ability to handle any situation that comes my way. During the winter I teach fifth-grade English and in the summer I drive a bus. I'm thinking of taking my skill to different locations."

A Special Place to Live and Work

🕐 **Camp Denali and North Face Lodge** (P.O. Box 67, Denali National Park, AK 99755; 907-683-2290; fax 907-683-1568; www.campdenali.com/employment/index.php; jobs@campdenali.com). Live and work at Camp Denali and North Face Lodge and become part of a unique community in an extraordinary setting that specializes in active learning adventures deep inside Denali National Park. Seasonal openings usually include positions as dinner cook, breakfast cook, assistant cook, baker, kitchen helper, or member of the waitstaff, operations crew, or housekeeping staff. Complete job descriptions are available on the Web site, and if you are interested in summer positions you have to apply by January.

You will need to submit a letter that explains how you heard of Camp Denali/North Face Lodge, why you are interested in working there, and how your experience applies to the position you are seeking. You need to describe your work ethic and your goals and provide references. You will also need to submit a résumé, and your dates of availability. A full season runs from the third week in May through mid-September, and preference is given to those who can work the entire season, or who can commit to two seasons. Wages are paid monthly, based on a 10-hour day and a 5-day workweek. Your employment will include room and board, and a travel stipend for out-of-state-employees.

You will have the opportunity to explore Denali National Park, interact with guests from all over the country and beyond, and be a part of a team that lives, works, and plays together, forming long-lasting friendships and growing personally and professionally. Find out more about the area by going to the Denali National Park Web site (www.denali.national-park.com), which also has links to information about Alaska.

Robert's Story

Kantishna is the last stop at the end of the 95-mile road through Denali National Park. There are only two ways to get to Kantishna, by bus or small aircraft to Kantishna Airstrip. After gold was discovered in Glacier Creek in 1905, Kantishna's population grew from a handful to two thousand. As the gold dwindled, so did interest in mining. Most visitors, and people applying for summer positions, just can't imagine the difference between living and working near the entrance to Denali or really going for it and discovering the true beauty of the park.

The majority of visitors to Denali during the peak of the season take the Tundra Wilderness Tour, a one-day, eight-hour bus trip about 33 miles into the park. That's an okay way to see the park, but the greatest views and most spectacular experiences are available to those who venture farther and allow sufficient time to make it to Kantishna and stay for awhile.

My first summer working in Denali I took a day
trip to Kantishna and could not believe the number of bear we saw and the loons on Wonder Lake,
and the red fox protecting her den. It was such an
incredible day that I decided to return
the next year to work at one of the lodges in
Kantishna. I'm glad I did. Every minute I wasn't
working I was hiking or viewing wildlife. Every day
was a phenomenal experience filled with the joy,
beauty, and wonder of Denali National Park.

Learn to Earn

**The Culinary Institute of America: Career Discovery
Programs** (Continuing Education Office, 1946 Campus
Drive, Hyde Park, NY 12538; 1-800-888-7850; 845-452-
2230; www.ciachef.edu/enthusiasts/programs/gs_
discovery.asp; ciachef@culinary.edu; courses range from
$650–$1,800). The Culinary Institute of America (CIA)
offers a career discovery program at its Greystone campus, in St. Helena, in the Napa Valley region of California.
If you love to cook and are considering turning your passion into a career, the CIA has classes designed specifically for you. You will learn about the food and hospitality
industry, attend lectures, demonstrations, hands-on
classes, and tastings.

Current course offerings include an introductory
course in Career Discovery, Baking and Pastry, the Flavors
of Napa Valley, and the Professional World of Wine. In the
weeklong Introductory course, you will find out what it's
like to be a chef and learn the basics of cooking, including
knife skills, kitchen terminology, and cooking methods.

You will explore the cuisines of the Caribbean, Asia, Mexico, and the Mediterranean. In the weeklong baking and pastry program, you will learn about opportunities in the field, ingredients, equipment, terminology, recipes, and techniques, and gain experience producing a variety of baked goods.

The Flavors of Napa Valley has an extended curriculum that includes four dinners in local Napa Valley restaurants. In the four-day program, you will learn the basics of food preparation and presentation, wine and food pairing, knife skills, kitchen terminology, and food storage and handling. The Professional World of Wine course will teach you everything you need to know: how wine is made, how to taste and evaluate wines, wine terminology, how to pair wine with food, proper wine etiquette, and how the business of wine works.

Go to the CIA Web site to download the Career Discover Programs brochure and check current course offerings and prices. Make your reservations online or call the Continuing Education office. For short-term housing contact Napa Valley Reservations Unlimited at 1-800-251-6272 or visit their Web site at www.napavalleyreserva tions.com or the Napa Valley Visitor's Bureau Web site at www.napavalley.com. Try being a professional chef or baker in a professional setting. You might like it and might even make a viable plan to trade in your day job.

Tasty Treats

Culinary Institute of America: Boot Camps
(Continuing Education Office, 1946 Campus Drive, Hyde Park, NY 12538; 1-800-888-7850; 845-452-2230; www.cia chef.edu/enthusiasts/programs/hp_bootcamps; ciachef @culinary.edu; 1-day boot camp, $325; 2-day boot camp, $850; 4-day boot camp, $1,625–$1,695; 5-day boot camp, $2,095). Attend boot camp at the Culinary Institute of

America (CIA) and experience an immersion adventure in cooking at one of the premier cooking schools in the world. Whether you are looking for an unusual culinary vacation, taking your skills to the next level, or exploring the culinary arts as a career option, boot camp at the CIA will whet your appetite.

You will work in the CIA kitchens at the school's main campus in Hyde Park, New York. You will learn to think about cooking in a whole new way, in an all-day program that gives you a taste of boot camp or in two- to five-day programs that teach many different cuisines, skills, techniques, and methods.

A Taste of Boot Camp includes courses in Spanish tapas, Italian American classic recipes, flavors of Asia, and American regional food. The two-day boot camp offers classes in hors d'oeurves, skills development, BBQ, and holiday cooking. The four-day boot camp includes classes in bistro food, baking, entertaining, Italian cuisine, and healthy cooking. In five-day boot camps you will learn about Asian cuisine, French cuisine, gourmet meals in minutes, and have a choice of either basic or advanced training.

Visit the CIA Web site for course details, directions, where to stay, and information about the Hudson Valley, as well as CIA recipes.

Girlfriends Who Cook Together

Three of us enrolled in the CIA's Italian cooking boot camp. We wanted to seriously figure out a few things. One, were we really exceptional cooks? Two, did we like cooking enough to do it correctly and produce recognizable saleable products or were we only happy cooking what we wanted to make whenever we felt like it? We all work at jobs we're not thrilled with and dream about owning our own catering business. That first course, literally and figuratively, whetted our appetites, and subsequent courses have taught us more of what we need to know. We've started catering on a small scale, with dessert or appetizer spreads and we're handling that well. So far we're enjoying what we're doing, having a lot of fun, and we're still good friends.

Talented Natural Builders and Teachers Needed

Cob Cottage Company (P.O. Box 942, Coquille, OR 97423; 541-396-1825; www.cobcottage.com). This company is looking for experienced natural builders to teach at the North American Retreat Center for Natural Building with people who enjoy working and living together. They offer workshops, present talks and slideshows, and produce publications.

Cob Cottage Company Apprentice Program (P.O. Box 942, Coquille, OR 97423; 541-396-1825; www.cobcottage .com; $4,400 fee covers instruction, meals, and camping). The apprentice program is open to people interested in making natural building their livelihood. Participants work one-on-one with a professional instructor on all phases of a house, completing buildings already in progress at the school and beginning new buildings elsewhere.

Grants for Students Considering Engineering Careers

✉ **The Exploration Systems Mission Directorate (ESMD) Space Grant Student Project** (Kennedy Space Center, Cape Canaveral, FL 32899; 321-867-8937; www.nasa.gov/audience/forstudents/postsecondary/programs/ESMD_Space_Grant_Student_Project.html; gloria.a.murphy@nasa.gov). The ESMD Space Grant Student Project offers three exploration-related internships at NASA centers or with space-related industry, senior design projects, and a systems engineering paper competition. The goal is to involve a diverse group of students in hands-on engineering experiences to prepare them for future careers in space. Application deadlines are in January for summer programs and in May for fall programs.

Hands-On Learning

🕐 **(or College Credits) National Wildlife Federation** (11100 Wildlife Center Dr., Reston, VA 20190; 1-800-822-9919; www.nwf.org). The National Wildlife Federation (NWF) offers many internships and opportunities for professional development within its organization, available to college or university undergraduate juniors or seniors, recent graduates, and graduate students from all fields of study. Applicants are selected on the basis of professional goals, course work, previous experience, résumé and cover letter, GPA, and professional and academic references. Internships allow students and graduates to work with a variety of NWF's skilled professionals, including working to protect endangered species, in land stewardship, education, fundraising, and communications.

A paid salary with medical benefits is available for interns who work 20 hours per week and complete a 24-week commitment. Sometimes college credit is substituted for a paid salary, and those internships do not have health benefits. Research current openings on the NWF Web site, as well as employment and volunteer opportunities.

College Students Needed

✉ **Living History Farms** (2600 111th St., Urbandale, IA 50322; 515-278-5286; www.lhf.org; info@lhf.org; daily May 1 to Sept. 3, Wed.–Sun. and Sept. 5 through Oct. 21, 9–5; three working farms from 1700, 1850, and 1900, Wallace exhibit center, and 1875 Walnut Hill town). This is an outdoor historical educational museum near Des Moines. A 13-week summer internship program is offered for 26 college students, sophomore year and up, working as living history performers, day-camp counselors, or marketing assistants. Earn a $2,250 stipend, six hours of tuition-free history credit, and valuable work experience. College credits are provided through Graceland University, costs paid by Living History Farms, and students can transfer the credit hours to their own program. This internship is a good supplement for students majoring in history, education, agriculture, child development, museum studies, folk art, leisure studies, journalism, marketing, or public relations.

Raising Sheep

⑤ **Bar VW Ranch** (P.O. Box 1379, Cut Bank, MT 59427; vwhmstd@hotmail.com). This is a historic site that was first homesteaded over one hundred years ago, located an hour east of the Rocky Mountains and Glacier National Park. Interns interested in learning about raising sheep and acquiring experience in land management techniques, wildlife habitat plantings, and general building tasks can trade a minimum of three weeks' work for room, board, and experience.

Get Truckin'

Swift Transportation Corporation (2200 South 75th Ave., Phoenix, AZ 85043; 1-800-800-2200; 602-269-9700; www.swifttrans.com; Info@swifttrans.com). Here's the perfect job for immersion travelers who love going to new places and driving. The trucking business is projected to grow 30 percent yearly and employers are guaranteeing jobs while you're in training. It's the new big career for baby boomers. Husband-and-wife teams have never been more popular, according to an industry spokesperson.

There are certainly a lot of skills to master to become a great trucker, but the income is substantial and steady. There are driving and nondriving positions available throughout the industry. Swift's Web site is helpful, informative, and insightful with oral blogs that provide firsthand stories to prospective drivers along with the necessary qualifications and how to apply.

Sean's Working Story

I was the typical kid growing up in Texas playing with trucks, driving the truckers crazy to blow their horns, and imagining myself flying down the highway with a big rig. Now that I've grown up I surprised myself. I'm not a truck driver. I'm a dispatcher, which suits me better. I'm around trucks and truck drivers, but I like talking to everybody and telling them what to do and where to go.

A shortage of drivers has helped improve the industry. Employers are far more aware than ever before of people needing to know their route and scheduling beforehand. The business is getting better and better and more open to more people. I still love playing with trucks and driving the truckers crazy to blow the horn.

Hit the Trail

Appalachian Mountain Club (AMC Main Office, 5 Joy St., Boston, MA 02108; 617-523-0636; fax 617-523-0722; www.outdoors.org). AMC is the nation's oldest and largest recreation and conservation organization. They need volunteers, interns, and seasonal workers. Seasonal crews work in the White Mountain National Forest in New Hampshire, Mount Desert Island in Maine, or in the Delaware Water Gap in New Jersey, among many other locations. Job opportunities are posted on their Web site and usually include caretakers, food service, instructors, naturalist, trail crew, lodging, and housekeeping.

On with the Show

Kentucky Shakespeare Festival (1387 South Fourth St., Louisville, KY 40208; 502-637-4933; www.ShakespeareInAmericanCommunities.org; www.kyshakes.org; info@shakes.org; technical positions, contact mgbombe@aol.com; managing director, doug@kyshakes.org). This program, supported by grants from the National Endowment for the Arts in cooperation with Arts Midwest, provides professional Shakespeare performances and educational programs to high school and middle school students nationally. The Kentucky Shakespeare Festival is the oldest professional Shakespeare company in North America, providing summer theater for everyone. The productions are performed at the C. Douglas Ramey Amphitheatre in Central Park in Louisville, Kentucky, in the heart of Old Louisville's historic preservation district. Free dormitory housing is provided for performers and interns. Acting auditions for the professional acting company are conducted in January, February, and March in a variety of locations such as Louisville, Kentucky; Memphis, Tennessee; and St. Louis, Missouri. Acting, technical, administrative, and education internships are also available. Salaries and contact information are posted on the Web site www.kyshakes.org. Depending on the position, this is a 9- to 14-week commitment.

Living a Sustainable Lifestyle

Beneficial Farm (286 Arroyo Salado, Santa Fe, NM 87508; 505-422-2238; www.BeneficialFarm.com; stevew@plateautel.net; working guests are asked to contribute $25 per day for 3–5 nights, $20 per day for 6–10 nights, and $18 per day for 11–21 nights, negotiable with discount for families). Beneficial Farm is off the grid in a pinyon-juniper wilderness area at 7000 feet in elevation, 20 miles southeast of Santa Fe. The farm practices sustainable farming to enrich the soil and produce an abundance of wholesome foods by natural means. They raise 500 laying hens, grass-fed beef, cows, llamas, vegetables, and herbs. The emphasis is on watershed restoration and restorative range management practices. Plan a vacation with the entire family (over age nine) to work the farm for

Beneficial Farm grows salad mix that looks good enough to eat right from the ground.

a week in exchange for room and board. Comfortable housing, common meals, weekly farm education classes, and visiting school groups add to the experience. Labor for room and board trades are also available to those who want to learn the business of farming for a year or longer commitment.

Steve's Story

Why working on a farm is terrific for everyone regardless of whether you intend to become a farmer or not:

- Develop your physical fitness and increase muscle strength, endurance, and stamina.

- Increase your ability to focus on tasks at hand and attention to detail.

- Eat nutritious, organic, healthy, and tasty food with a farmer's appetite.

- Experience living with solar power and attending to careful water use.

- Experience working closely with animals and plants.

- Increase your experiences of teamwork, communication skills, and strategies.

- Add an unusual and compelling piece to your work résumé.

- Explore a corner of the unique Southwest.

Become an Organic Gardener

Wellspring (4382 Hickory Rd., West Bend, WI 53090; 262-675-6755; www.wellspringinc.org; wellspring@hnet.net; private rooms, $45 for single, $55 for double occupancy; $25 per night in cottage or barn loft dormitories). Wellspring has volunteer positions, internships, and trade-off-of-work possibilities on their 36-acre estate. They need nature trails trimmed, flower gardens maintained, and housekeeping help.

A nonprofit educational organization, Wellspring is located in the Milwaukee River Valley, only 35 minutes from downtown Milwaukee. It has 6 acres of organic gardens, nature trails, woods, meadows, ponds, and an outdoor labyrinth. It is the ideal immersion excursion for those wanting to refresh and rejuvenate, while benefiting from programs in wellness education, ecology, and gardening.

Wellspring participates in Community Supported Agriculture (CSA), which is a direct partnership between the farmer and the consumer. People who join a CSA want to know where their food comes from and how it is grown. They pay up front for food that is delivered weekly to local drop-off sites, or picked up at the farm, from early June to mid-November, along with recipes and tips on how to handle and prepare fresh food. Some farms offer "worker shares," exchanging work for a share of the produce, allowing you to become involved in the food you choose to eat. Contact Wellspring for more information.

Wellspring also teaches organic gardening. Interns live at the farm and work in the gardens from early April to mid-November, learning about a full growing season. Applications for internships open in the fall for the following season. Full-year internships are also available. Volunteers, and guests who want to learn how to grow their own food, work along with the interns. Guests may make reservations to stay in the main house with private rooms or a cottage or barn loft with dormitory accommodations. Linens are provided. Vegetarian meals are available on request, or guests may use a fully equipped kitchen or choose to visit nearby restaurants. Arrangements for groups must be made six months in advance, and there is a facilities charge.

There are farm festivals and other special events, including an Earth Day celebration and herb sale in spring, a summer picnic, and a fall Harvest Fest that showcases A Taste of Wellspring and offers hayrides, live music, river walks, and garden tours. Consult the events calendar and newsletter on the Wellspring Web site for a complete schedule, information on organic food, and environmental news. You will also find directions, things to do in the area, how to apply for a garden share, and a list of garden produce on the Web site.

Captain Your Own Wooden Boat

Glacier Park Boat Company (P.O. Box 5262, Kalispell, MT 59903; 406-257-2426; www.glacierpark boats.com; info@glacierparkboats.com). Seasonal boat captains are needed to staff historic wooden boats, carrying from 45 to 80 passengers, from the first part of June until the end of September. Applicants must be 18 years of age or older, possess current CPR and first-aid certificates, and pass a physical exam, but do not need prior experience. You will be trained to drive the boats and give commentary about the historic, cultural, and geographic highlights of Glacier Park. It's an opportunity to both learn and teach others, as you earn $8 an hour, with increases for experience. Housing is family style and included in the compensation package, but you provide your own food. E-mail your résumé, along with a cover letter explaining why you would like to have this job and what qualities you will bring to the work, to Denise VanArtsdale at DeSmet1@centurytel.net.

Seasonal Employment

Oakland House Seaside Resort (435 Herricks Landing, Brooksville, ME 04617; phone inquiries to Jim Littlefield at 207-359-8521; www.oaklandhouse.com/summer_job_employment.html; jim@oaklandhouse.com). Summer and fall seasonal positions include chef, dining room manager, pastry chef, bakery assistant, breakfast cook, line cooks, waitstaff, front office/reservations/

hospitality assistants, housekeeping, maintenance, and grounds assistant. There are also horticulture internships available.

The culinary program has openings throughout the season, which runs from mid-May through mid-October, with a concentration of need in July and August. Join the staff of an upscale coastal inn and work a 40-hour week, with two consecutive days off. Room and board are available on-site for a minimal charge. Wages are commensurate with skills. Download an application from the Web site.

Apply for a horticulture internship and gain experience in vegetable garden production, floraculture, property maintenance, and shrubs and small trees. The schedule is flexible with hours over five or six days, depending on daylight and guest requirements. Days off are rotated, and work beyond 40 hours is paid time and a half. Wages are commensurate with skills, with room and board available on-site, for a minimal charge.

Oakland House is a family-owned seaside resort located on the rural coast of Maine. It offers a relaxing setting for guests, many who return each year. June is the training period for staff, when the workload is light. Extra staff is needed in August. The longer an applicant is able to stay, the greater the possibility of employment. There is also the option of spring- or fall-only employment.

Applicants should be friendly, neat, have a positive attitude, and take pleasure in serving guests. Prior experience (except for professional positions) is not necessary, but some experience or a strong interest is helpful. On the job, life/safety, and hospitality training are all provided. Salaries are competitive for professional staff, and general staff positions start at $7 an hour, depending on experience and position. There is a weekly merit bonus of up to $40, paid when your date commitment is fulfilled.

A Working Connection

The Web site CoolWorks.com is the place to go to find short- or longer-term, seasonal or permanent jobs all over the country. The categories include immersion excursions in every location you can imagine: national park jobs, conservation corps, resort jobs, state park jobs, camp jobs, theme park jobs, ranch jobs, guide jobs, jobs on water, ski resort jobs, internships, volunteer positions, teen jobs, and older and bolder. Click on what interests you to read more detailed information, conduct your own research and, in most cases, apply directly online to the employer.

Tips are yours. Waitstaff salaries range from $6.75 to $7.15 per hour, depending on guest rating. Waitstaff also receives a weekly bonus paid at the end of your date commitment, and tips are yours to keep.

Be a Wrangler

Allen's Diamond Four Ranch (P.O. Box 243, Lander, WY 82520; 307-332-2995; summer cell 307-330-8625; www.diamond4ranch.com; diamond4@wyoming .com). Allen's Diamond Four is the highest alpine ranch in Wyoming. They specialize in wilderness pack trips and rustic ranch vacations. It's off the grid and promises real ranch work, physically and emotionally demanding. They hire about 10–15 employees who work and live together on a 24-hour basis per season and typically need wranglers, ranch cooks, and cabin and housekeeping staff. The summer season runs June 23–August 31, and the fall hunting season runs September 1–October 25. Applicants who are available to work both summer and fall seasons are given hiring priority.

Adventure Ridge at Eagle's Nest Is Vail's Mountaintop Activity Center

The gondola is free for nonskiers after 2 PM. There's ice skating, tubing, and other fun activities, like horse-drawn sleigh rides and singing cowboys. Restaurants are open late with both indoor and outdoor eating options at 10,000 feet. Pazzo's Pizza and Los Amigos are great choices for families with children.

Betsy's Story

I'm a 45-year-old elementary school teacher who went on a spring break horse-packing trip and enjoyed it so much that I applied for the adventure job of my dreams, packing horses and cooking on Allen's Diamond Four Ranch in the Wind River Mountain Range. They specialize in horses, fly-fishing, pack trips, and elk hunting in Shoshone National Forest.

I was thrilled. People thought I was crazy because the ranch wanted a commitment to both seasons so I gave up my house and teaching job to go, and I went. One of the first things I did was break my wrist falling off a hayloft. I had to return home for medical coverage and care. It was pretty disappointing and embarrassing. I'd told everyone I was moving out West. I did what I had to do to heal my wrist and then I went back to finish out the season.

It wasn't easy running a camp at 10,000 feet without electricity or conveniences, but I loved it. It's such a beautiful place to live and be. Having an adventure like that helps you see new potential in what you've been doing all along and develop greater appreciation than ever before for the job you've always done.

Live, Work, and Play at a Ski Resort

Ski resorts need employees on the slopes and in hotel, restaurant, and other service positions. Jobs include reservations, check-in, valets, cooks, waitstaff, bartending, ski shop, maintenance and janitorial, among others. Employers look for dependability, positive attitude, team players, and availability for the dates needed. Definitely inquire about the perks of the job, which often include seasonal ski or snowboarding passes and discounts on equipment and lessons. Job resources include: www.skiing thenet.com, www.skijob1.com, and www.jobmonkey.com/ski/html/instructors.

Great Job Perks

Breckenridge Resort (P.O. Box 1058, Breckenridge, CO 80424; 1-800-789-7669; www.skijob1.snow.com/info/or.b.asp; Breckinfo@vailresorts.com). Types of jobs include administration and professional, food and beverage, golf, hospitality, mountain operations, ski and ride school, and resort services. Specific jobs are posted on their Web site seasonally, year-round, and midseason as needed. Some positions require in-person interviews. Not all jobs come with housing. Hourly wages depend on position and experience, with fees for room and board.

Bess Teaches Snowboarding

I moved to Breckenridge, Colorado, after teaching at Hunter Mountain in New York. I wanted to live in a community with year-round employment opportunities. I work for the town of Breckenridge during the summer. In the winter my employer is Vail Resorts. I teach snowboarding at Breckenridge Ski Resort for the winter season, a fabulous 160 days on snow. When I'm not teaching others how to board I'm out there doing it myself. I don't make a ton of money and rely on tips to survive, but it's like being on vacation every day, enjoying skiing, mountain biking, kayaking, and hiking. I can see how doing what I love will support me professionally too. I plan to pursue further training and certification in snowboarding instruction and become an examiner to review other instructors. Lucky me, I live in outdoor heaven.

The Christie Lodge Motto: Having Fun Helping Our Guests Have Fun

🕐 **The Christie Lodge** (47 E. Beaver Creek Blvd., Avon, CO 81620; 1-800-551-4326; 970-845-4504; www.christielodge.com; careers@christielodge.com). The Christie Lodge actively recruits and hires people for both year-round and seasonal positions in the hospitality industry. To apply for a vacancy, send a cover letter and résumé to careers@christielodge.com. If you're in the area, applications are also available in the lodge's administrative offices.

Vermont Ski Jobs

🕐 **Smugglers' Notch** (Human Resources, 4323 VT 108 South, Smugglers' Notch, VT 05464-9537; 1-888-754-7684; fax 802-644-8580; www.smuggs.com/pages/universal/jobs/index.php; employment@smuggs.com). They offer bonuses to employees who refer future employees. There is also an ongoing internship program in hotel management where students can earn experience and income. Typical winter positions include childcare, snow-sports instruction, hotel management, housekeeping, and food preparation. Online and printable application forms are available.

Become a Certified Yoga Instructor

Kripalu Yoga Teacher Training (Kripalu Center, P.O. Box 309, Stockbridge, MA 01262; 1-800-848-8702; fax 413-448-3384; www.kripalu.org/article/214/; professional-training@kripalu.org). Kripalu offers 200- and 500-hour training certification programs. Immersion learning with their skilled faculty prepares you to teach yoga as it encourages personal growth and improves your breathing and posture practices. Building support networks and relationships with fellow practitioners enhances the experience and can lead to lifelong friendships. The 200-hour training is offered either in a one-month intensive format or in two 12-day sessions. The 500-hour course, which builds on the 200-hour training, is offered in four 9-day modules and includes 75 hours of instruction and in-depth practice. For information on financial aid and scholarships, contact Kripalu at 413-448-3400. You may also download an application from their Web site.

Chris's Story

I chose Kripalu for my yoga training based on a number of criteria. I live in Connecticut and it's in Massachusetts. I knew that once I had my certification I'd be returning periodically for coursework, so the accessible location was important. The program is really dynamic and matched my philosophy and needs. I had discovered that Stamford, Connecticut, did not have a yoga studio at that time, and was convinced opening one was the right move for me. Kripalu helped me on every level, figuring out what I needed and how to get it all done. It's been a very rewarding experience opening my studio and filling a need in the community. Of course, now that I've opened up, many studios

have followed my lead. But that's just fine. I'm
really pleased with what I've been able to create here. It's very rewarding, challenging, and
stimulating too.

Learn How to Own and Run Your Own Bed & Breakfast

Wedgwood Inn (111 W. Bridge St., New Hope, PA 18938;
215-862-2570; www.new-hope-inn.com/innkeeping.html;
stay@wedgwoodinn.com; courses range from $275–$500).
Nadine and Carl Glassman own and run three bed & breakfast inns. Carl coauthored a book for aspiring innkeepers,
How to Start and Run Your Own Bed and Breakfast Inn,
and teaches a workshop by that name. Courses are
offered in March, April, November, and December.
Participants experience hands-on activities in every
aspect of locating, purchasing, designing, running and
maintaining a successful bed & breakfast.

Homes Away from Home

The Caretaker Gazette (3 Estancia La.,
Boerne, TX 78006; 830-755-2300; www.caretaker.org;
caretaker@caretaker.org; Blog: http://caretakergazette
.blogspot.com). This is a bimonthly newsletter with
Internet listings of homes in every state with property
owners looking for people to live in them as caretakers,
pet sitters, and house sitters. Some openings offer com-
pensation in addition to the free housing provided. Short-,
medium-, and long-term property caretaking assignments
are in every issue. Subscriptions run $29.95 per year.

Swap-a-Vacation House

Home Exchange, Inc. (P.O. Box 787, Hermosa Beach, CA 90254; 1-800-877-8723; 310-798-3864; www.HomeExchange.com). This is the place where people say, "I'll swap you my house for your house." There is a one-year membership fee of $100 with the guarantee that if you don't exchange in the first year, the second year is free.

4

Caring

Immersion Travel for Animal Lovers,

Caretakers, and Activists

I am only one, but still I am one. I cannot do everything, but still I can do something; and because I cannot do everything, I will not refuse to do something that I can do.

—HELEN KELLER, *activist and lecturer*

Whether your cause is returning the wolf to its natural environment, encouraging new ways of conservation, or discovering new energy sources, these selections will help you achieve your personal goals. What touches your heart? What's important to you and what do you really care about?

Kathleen's voice breaks when she describes birds she used to see that no longer visit her feeder. Annette was moved when swimming with the manatees. She cried into her goggles while touching the animals' scars from motorboats.

"If each and every one of us had a cause we cared about and worked for," says Judy, who raised two sons and three adopted daughters along with dozens of cats and dogs saved from a variety of unspeakable conditions, "then probably no one, including animals, would be in need."

Protecting the Endangered

Sky Island Alliance (738 N. 5th St., Suite 201, Tucson, AZ 85717; 520-624-7080; fax 520-791-7709; www.sky islandalliance.org; info@skyislandalliance.org). Here's an opportunity to protect and restore the habitats of jaguars and Chiricahua leopard frogs, and other unique species, in the Sky Island region of the Southwest. Helpers assist by planting native vegetation and assisting with data entry, which benefits endangered fish, reptiles, and

Volunteers at riparian habitat assessment training through the Sky Island Alliance, Sycamore Canyon, Pajarita Wilderness. *Trevor Hare*

amphibians. Consider visiting Arizona to become part of a team that documents six different species every six weeks, or map out and document illegal roads on public lands.

The Sky Island Alliance is a coalition of scientists, land managers, and citizens that plans, promotes, and implements conservation policy and action. The Alliance believes that isolated wilderness areas and national parks alone are not enough to protect species and biodiversity. Its conservation plan calls for linking wildlands by protected corridors so that animals that need room to roam, like the bear and mountain lion, can continue to survive.

Sky Island Alliance sponsors many events that are just a day trip out of Tucson, which could fit almost anyone's schedule. There are also monthly field weekends that are physically demanding, but there are tasks to suit different fitness and skill levels. Road closures necessitate the placement of barriers and signs, and the road surfaces may need to be broken up to allow water to penetrate and seeds to take hold when restoring native vegetation. The goal is to replace illegal roads with natural habitats. If you are interested in participating, e-mail sarah@skyisland alliance.org for more information.

Committed "citizen scientists" can attend a five-day training workshop, held over two weekends. You will be taught tracking techniques and wildlife sign recognition, and ecology and behavior of local mammal species, in the classroom and on field trips. Teams of three to four volunteers commit to a full day of monitoring once every six weeks. Two training workshops are offered each year, for 15 volunteers. If you are interested, e-mail janice@sky islandalliance.org for workshops dates and an application.

You'll find a volunteer interest form on the Sky Island Alliance Web site, and a list of current projects with dates, descriptions, and sign-up links. There's also a current newsletter, a Sky Island map, and an e-mail list if you would like to be informed about news, events, and volunteer opportunities on a regular basis.

Gene's Camping Experience

I was never really big into ecology or camping out, but volunteering with this group is not only fun, it's worthwhile, physically challenging, and meaningful work. A few weeks ago there was a notice on the Sky Island Alliance Web site that the Bureau of Land Management and the Forest Service was asking our organization for volunteers to close roads in the Las Cienegas National Conservation Area, about 50 miles from Tucson, near Sonoita, Arizona, that people riding on ATVs had opened up. Making roads where they weren't meant to be was causing erosion. A group of 12 went out last Friday night, camped in the wilderness, and worked all day Saturday closing the road. We dug it up and put plants in so that it didn't look like a road anymore. We camped that night and the next day and added a few finishing touches. The camaraderie of the camp, and being out there and doing something important, was really remarkable. I was surrounded by people with two or three academic degrees, who all lead very busy lives, and it was amazing. There was so much to learn and do together. Every time I volunteer for a project it's a whole different group of people with a whole new social dynamic. Each person has a different reason for going, and I've never met anyone who has volunteered three days like that who didn't enjoy it.

Visit the Wild in the Wild

National Wildlife Federation (11100 Wildlife Center Dr., Reston, VA 20190; 1-800-822-9919; www.nwf.org; expedition prices vary with length of trip and destination). The mission of the National Wildlife Federation (NWF) is to inspire Americans to preserve wildlife for our children's future. NWF supports conservation and education programs, offers nature travel opportunities, and encourages people to speak up for wildlife. The Web site and newsletter keep citizens informed about government decisions and policy that affects natural habitats and asks its members to take action. Concerned about global warming, which it believes is the single biggest threat to wildlife today, NWF works to reduce global warming pollution through education, action, by demanding policy change and legislation, and by dedicating funding to address the impacts of global warming on America's natural resources. NWF also asks that each and every person be part of the solution.

NWF expeditions are environmentally sensitive, and expert guides teach you to travel responsibly. NWF has teamed up with NativeEnergy, a private, Native American-owned renewable energy company, to offset the carbon releases from NWF trips. For more information on NativeEnergy, visit www.nativeenergy.com/traveloffsets.

NWF is committed to connecting people with nature and providing opportunities for travelers to explore wildlife areas. Some current travel programs include Wolves, Bears, Geysers in Yellowstone National Park. There's wildlife viewing, educational presentations, and great hikes, all accompanied by naturalists. The small group size makes it easy to stop very quickly whenever wildlife presents itself. Be sure to bring along your binoculars and high-powered camera lenses.

A popular May offering is Walking Acadia National Park, in Maine. Acadia is made for walking. Evenings are spent in a traditional New England inn and days are used for hiking the park's trails and carriage paths with a naturalist who informs you about the ecosystems, wildlife, and springtime wildflowers. Additional activities include boat excursions, village exploration, and a lobster dinner.

A true American safari is NWF's Where the Buffalo Roam in South Dakota. You will be escorted through the American prairie to see one of the world's largest herds of bison. You'll also appreciate the phenomenal views of South Dakota's Black Hills while observing coyote, pronghorn antelope, and buffalo. For dates, detailed itineraries, costs, and other information, check the NWF Web site or request a brochure.

Most Careful Observers

Marine Resources Council of East Florida (MRC Headquarters, 3275 Dixie Hwy. NE, Palm Bay, FL 32905; 321-725-7775; fax 321-725-3554; www.mrcirl.org; council @mrcirl.org; North Atlantic Right Whale Monitoring Network Hotline is active Nov.–Apr.; 1-888-97-WHALE). People who live in high-rises along the coast and beaches have the greatest chance of seeing whales. Marine Resources Council (MRC) encourages shoreline users, residents, beach patrol, lifeguards, store owners, shoppers,

Provide Caring Opportunities for Children

"Teach children when they are young how to participate in volunteer settings and they will carry on this meaningful work into adulthood."
—Julie Albert, Right Whale Volunteer Program Coordinator

contractors, beach walkers, and sunbathers to immediately call the whale-sighting hotline at 1-888-97-WHALE whenever they see a North Atlantic right whale. They ask observers to report where and when the sighting is taking

North Atlantic right whale #1622 and her fourth calf frolic off Satellite Beach, Florida. She has been seen with previous calves as well. *Julie Albert/MRC*

place, the direction the animal is moving, distance off-shore, and if possible to photograph the sighting, all while keeping the mandatory 500 yards distance, which is a federal law.

Training sessions are organized in the fall to teach people how to identify these endangered whales. The whales come so close to shore that identifying marks can be seen on the head and body. When a call comes into the whale hotline, a response team goes out to document the sighting and make sure the whale is not injured or entangled.

Julie's Story

Aerial surveys are not regularly conducted south of Crescent Beach, near St. Augustine, Florida. MRC relies on a volunteer network of ordinary people sitting in their houses or out on the beaches spotting whales to provide the documentation needed to extend the current federally designated critical habitat area. The biggest cause of death of the North Atlantic right whale is collisions with ships.

The right whale comes to Florida and Georgia to give birth in the winter months and spends summer in and around the Bay of Fundy in Canada. We are very lucky to be able to see mothers with their calves so close to shore, especially when only about 15 are born each year. The numbers of births have been increasing recently. We work very

hard to make sure they stay safe while visiting
our waters.

Adopt a Turtle

Loggerhead Marine Life Center of Juno Beach
(14200 US Hwy. One, Juno Beach, FL 33408; 561-627-8280;
fax 561-627-8305; www.marinelife.org; info@marinelife
.org). The center is almost completely run by volunteers
who assist in the documentation of nesting activity on a
6-mile stretch of beach in Juno and Jupiter. Turtle adop-
tions provide funding for medications, tank maintenance,
food, and veterinary care. A yearly Turtlefest fundraiser
supports the center's sea turtle rehabilitation and youth
education programs. Medical costs exceed $20,000 a year
for injured sea turtles, with 50 to 60 being treated and
released.

Beverly and Sheryl on Juno Beach

There were over 100 wooden stakes, some with
red strips of plastic tied to the tops, some with
yellow, dotting 6 miles of Juno Beach (Florida)
marking loggerhead sea turtles' nests. The females
leave tracks, called crawls, from the water into the
dunes to dig nests and lay their eggs. Signs warn
visitors not to disturb the nests at the risk of
breaking the law.

We arrived early at the beach to walk as the
sun rose. Workers from the Loggerhead Marine
Life Center rode along the beach in all-terrain

vehicles documenting the newest crawls and nests. About 60 days after the eggs are laid, baby turtles will hatch deep in the sand, knowing their mission: to climb up toward the light and then to make their way directly to the water.

We paused to photograph the turtle crawls and nests when suddenly Beverly grabbed my arm and pointed to where my foot was about to tram-

Injured in a boating accident, this loggerhead turtle is being rehabilitated at the Loggerhead Marine Life Center in Juno Beach, Florida.

ple a struggling new hatchling. The tiniest of turtles, smaller than the length of my big toe, was scurrying across the sand when suddenly it was pushed back by a mighty wave. The hatchling came out of it to push forward again but was thrown by another, bigger wave.

The tiny turtle had climbed its way out of the sand and down the 20 feet of beach to the edge of the water, and with seemingly unrelenting determination and confidence, rode the next wave out into the ocean.

Caring Volunteers Monitor Hatchlings

Caretta Research Project (P.O. Box 9841, Savannah, GA 31412-0041; 912-447-8655; fax 912-447-8656; www.carettaresearchproject.org; WassawCRP@aol.com; $725 per person per week, includes transportation to and from Wassaw Island on the designated dates, food, and rustic housing; for adults over age 18). Protecting Georgia's loggerhead turtles since 1973, the Caretta Research Project relies on volunteers to monitor egg-laying activity and hatchling rates. The goals of the project are to learn more about the population levels and nesting habits of loggerhead turtles, increase the survival rate of eggs and hatchings, and to involve people in turtle preservation.

During egg-laying season, mid-May through early August, volunteers patrol 6 miles of beach on Wassaw Island, to observe and tag female turtles that have emerged from the ocean to lay their eggs. Some nests need to be relocated to safer areas, and all nests are protected with screens. Since turtles lay eggs at night, volunteers can sleep and relax, swim, and explore the island during the day. Throughout the hatchling season, July to September, volunteers monitor nests and, when hatchlings emerge, escort the tiny turtles to the ocean and record data. Later they excavate the nest and count unhatched eggs to determine the hatchling success rate. Again, most activity takes place during the night so volunteers have their days free.

In addition to contributing to the protection of the turtles, participants signed up for a week or more in the 16-week program have the opportunity to explore a beautiful Georgia sea island, take part in a hands-on learning experience, and make new friends. No special gear is required; just bring a positive attitude and sense of adventure. Accommodations are two small cabins in the center of Wassaw Island. Meals are included in the registration fee and team members are expected to help with daily housekeeping and dinner preparation. Each team has six members, so sign up with friends or come on your own to meet new people and engage in a unique immersion travel experience.

Return Wolves to Their Natural Habitats

 The Grand Canyon Wolf Recovery Project (P.O. Box 1594, Flagstaff, AZ 86002; 928-202-1325; www.gc wolfrecovery.org; info@gcwolfrecovery.org). This is a grassroots, nonprofit group working to educate people and garner support to reintroduce the wolf into its natural habitat on both the North and South Rims of the Grand Canyon, where it once thrived before being hunted to extinction. People who care deeply about this important cause receive about two hours of training and education in order to donate, from May through August, an hour or a few days of their time or to receive a stipend for volunteering five or more days.

Erin's Grand Canyon Family Mission

I, along with my husband Miguel and our two-year-old son Aiden, my cousin, Miguel's parents, his sister, and her toddler, camped out for four nights at the North Rim of the Grand Canyon and donated a few hours of our time, for three days, to the Grand Canyon Wolf Recovery Project. Miguel and I were previously trained by the director, Paula Lewis. She provided us with pamphlets, bumper stickers, a coyote's skull, a mold of a wolf's footprint, a huge stuffed wolf and dog, coyote, and wolf scat.

Kids of all ages were drawn to our table. I was impressed with the parents who followed their kids' leads, asking questions and engaging in a lively dialogue about the issues. Many people wanted to do more. A professional wildlife photographer offered to create a new brochure. Others signed up for our e-mail list to receive action alerts on pending legislation, make phone calls, come to another event, help stuff envelopes, give donations, or educate others. We've already decided we're doing it again next year.

The experience really impacted my 14-year-old cousin Carly from White Plains, New York. She told me that none of her friends at home ever did anything like camping out in the Grand Canyon. She thought it was really cool learning things she never knew about, talking to other visitors and the park rangers.

Visiting the South Rim of the Grand Canyon

Xanterra South Rim, LLC (6312 South Fiddlers Green Cir., Suite 600N, Greenwood Village, CO 80111; 1-888-297-2757; 303-297-2757; fax 303-297-3175; www.grand canyonlodges.com; reserve-gcsr@xanterra.com). Xanterra operates lodging inside the Grand Canyon on the South Rim. Accommodations are also available along the road to the park's entrance and in surrounding towns, but it's exciting to stay inside the park and worth planning ahead with reservations, particularly in summer.

⑤–⑤⑤ **Bright Angel Lodge** (West Rim Dr., Grand Canyon Village, AZ 86023; 928-638-2631; 39 rooms, 50 historic cabins). The transportation information desk in the lobby takes reservations for mule rides, bus tours, plane tours, Phantom Ranch, and more, 6 AM–8 PM daily. Watch the sunset from your table in the lodge's popular

Wolf Facts

- Wolf pups weigh 1 pound at birth, and open their eyes at about two weeks old.
- The wolf was placed on the endangered species list in 1973.
- A 1998 National Wildlife Federation poll found that 76 percent of Americans support wolf restoration.

Arizona Room rather than outside along the rim to avoid the long line.

$ $–$ $ $ **El Tovar Hotel** (West Rim Dr., Grand Canyon Village, P.O. Box 699, Grand Canyon, AZ 86023; 303-297-3175). Built in 1905 and a registered National Historic Landmark, the hotel requires advance reservations, particularly for suites and rooms with full canyon views. It's also known for its restaurant, which accepts reservations.

$ $ **Yavapai Lodge** (1 Main St., Grand Canyon Village, AZ 86023; 303-29PARKS). Just 0.5 mile from the rim, Yavapai is the largest facility in the area with motel-style rooms and adjacent parking. Convenient to shopping, coin-operated laundry, bus route, and visitor center, Yavapai East has 198 air-conditioned rooms with refrigerators. Yavapai West offers 160 rooms with ceiling fans.

$ **Phantom Ranch** (Grand Canyon, AZ 86023; for required reservations, call 303-29PARKS). This is the only lodge facility below the rim. It's at the bottom of the canyon, accessed by foot, raft, or mule trip, with designated male and female dormitories, a few cabins, or campsites on the canyon's floor. Meals can be purchased.

$ **Trailer Village** (1-800-858-2808; www.grandcanyon.com or www.nps.gov/grca). A full-service RV park that is open year-round.

North Rim Lodging

The North Rim is a totally different experience from the South Rim, with fewer tourists, cooler temperatures, ponderosa pine forests, and fabulous views into the side canyons.

$ $ **Grand Canyon Lodge** (North Rim, 1-877-386-4383; www.grandcanyonlodgenorth.com). Forever Resorts

(Scottsdale, Arizona) manages these basic cabins, which are open mid-May to mid-October.

The Farthest American Outpost

Midway Atoll National Wildlife Refuge (P.O. Box 50167, Honolulu, HI 96850; 808-674-8237, ext 100; www.fws.gov/midway; Barry_Christenson@fws.gov). People who are able to provide their own transportation to Midway Island should contact the refuge manager for more information about visiting.

Laysan and black-footed albatrosses on Eastern Island, Midway Atoll National Wildlife Refuge. Midway hosts the world's largest nesting colony of both species. *Barbara Maxfield/USFWS*

Getting to Midway

Oceanic Society (Fort Mason Quarters 35 N, San Francisco, CA 94123; 1-800-326-7491; 415-474-3385; www.oceanic-society.org; menglund@oceanic-society.org; Midway Atoll National Wildlife Refuge, 1 week, limited to 16 participants, $4,890 each, includes airfare from Honolulu, Hawaii, and all accommodations). The Oceanic Society, a nonprofit group, has taken more than 5,000 people on participatory research expeditions, natural history expeditions, and other volunteer activities. Located in the middle of the North Pacific Ocean, Midway Atoll National Wildlife Refuge is a coral atoll, a historical site, and home to Hawaiian monk seals, gooney birds, green sea turtles, spinner dolphins, and many other species. The U.S. Fish & Wildlife Service oversees the site.

This is a must-see for those who care deeply about the environment and want to learn more. Midway Atoll consists of three islands and a shallow white-sand lagoon,

Hawaiian monk seal and pup on Midway Atoll. The refuge provides a habitat for about 65 of these highly endangered marine mammals. *Robert Shallenberger/USFWS*

sheltered from the surrounding Pacific Ocean by a coral reef. The atoll supports over two million seabirds, including the world's largest colonies of Laysan and black-footed albatrosses. The lagoon is great for snorkeling and green sea turtles, and spinner dolphins often visit.

The Oceanic Society charters the aircraft that takes people to Midway, which is included in the cost of the expedition. The itinerary includes guided wildlife and historical excursions, Eastern Island tour, snorkeling, and optional service projects.

Going Batty

Bat Watch (Wildlife Diversity Program, P.O. Box 53465, Oklahoma City, OK 73152; 405-424-0099; www.wildlife department.com/BatWatchWeb/AboutSelman.html; mhickman@zoo.odwc.state.ok.us). Here's a great immersion excursion that also sounds a lot like an Alfred Hitchcock movie set. Hitchcock would have loved the highlight of this bat watch, with a multitude of bats flying out of their roost and overhead.

You can experience this scene. The Selman Wildlife Management Area (WMA), located in Woodward, Oklahoma, protects and monitors one of the state's largest colonies of Mexican free-tailed bats. The bats migrate to Oklahoma each summer.

Not only will you get to view the evening flights, you'll also learn all about this flying mammal's contribution to local farmers and ranchers. Bats eat an estimated 22,000 pounds of mosquitoes, moths, and beetles each night. And don't worry. It's a myth that bats aim for human heads to deliberately entangle themselves in human hair. Bats don't like hair, but they do like bugs.

A Wildlife Department biologist escorts all visitors. The guide helps you to understand and appreciate the prairie area, also the home of the great-crested flycatcher, western meadowlark, porcupine, dickcissel, common nighthawk, canyon wren, glass lizard, Chuck-wills-widow, Swainson's hawk, turkey vulture, Texas horned lizard, and rufous-crowned and grasshopper sparrows. The area is closed to the public except during bat watch evenings, so check summer viewing dates on the calendar on the Web site and download the registration form as bat watches are limited to 75 viewers.

Bat Volunteers Wanted

Volunteers are needed to greet visitors, assist with tours, and answer visitors' questions. There is a one-day training and field workshop offered in June, and volunteers must be at least 18 years old and be willing to contribute 10 hours a year assisting with trail maintenance in the Selman WMA.

An Observatory for Stargazing

You can also enjoy stargazing after the bat watch on Friday and Saturday nights, at the University of Oklahoma's Selma Living Laboratory Observatory, and learn about constellations, star clusters, and binary stars, and perhaps catch a view of the International Space Station. Telescopes are provided and a knowledgeable staff will assist you.

Robin's Bat Story

Growing up, just the idea of bats made me shake. I believed the stories that they liked to get tangled up in human hair and thought they bit humans.

When one appeared in our old house one night, my parents, brothers, and I all screamed at the whooshing black figure that flew up and down the stairs and twice around my head. No one knew what to do so I looked in the Yellow Pages under "exterminators" and then "pest control" and found a wildlife removal service. I was so relieved when Harry answered the phone and calmly told me to check the upstairs walls until I found the bat and then to cover it with a plastic container, slide a

Bat Facts

- Bats are the only true flying mammal.
- The bones in a bat's wing are the same as those in a human arm and hand. The difference is that the bat's finger bones are elongated and support the membrane used for flight.
- Bats are not blind, but have small eyes that are sensitive to light.
- Bats have large ears to aid them in echolocation, emitting pulses of high-frequency sound waves that echo back to them.
- Bats are able to fly within two to five weeks after birth.
- Newly born bats use their feet and claws to cling to their mothers or roost when their mothers hunt.
- Bats prefer to avoid humans and are not deliberately aggressive.
- Oklahoma bats either hibernate during the winter or migrate to warmer areas.
- Vampire bats do exist, but they don't live in Oklahoma.

piece of cardboard under the bat and over the opening, and remove it to the outside.

I took care of the whole thing, which inspired me to study and learn all about bats. They are very useful creatures, protecting us from swarms of insects and helping farmers grow their crops. I attended bat classes and became obsessed with tracking their sounds using bat detectors, which are electronic devices that pick up the bats' inaudible ultrasonic echolocation calls and make them audible to humans. Eight years following this experience, and after receiving a degree in biology and education, I work as a park ranger specializing in educating the public all about bats.

One Enormous Cave

Alabaster Caverns State Park (Hwy. 50 & 50-A, Freedom, OK 73842; 580-621-3381; fax 580-621-3572; www.stateparks.com/alabaster_caverns.html; Alabaster caverns@OklahomaParks.com). Alabaster Caverns is located 6 miles from Freedom, Oklahoma, and you can explore this 200-acre park with a 0.75-mile cavern formed out of alabaster, a rare form of gypsum. There are daily tours on the hour, from 9 AM to 4 PM Group tour reservations are required at least two weeks in advance. A horseshoe pit, volleyball court, hiking trails, RV & other camping areas, picnic tables and shelters, group shelters with electricity, water, and grills are all available at the park. Wild caving is also available. Check the park Web site for directions and other information.

Hiking Exit Glacier in Alaska. *Wendy Doughty*

Saddle Up for the Rodeo

Plan your trip to include the annual **Open Rodeo and Old Cowhand Reunion** in Freedom, Oklahoma (www.freedomokla.com/rodeo.htm), situated on the banks of the Cimarron River. The Old West still lives in this small city, with nearly every building on its main street covered with native cedarwood in typical cow-town designs. The rodeo takes place the third weekend in August, and includes nightly rodeo events, western music and dancing, western art and country crafts, and a chuckwagon feed. Local residents stage a Great Freedom Bank Robbery and Shootout on Saturday afternoon.

Hug a Glacier

Kayak Adventures Worldwide (P.O. Box 2249, 328 3rd Ave., Seward, AK 99664; 907-224-3960; fax 907-224-2255; www.kayakak.com; fun@kayakak.com; office hours mid-May to mid-Sept., daily 8 AM–7 PM; Kayaking and Glacier-Hiking Package, $220 per person; Aialik Bay day-trip paddling to glaciers, $483.50 per person). Every person needs to see and touch a glacier. Walking and climbing on a glacier will increase your awareness of global warming and perhaps redefine what your role can and should be.

Hiking on Exit Glacier is a five-hour excursion. It starts with a 1.6-mile hike up the Harding Icefield Trail before dropping to the glacier. Helmets and ice gear are provided for safe navigation. Exit Glacier guides educate visitors about glacial geology and identify wildlife and plants. This hike can be physically challenging; ask questions before signing up. For those who want to paddle to a glacier, there is an Aialik Bay day trip for all ability levels.

Wendy's Story

It's awesome paddling up to Aialik Glacier to see

the giant face, over a mile across, of this tidewater

glacier. When it is actively calving, large chunks of

ice fall into the ocean with the most amazing

sound.

Paddling up to Aialik Glacier in Aialik Bay in Kenai Fjords National Park, Alaska. *Wendy Doughty*

You can't help caring about what's happening to all of the beautiful life around you. Aialik Glacier is holding relatively stable, receding slightly over time. The changes in Exit Glacier can be seen each year. There are markers along the pathway to the glacier showing where it has been to emphasize this rapid change. It makes you painfully aware of our changing and fragile environment.

Where to Stay

$⑤⑤–⑤⑤⑤ **Kayak Adventures' Bear Paw Lodge** (10411 Bear Paw Dr., Seward, AK 99664; 907-224-3960; fax 907-224-2255; www.kayakak.com/bear_paw_lodge.cfm; fun@kayakak.com; the entire lodge can be rented for $495 a night for groups of up to 13 people). Stay in this custom, hand-built log home. Filled with conveniences and charm, it's 4.5 miles from downtown Seward. Breakfast, kitchen privileges, fireplace, high-speed Internet, and hot tub are all included.

Vacation Rental

HomeAway, Inc. (3801 S. Capital of Texas Hwy., Suite 150, Austin, TX 78704; www.homeaway.com; 512-493-0375). Their Web site lists vacation rentals all over the country. Renting a home can be cost efficient compared with hotel suites or multiple rooms, particularly if you are traveling with a family or an extended group.

⑤⑤–⑤⑤⑤ **A Swan Nest Inn** (504 Adams St., Seward, AK 99664; 907-224-3080). Rooms are furnished with hand-crafted Alaskan furniture and accessories from local artists. There are beautiful views of Resurrection Bay, and shops and restaurants in the downtown area are within walking distance.

See Puffins Up Close and Personal

Kenai Fjords National Park (Alaska Heritage Tours Reservations, 509 W. 4th Ave., Anchorage, AK; 1-877-777-2805; 907-265-4501; fax 907-777-2888; www.kenai fjords.com; info@alaskaheritagetours.com; 6-hour tours include lunch, onboard wildlife guide, and free parking, $129–$139 for adults; $64.50–$69.50 for children). There are a number of different tour companies to select from. Be sure to plan a full one-day boat excursion in the Kenai Fjords National Park. It is not to be missed. You'll see abundant wildlife, spectacular fjords, glaciers, whales, sea otters, sea lions, harbor seals, and an occasional black bear. People of all ages gasp and giggle at the puffins floating by. Their antics are charming and epitomize the Alaskan experience, particularly when they seem to be waving at a bald eagle overhead or an osprey passing by. The Kenai Fjords are a highlight of any Alaska trip, and perfect for visitors of all ages and nationalities.

An Integrated Ecosystem

Tallgrass Prairie National Preserve (P.O. Box 585, 226 Broadway, Cottonwood Falls, KS 66845; 620-273-6034; fax 620-273-6099; www.nps.gov/archive/tapr/home.htm; open daily from 9 AM to 4:30 PM except Thanksgiving, Christmas, and New Year's Day). Less than 4 percent of the 400,000 square miles of tallgrass prairie that spanned North America remains, and most of it is in the Flint Hills of Kansas. The Preserve protects this ecosystem and the history of the area, and is managed jointly by the National Park Service and the Nature Conservancy (www.nature.org /wherewework/northamerica/states/kansas). It is located 2 miles north of Strong City, 18 miles west of Emporia, 16 miles south of Council Grove, and 85 miles northeast of Wichita.

Two nature trails are open daily, and three backcountry hiking trails open on weekends during the off-season, and daily during the summer. There are hundreds of varieties of prairie grass, and a variety of wildlife such as deer, fox, bobcats, and coyotes. Birds in the Preserve include hawks, wild turkey, falcons, and prairie chickens. Open to the public is an 1881 ranch house, a limestone barn, outbuildings, and a one-room schoolhouse. National Park Service (NPS) rangers give daily guided house tours, free of charge.

There are also prairie bus tours led by NPS rangers that last about an hour and a half, available daily from the last Saturday in April through the last Sunday in October. You will learn about the tallgrass prairie ecosystem, the geology that formed the Flint Hills, Native Americans, and historic ranching. For more information, e-mail tapr_interpretation@nps.gov or call 620-273-8494 for reservations.

Birds of a Feather

Connecticut Audubon Society EcoTravel (35 Pratt St., Suite 201, Essex, CT 06426; 1-800-996-8747; 860-767-0660; www.ctaudubon.org; www.ecotravel.ctaudubon.org; ecotravel@ctaudubon.org; fees dependant upon distance and size of group). EcoTravel Rarities Expeditions is a service of Connecticut Audubon that provides transportation, a driver, and a group of similarly interested people when a bird of significance or particular interest to you is spotted in a surrounding state. EcoTravel makes the arrangements and invites you to join the adventure. All you have to do is register.

Block Island is a national treasure with 17 miles of beaches, 32 miles of natural trails, and 365 fresh-water ponds off the coast of southern Rhode Island. An Audubon guide will accompany you, explaining what you see as you bike the island and view the diverse habitats. Bring your own bike or rent one (not included in fee). Fees include the guided tour and a round-trip passenger ticket for the high-speed ferry; $60 CAS members, $70 nonmembers.

Aransas National Wildlife Refuge (U.S. Fish & Wildlife Service, 1 Wildlife Cir., Austwell, TX 77950; 361-286-3559; fax 361-286-3722; www.fws.gov/southwest/REFUGES /texas/aransas/contact.html; fw2_rw_aransas@fws.gov; open daily except Thanksgiving and Christmas, 8:30 AM–4:30 PM). The Aransas National Wildlife Refuge is the winter home (from late October to mid-April) of the endangered whooping crane. The refuge is teeming with wildlife: alligators, bobcats, grizzly bear, red fox, and deer coexist with pelicans, herons, egrets, roseate spoon-bills, ducks, and geese. Commercial boat tours from Rockport are a nice way to view the cranes and 350 other bird species.

Jim's Story

I went with EcoTravel to Kent, Connecticut, on the River Road trip, which is a tremendously impor-tant and unique birding site. Many migrating war-blers come through there and you can see them relatively unencumbered. I spotted a cerulean warbler, Louisiana and northern water thrush, rough-winged swallows, solitary vireo, and wood ducks. The guide was excellent, with a lot of local knowledge. He'd been in the area numerous times and knew all of the streets, if not by name, by heart. Before actually spotting a bird he could identify it by its call.

The most exciting spotting I've ever had was when I saw the whooping crane in 1974 in Texas, at the Aransas Wildlife Refuge. I'm planning, after all these years, to return to Aransas with EcoTravel for a 10-day trip. The whooping crane winters there and I'm very excited about going.

Learning How to Ride

The Ranch (Forest Home Rd., P.O. Box 128, Lake Clear, NY 12945; 1-800-613-6033; 518-891-5684; fax 518-891-6350; www.childrenscamps.com; marleen@childrenscamps.com; winter address: P.O. Box 212, Indian Rocks Beach, FL 33785). The Ranch is a summer horse camp for girls ages 7–12. The emphasis is on creating skilled horsewomen. Campers take responsibility for the daily care of the horses. Instruction is given in western and English saddles, trail riding, jumping, and more. Special offerings include 2- to 8-week overnight programs, a mother-and-daughter week, teen travel, and golf camps.

Lovely Llamas

El Paseo Llama Expeditions (P.O. Box 2672, Taos, NM 87571; 1-800-LLAMAS; 575-758-3111; www.elpaseo llama.com; adventurer2008@elpaseollama.com; half-day fun hike, $74 per person; custom half-day hike, $84 per person; custom full-day hike, $94 per person; 2- to 8-day expeditions, from $299–$1,199 per person; children under 10, half price). All ages are welcome on llama-trekking day hikes and llama-packing treks. There are full and half-day hikes and many trails to choose from depending on the level of difficulty and location preference. Children too small to hike may ride llamas, and llamas also carry the hiking gear. El Paseo hikes and treks, in the Sangre de Cristo Mountains and the Wild River Recreation Area of northern New Mexico, are convenient to Taos, Red River, Angel Fire, and Santa Fe.

Llamas are gentle, intelligent animals that are eager to please. Children and llamas tend to get along very well together. This is an immersion excursion that encourages participants to experience and understand the llama and the environment in a broader way than one had considered them before. It includes learning about an animal many of us know little about, appreciating its background, history, and contributions. Llamas are easily trained, low maintenance, and enjoyable to be around.

Select the experience that will work best for you and your family or group. Try an easy half-day llama fun hike, which includes a picnic gourmet lunch. If you want a bit more of a challenge there are custom half-day and all-day hikes. Check the El Paseo Web site for trail descriptions and choose the one that interests you. If you want to take a multiday llama pack trek, you can choose either family or adult adventures. Air mattresses, tents, cooking equipment, food, and water are provided, and remember, the llamas, not you, carry all the gear.

Half- and full-day hikes are offered year-round. Two- to three-day expeditions operate from April to mid-November; four- to eight-day hikes are available from June to mid-October. Expeditions include gourmet meals, with ingredients from El Paseo's organic garden in season.

Click on Food for Thought on the Web site to see incredible meal and dessert selections. Call or e-mail for more information on hikes, expeditions, llamas, directions, and reservations.

Whale-Watching

San Juan Safaris (2 Spring St. Landing, Suite 6, Friday Harbor, WA 98250; 1-800-450-6858; 360-378-1323; www.sanjuansafaris.com; reservations@sanjuansafaris .com; whale-watch tours, $59 adult and $39 children). Whale-watching and wildlife tours depart daily from Friday Harbor on San Juan Island from April to October. San Juan Safaris is known for its knowledgeable and enthusiastic naturalists and small personalized tours. Guests will enjoy watching the antics of orcas in their natural habitat along with dolphins, seals, seabirds, kelp forests, lighthouses, and the beautiful shorelines of the San Juan Islands. The San Juan Safaris check-in desk is directly across the street from the ferry landing.

How to Get to Friday Harbor

Off the coast of Seattle, Washington, state ferries run from Anacortes to all of the San Juan Islands. The ferry ride from Anacortes to Friday Harbor, on the east side of San Juan Island, takes approximately one hour. Book ahead to have a place to stay.

ⓢⓢⓢ–ⓢⓢⓢⓢ **Harrison House Suites Bed & Breakfast** (235 C St., Friday Harbor, WA 98250; 1-800-407-7933; 360-378-3587; fax 360-378-2270; www .harrisonhousesuites.com; innkeeper@harrisonhouse suites.com). Nonsmoking suites with Jacuzzi, fireplace, private deck, grill, cable TV, VCR, CD player, wireless Internet, and gourmet breakfast included.

San Juan Safaris of Friday Harbor, Washington, sponsors photo contests for guests who have enjoyed whale-watching trips with them. *Claude Steelman*

Ⓢ Ⓢ **Discovery Inn** (1016 Guard St., Friday Harbor, WA 98250; 1-888-754-1016; 360-378-2000; www.rockisland .com; dinn@rockisland.com). Conveniently located 0.75 mile from the ferry landing, the inn is great for families or business travelers. It's a good value and is central to the island's beaches, hiking trails, and historical sites.

Dolphin Fun Facts

- There are 32 different species of oceanic dolphins, and five species of river dolphins.
- The average life span of bottlenose dolphins is approximately 35–55 years.
- The dolphin uses its dorsal fin for stability and thermoregulation; no two dorsal fins are exactly identical.
- The pectoral fin aids a dolphin in stopping and steering.
- The flukes are for propulsion through the water and allow the dolphin to swim upward of 20 mph.
- Dolphins have a layer of blubber below their smooth, rubbery skin.
- Dolphins breathe through a nasal opening called the blowhole, located on the top of the head. When resting, their blowhole remains tightly shut. They are able to hold their breath for an average of 4–5 minutes and a maximum of about 10 minutes.
- An adult male dolphin eats about 20 pounds of fish a day, while a nursing mother can eat 40 or more pounds daily.
- Dolphins have 20/20 vision both above and below the water and are able to see stereoscopically, focusing both eyes downward toward their stomach.
- Bottlenose dolphins are capable of distinguishing an object the size of a Ping-Pong ball from a football field away.
- Dolphins use echolocation to emit sounds, or clicks, which bounce off objects and are received by the dolphin's lower jaw as an echo.

ⓢⓢ–ⓢⓢⓢ **Friday Harbor House** (130 West St., Friday Harbor, WA 98250; 1-866-722-7356; 360-378-8455; fax 360-378-8453; www.fridayharborhouse.com; Berit@ FridayHarborHouse.com). Friday Harbor House is next door to the Whale Museum, a must stop.

Eat with the Locals

⑤ **Rocky Bay Café** (225 Spring St., Friday Harbor, WA 98250; 360-378-5051). The locals call this the doughnut shop for the perfect breakfast stop.

⑤–⑤⑤ **Friday's Crabhouse** (65 Front St., Friday Harbor, WA 98250, 360-378-5258; www.fridayscrabhouse .com; sales@fridayscrabhouse.com). A local favorite known for its great seafood and sea views.

⑤⑤–⑤⑤ **Downriggers Restaurant** (10 Front St., Friday Harbor, WA 98250; 360-378-2700; www.downriggerssan juan.com; downriggers@rockisland.com). Dining on the waterfront for breakfast, lunch, and dinner; the specialty is Pacific Northwest seafood.

Dolphins and Sea Lions, Oh My!

Dolphins Plus (31 Corrine Pl., Key Largo, FL 33037; 305-451-1993; 1-866-860-7946; fax 305-451-3710; www .dolphinsplus.com; info@dolphinsplus.com; observers and guests 7–17 years old, $5; adults, $10; under 7 years old, free; Natural Dolphin Swim, $125 per swimmer for 30 minutes in water, $210 per swimmer for 60 minutes in water; Sea Lion Encounter $100, with any dolphin swim, $80; Structured Dolphin Swim, $165 per swimmer, non-peak season, $185 per swimmer, peak season; booking office, 305-451-1993 or 1-866-860-SWIM). Imagine swimming with dolphins, encounters with sea lions, and an exciting opportunity to get up close and personal with these amazing marine mammals.

Dolphins Plus offers Natural Dolphin Swims, Structured Dolphin Swims, and Sea Lion Encounters in Key Largo, an hour south of Miami. The facility is located on a canal adjacent to the Atlantic Ocean, which creates a natural seawater home for Atlantic bottlenose dolphins and California sea lions. Dolphins Plus is also an educational and research facility, working with the Marine Mammal Conservancy and the Southeast Marine Mammal Stranding Network (305-451-4774).

Visitors learn about dolphin and sea lion natural history, anatomy, social behavior, reproductive biology, echolocation, and conservation, and follow the briefing with an in-water program. During structured dolphin swims and sea lion encounters, individuals participate in a variety of trained behaviors, such as belly rubs, kisses, and dorsal tows. For the natural dolphin swims, participants enter the water with mask, fins, and snorkel, and swim along with the dolphins, but without direct contact.

Dolphin and sea lion swims are by appointment only and reservations are not accepted online. Call the booking office for reservations, program details, and directions. An extensive list of local hotels, motels, condos, campgrounds, and nearby attractions can be found on the Dolphins Plus Web site.

A Mother and Daughter's Wonderfully Wet Tale

When my children and I were visiting Maui, I wanted to do something memorable together. I booked a "swim with the dolphins" boat trip for a morning. We arrived and were outfitted with wetsuits, goggles, and flippers. After about a half-hour traveling from the shore someone spotted our first school of dolphin. The captain stopped the boat, threw a ladder over the side, and people began descending into the water. My daughter jumped off the ladder and within seconds yelled up at me, "Look, over there! A herd of dolphin!

Living Green

Campaign Earth (P.O. Box 7672, 8 Pier Rd., Cape Porpoise, ME 04014; 207-459-0419; www.campaignearth.org; general@campaignearth.org). Campaign Earth is a user-friendly Web site geared toward enabling people interested in developing a living green consciousness.

Let's go!" She began swimming across the ocean with such lightning speed she appeared dolphin-like. All I could think was how vast the ocean is and how slight she is. She competed in the front crawl with her high school swim team. I swam faster than I've ever swum in my life. She enjoyed the dolphin; I had a workout keeping up with them, and my eye on her. It truly was very exciting swimming out in the deep, expansive water as free as the dolphin.

It Can Be Fun and Easy Being Green

Green Festivals (www.greenfestivals.org; Alesha Reardon, National Volunteer Director, 828-236-0324, ext. 122; www.greenfestivals.org; volunteer@green festivals.org). This organization, a joint project of Global Exchange and Co-op America, produces annual Green Festivals in Chicago, Seattle, San Francisco, and Washington, D.C.

Global Exchange (www.globalexchange.org) and Co-op America (www.coopamerica.org) are nonprofit action and resource centers that emphasize creating an

Not All Accommodations Are the Same

Green Hotels Association (P.O. Box 420212, Houston, TX 77242-0212; 713-789-8889; fax 713-789-9786; www.greenhotels.com; info@greenhotels.com). This organization supports and encourages eco-consciousness in travel and hospitality. Abundant information and resources enable travelers to go green, creating entire immersion excursions and respecting local culture, resources, and ways of life.

environmentally sustainable world. Green Festivals are a celebration of the successful efforts of businesses, organizations, community groups, and concerned individuals. They are called "parties with a purpose," with the aim of educating the public about greener ways of living. Organizations and businesses promote their green services and products, speakers offer relevant and dynamic presentations, and issues of personal, local, national, and global concern are discussed. The festivals also offer music, art, food, and other local cultural attractions. There are how-to workshops, green films, yoga and movement classes, and green careers sessions.

Speakers and exhibitors can find applications on the Web site. Hundreds of volunteers are needed at each event, and are an essential part of Green Festivals. Become a member of the Volunteer Media Team and record the event through photography, video, and audio technology. Professionals, students, and those interested in helping to share Green Festivals with the rest of the world are welcome. Join the Volunteer Street Team and assist with volunteer outreach and recruitment before an event, or help out at the festival.

Volunteers who are able to commit to at least one 4½-hour shift, or help set up the event, will receive free admission each day, an organic and sweatshop-free Green Festival T-shirt, a 10 percent discount for the Global Exchange Store, and a free one-year membership in either Co-op America or Global Exchange. This offer is available to new members only. Make a Green Festival a stop on your next planned vacation or find out if there is one scheduled in your area. Meet new people, have fun, learn what you can do to make a difference, and support a great cause. It's pretty amazing how much most of us need to learn and fantastic that an organization like this is so accessible with the information and know-how. Bring the whole family and get, and stay, involved.

Ichthyology

Gray's Reef National Marine Sanctuary (10 Ocean Science Circle, Savannah, GA 31411; 912-598-2345; fax 912-598-2367; www.graysreef.noaa.gov). Gray's Reef National Marine Sanctuary is one of the largest near-shore, live-bottom reefs in the country. It is 17 square miles (about 11,000 acres) of protected natural area off the Georgia coast, accessible only by private boats. Gray's Reef is a rock outcropping that stands above the shifting sands of the continental shelf. It supports a wide variety of invertebrates, soft corals, and sponges, which sustain a wide variety of reef and pelagic fish, making it a popular spot for diving and recreational fishing. The sanctuary is used as a living classroom by educators, and scientists conduct marine research projects there.

The Dolphin Project, Inc. (P.O. Box 10323, Savannah, GA 31412; www.thedolphinproject.org). The Dolphin Project (TDP) is a nonprofit group that uses volunteers to conduct a long-term, scientific study counting Atlantic bottlenose dolphins quarterly along the East Coast. Anyone can join. Their mission is to educate the public about marine mammals and expand knowledge and concern for the environment. TDP actively collects data to broaden the understanding of bottlenose dolphins. Members conduct field research using 16- to 35-foot boats in sounds and tidal rivers from Hilton Head, South Carolina, to Fernandina Beach, Florida.

Training sessions are offered four times a year in Atlanta and Savannah to teach people how to conduct surveys. There's no charge for the four-hour orientation and training; however, members do pay their own expenses while conducting surveys. Participants come from all over the United States and abroad. This study is unique among dolphin research programs for its longevity, quarterly abundance surveys, and self-funding.

The Dolphin Project seeks members who:

- Love dolphins
- Enjoy the Georgia coastline and marine environment
- Relish being outdoors
- Wish to participate in scientific field research

Energy Planning for the Future

The Chewonki Foundation (485 Chewonki Neck Rd., Wiscasset, ME 04578; 207-882-7323; 207-882-4074; www.chewonki.org; info@chewonki.org; fees vary according to trip). The Chewonki philosophy is that there are no limits to opportunities for life-changing experiences. Caring about the environment begins with knowledge and experience. The Foundation conducts tours and seminars for children and adults on hydrogen, solar heat, electricity, energy, and aggressive conservation techniques.

Seasonal programming is diverse. In the winter you can live in the forest for a week in a wood-heated yurt and take daily hikes with a guide. Summer trips include canoeing and whitewater rafting.

Chewonki has operated its vehicles and buildings on biodiesel fuel created from vegetable oil since 2000. A part of the energy and sustainability workshops is experiencing firsthand the biodiesel production facility and actively discussing energy issues facing future generations.

Dishwashing Detergent Dawn Really Does Cut Through Oily Grease

International Bird Rescue Research Center (IBRRC) locations:

- **San Francisco Oiled Wildlife Care and Education Center** (SFBOCEC, 4369 Cordelia Rd., 707-207-0380, www.ibrrc.org; info@ibrrc.org).

- **Southern California Bird Center** (3601 South Gaffey St., San Pedro, CA 90731; 310-514-2573; www.ibrrc.org; info@ibrrc.org).

Simone, a corn snake, is comfortably wrapped around Dan Clere's arm as he educates visitors about area snakes at the Western North Carolina Nature Center in Asheville, North Carolina.

Jonathan Engle with Art, a barred owl. Art was hit by a car and cannot live in the wild. He permanently resides in the Western North Carolina Nature Center.

- **Alaska Wildlife Response Center** (6132 Nielson Way, Anchorage, AK 99518; 907-562-1329; www.ibrrc.org/alaska_center.html; info@ibrrc.org).

When disaster strikes and birds are threatened by the effects of oil spills, this organization depends upon the caring, time, and training of people to provide the needed services. When 50 bald eagles feasted at a Kodiak, Alaska, fish-processing plant, about 20 died in the fish-gut sludge and the survivors needed to be bathed, according to Barbara Callahan of the International Bird Rescue Research Center. A total of 31 bald eagles were transported by the U.S. Coast Guard from Kodiak to Anchorage for cleaning, care, and rehabilitation. The 60 trained volunteers had to scrub each eagle with unscented Dawn dish detergent to remove the fish oil and slime that soaked their feathers, then rinse them in a wood-framed structure covered in plastic to keep the air hot and humid. Then the birds were placed in a warming room with hair dryers blowing hot air on them. Traumatizing for the birds and exhausting for the workers, emergency situations like this illustrate how important it is for people who care to give of themselves in times of need.

Back to Nature

Western North Carolina Nature Center (75 Gashes Creek Rd., Asheville, NC 28805; 828-298-5600; fax 828-298-2644; www.wildwnc.org; kmastin@ashevillenc.gov). Google "nature centers in the United States" and 4,570,000 appear in 20 seconds. That's a lot of nature centers and they truly are all over the country. Nature centers are a great way to teach children to care for and appreciate the environment and wildlife in their lives and all around them. It is not unusual for local nature centers to offer nursery school or outreach education programs. Inquire what's available in your town, county, and state. Perhaps there's a nature center nearby that could enhance your life and knowledge by becoming an ongoing immersion experience.

Go to Visit the Resident Otter

The Western North Carolina Nature Center (WNCNC) is a living museum of plants and animals native to the Appalachian region. They offer diverse programs to increase public awareness and understanding of the natural environment through hands-on and sensory experiences. There are approximately 160 animals living in WNCNC, many of which have been injured or imprinted by humans and cannot be released back into the wild. WNCNC is part of the endangered species program, serving as a breeding facility for the red wolf. Alligator River National Wildlife Refuge, on the east coast of North Carolina, is the release site for the red wolves.

Caring Through Personal Experience

North Cascades Institute and North Cascades Environmental Learning Center (810 State Rt. 20, Sedro Woolley, WA 98284; 360-856-5700; www.ncascades .org; www.ncascades.org/learning_center; nci@ncascades .org). The North Cascades Institute and North Cascades Environmental Learning Center are located on State Route 20, less than three hours northeast of Seattle in the North Cascades National Park. Dedicated to the idea that learning together inspires stewardship, programming aims to connect people to the land through education and experience exploring the history and science of the Northwest. Trails lead hikers up the Skagit River deep into the mountains. Choose to paddle a canoe on glacier-fed Diablo Lake or study salmon and songbirds with naturalists. Family getaways, summer camp, and mountain school are a few of the offerings.

Stellwagen Bank National Marine Sanctuary (SBNMS, 175 Edward Foster Rd., Scituate, MA 02066; 781-545-8026; www.stellwagen.noaa.gov). Using geographic information systems, the sanctuary determined that a great majority of right whales were feeding in the direct path of the Boston shipping lanes. By moving the shipping lanes 5 miles north there was an 85 percent reduction in ship strikes on right whales. Whale-watching, fishing, diving, and birding are just a few of the ongoing activities at the sanctuary. There are also fascinating projects and studies, including the mapping of the sea floor, the sounds and communications of whales, and contests to name the wildlife. Scientific exhibits and programs are available in surrounding centers in Massachusetts:

- New England Aquarium—Boston
- Gloucester Maritime Heritage Center—Gloucester
- Scituate Maritime and Irish Mossing Museum—Scituate
- Cape Cod National Seashore Province Lands Visitor Center—Provincetown
- Cape Cod Museum of Natural History—Brewster
- Woods Hole Aquarium—Woods Hole

Care to Contribute

Citizen Scientists (The Provincetown Center for Coastal Studies, 5 Holway Ave., Provincetown, MA 02657; 508-487-3623, ext. 107; www.coastalstudies.org; whalewatch @coastalstudies.org). The Provincetown Center for Coastal Studies (PCCS) conducts an active citizen scientists program to monitor the water quality of Cape Cod Bay. A minimum of 12 sites, from Provincetown to Plymouth, are sampled weekly from June through October during mid-ebb tide by the citizen scientists. These areas are not accessible by boat. Important data is collected on water

Animal Heading

"An animal's eyes have the power to speak a great language."

—Martin Buber, philosopher

temperature, salinity, turbidity, dissolved oxygen, pH, and nutrients.

The Sharks Are Free, Observers Are Caged

Cage Diver (national headquarters: 6604 Midnight Pass Rd., Sarasota, FL 34242; 941-346-2603; 1-800-644-7382; fax 941-346-2488; www.cagediver.com; info@cagediver .com; select Saturdays and Sundays, mid-Sept. through Nov.; $875 for cage diving, $373 for topside viewing). Cage dive with great white sharks, 30 miles off the coast of California, leaving early in the morning from Fisherman's Wharf in San Francisco. Boats will accommodate 18 cage divers and 10 topside viewers. If you are over age 18 you do not need to be dive certified, but

A diver awaits a shark sighting off the coast of California. Cage Diver boats leave from Fisherman's Wharf in San Francisco for the Gulf of the Farallones National Marine Sanctuary, which has one of the largest concentrations of white sharks in the world. *Tim Taylor*

Cage Diver takes you to the best viewing areas at the best time of the year to see the great white shark. *Incredible Adventures*

some underwater experience is preferred. Under age 18 you must be dive certified and accompanied by a parent or guardian. Topside viewing is open to anyone over age 10 with an adult.

The Gulf of the Farallones National Marine Sanctuary protects 948 square nautical miles off the northern and central California coast and has one of the largest concentrations of white sharks in the world. It is home to 27 endangered or threatened species, including the blue whale, and breeding seabirds.

A wet suit and equipment will be provided, and a suggested packing list will be sent to you before your day at sea. The shark viewing boat returns to Fisherman's Wharf before 5 PM. There is no guarantee you will see sharks, but you will be taken to the best viewing areas at the best time of year. A reservation form, shark policies, and a release of liability are available on the Web site. For visitor information and where to stay and dine, visit www.fishermanswharf.org.

Total Immersion with the Manatees

Cap'n Mike's Swim with the Manatees (5297 S. Cherokee Way Homosassa, FL 34448; 1-866-645-5727; www.swimwithmanatees.com; captainmike@sunshine rivertours.com; seasonal tours Nov.–Mar., 6 AM and 9 AM; $10 observers only, $50 to swim with the manatees for all ages, snorkel gear included). Manatees are gentle and enormous creatures. Directions are given to guests on appropriate interaction with the animals. Manatees not interested in human contact are able to maneuver below swimmers while the animals choosing to interact might rub noses or turn over for a belly rub. Check out the video on their Web site.

Cap'n Mike insists that the manatees are the most active in the early morning when they are feeding. The first run of the day is at 6 AM. The downside is that it's very early, but the upside is seeing the sun rise up and over the manatees floating all around you. Later in the day they tend to eat less and sleep more.

Homosassa Springs State Wildlife Park (4150 S. Suncoast Blvd., Homosassa, FL 34446; recorded information 352-628-2311; office Mon.–Fri., 8 AM–5 PM). This is a low-key nature park, easy to manage with young children. There are beautiful flamingos, herons, wood ducks, and egrets. A hands-on exhibit in the visitor center is a popular stop for kids of all ages. Homosassa Springs is home to the wintering manatee: large, lumbering, and loveable.

Where to Stay

$ $ $–$ $ $ $ **Homosassa Riverside Resort** (5297 S. Cherokee Way, Homosassa, FL 34448; 1-800-442-2040; 352-628-2474; fax 352-628-5208; www.homosassa riverside.net; info@RiversideResorts.com). Roll out of bed and onto Cap'n Mike's tour boat for the 6 AM run to watch the sun rise over the manatees. A restaurant and a monkey park are on the premises.

$ $–$ $ $ **Comfort Inn** (4486 N. Suncoast Blvd. US 19 N, Crystal River, FL 34428; 352-563-1500; fax 352-563-5426; www.comfortinn.com; info@comfortinn.com). A block from Homosassa Springs State Wildlife Park, 4 miles from Crystal River State Archaeological State Park, 12 minutes from Cap'n Mike's, and 75 miles from Walt Disney World.

Spring Bayou Inn (32 West Tarpon Ave., Tarpon Springs, FL 34689; 727-938-9333; www.springbayouinn .com; info@springbayouinn.com). This is a turn-of-the-century beauty with a wraparound front porch, heart-of-pine original woodwork, antiques, and six spacious rooms, each with private bath, wireless Internet, and breakfast included. Tarpon Springs is the sponge capital of the world, a place where Greek immigrants came to harvest natural sponges from the sea. Visit the original sponge docks, and enjoy the Greek history and ethnic cuisine.

Did You Know?

- Manatees are herbivores. They eat approximately 15 percent of their body weight daily.
- Manatees squeak and squeal when frightened, playing, or communicating.
- Manatees can grow to be 13 feet long and weigh more than 3,000 pounds.
- Calves are born weighing about 40 pounds and weigh about 740 pounds at their first birthday.

Annette's Story

Annette, a senior citizen, was the first one into the manatee-filled water. "It was absolute magic down there. I've never done anything like this. I read about swimming with the manatees in a magazine and knew I had to come. This isn't something I'm able to do back in my homeland of Australia. I drove in from the East Coast last night and slept in my car to be here for the 5:30 AM tour. The manatees were so gentle and beautiful. I could have stayed with them all day. They kept visiting me, rubbing against my face, looking into my eyes, being with me. It was amazing. I'll always remember their feel and touch."

5

Playing

Enjoy the Great Outdoors, Sports, and the Arts

You've got to get to the stage in life where going for it is more important than winning or losing.

—Arthur Ashe, *athlete*

People definitely need to play more. Great outdoor travel adventures are a means of refreshment and diversion, renewal, pleasure, and entertainment. In this chapter, many of the selections combine having fun with some very hard work, as anyone who has been on a cattle drive would agree. These immersion excursions have components that cross over into Learning, Caring, Helping, and Working, although the emphasis is on Playing and outdoor recreation. This is the real appeal of immersion travel—to be immersed in an environment that adds, in so many different ways, to the travel experience.

Playing also includes a diverse range of immersion travel excursions from the quietly sublime to the highly active and energetic. Let your playful spirit emerge and have fun!

Baseball Quote

"Baseball is America's game. It has the snap, go, fling of the American atmosphere."

—Walt Whitman, poet

Play Ball

New York Yankees Fantasy Camp (Tampa, Florida; 1-800-368-CAMP; 813-875-7753; www.newyork.yankees .mlb.com/nyy/fan_forum/fantasycamp.jsp; jkremer@ yankees.com; Nov. and Jan., one week each, $5,500). Share the field with a few of the greats from your childhood. Participants wear the authentic New York Yankees pinstripes, play an eight-game schedule, and receive signed souvenirs and team and camp photos. Accommodations are private rooms in a nearby suites hotel with transportation from the airport and daily bus to the field. Daytime meals provided.

Take Me Out to the Ball Game

The National Baseball Hall of Fame & Museum (25 Main St., Cooperstown, NY 13326; 1-888-HALL-OF-FAME; 607-547-7200; fax 607-547-2044; www.baseballhalloffame .org;). Take a brief immersion excursion into America's national pastime. Baseball unites a vast country by a game that the poet Walt Whitman described as America's game, belonging as much to the American way of life as its constitution and laws. Founded in the 1930s by a group of Cooperstown businessmen and officials of the major leagues, the National Baseball Hall of Fame is where memories and history reside.

The mission is to preserve history, honor excellence, and connect generations. Plaques of all Hall of Fame members line the walls of the Hall of Fame Gallery. Only 1 percent of all who have played in the major leagues are honored in the Hall of Fame. Begin your immersion into the world of baseball with a multimedia presentation called "The Baseball Experience." Enter the Baseball Timeline and explore the history of the game. Visit the Babe Ruth Room, the Women in Baseball exhibit, and the African American Baseball Experience. Salute No-Hitters, the Presidential Pastime, Youth Baseball, Baseball Cards, and Baseball at the Movies. End your tour of baseball on Sacred Ground, the exhibit that examines ballparks of the past. An interactive section commemorates music at the ballparks and traces the history of "Take Me Out to the Ball Game."

Contact the Cooperstown Chamber of Commerce (www.cooperstownchamber.org) for hotels, motels, and bed & breakfasts, where to dine, a calendar of events, and other attractions in Cooperstown. Check out the Fenimore Art Museum, the Glimmerglass Opera, and the Farmer's Museum. If you drive to Cooperstown consider bringing your bike, as Cooperstown is a beautiful village with scenic rides to enhance your immersion experience.

Plan the perfect family vacation or getaway with your baseball buddies at the National Baseball Hall of Fame & Museum. Located on Main Street in the center of Cooperstown, the museum is open daily from 9 AM to 5 PM (with the exception of Thanksgiving Day, Christmas Day, and New Year's Day) from the day after Labor Day through the Thursday before Memorial Day weekend, and from 9 AM to 9 PM from the Friday of Memorial Day through Labor Day Monday. Admission prices are $16.50 for adults (13 and over), $11 for seniors (65 and over), and $6 for juniors (ages 7–12). Group rates are available as well as AAA discounts, and admission is free for museum members and active or retired military personnel. The museum is handicapped accessible and video programs are captioned for the hearing impaired. And you're only about four hours away from the opportunity to watch major-league New York or Massachusetts teams play ball.

Ghostball Players

Field of Dreams (28963 Lansing Rd., Dyersville, IA; 1-800-443-8981; www.roadsideamerica.com/attract/IADYEdreams.html; open Apr.–Nov., 9 AM to 6 PM, free admission). It may have been a field of dreams in the movie, but it is in fact a field in Iowa, and a very popular tourist attraction. If you are a fan of the movie, Shoeless Joe, athletic ghosts, or anything baseball, be sure to make a "shortstop" here. Built on the adjoining property of two Iowa farmers, the off-the-beaten-path landmark has off-beat allure. Until September 2007, one farmer owned left and centerfield; the other the infield and bleachers. One half closed when the clock struck (out) six; the other

The Start of Something New

Alexander Cartwright loved to play town ball on Sundays in New York City with his friends. Town ball was played with a ball, paddles, posts that had to be touched, and up to 25 players on a team, all who had a chance to paddle before the other team had its turn. The story goes that Cartwright, who is often referred to as the father of organized baseball, created some rules and drew a baseball diamond and called his new version of the game "baseball" in 1845, with flat bases and nine players. The Knickerbocker Baseball Club was the first team, and they played the New York Nines in Hoboken, New Jersey, on June 19, 1846. The Nines won, 23 to 1.

stayed open until sunset. However, in September 2007, one farmer bought the other's property and now left and centerfield close at the same time the infield retires for the night.

So, if you are in the neighborhood, stop by with your mitt, bat, and ball, and catch, hit, and pitch to your heart's content until your baseball fantasy plays itself out. But don't wait for the ghost players to emerge from the cornfields. The semipro team that used to dress in turn-of-the-century uniforms and hide in the cornfields until game time has retired as well. Oh, and if you steal an ear of corn rather than a base, there is a sign, next to a box, asking you to please leave money for it. Batter up.

Fore!

Steve Dresser Golf Academy (80 Pinehurst Ln., Pawleys Island, SC 29585; 1-800-397-2678; www.dressergolf.com; info@dressergolf.com; 3-day "No Frills" Instruction Only Package, with no meals or accommodations, available year-round, $399; the most popular 3-day commuter package, including lunch and three golf rounds, $699 per person in spring and fall, $599 in summer and winter; accommodations packages based on a 4-day stay True Blue Condo Packages from $824 to $1,089 per person, depending on season and dates, and Hampton Inn Packages, which range from $784 to $954 per person depending on dates; customized packages available). Calling all golfers. Whether you are a beginner or an advanced player, you will benefit from instruction at the Golf Academy, with its building-block approach and the latest technology.

There are two-, three-, and five-day programs available, as well as private lessons, clinics, and playing lessons. The Academy offers computerized club fitting and laser putter fitting, as well as video swing analysis.

17-Mile Drive, Pebble Beach, California

View the stunning vistas along the 17-Mile Drive, guided by a map given to you when you pay the under-$10 admission fee. There are about 20 marked stops, as well as road signs, so you will be sure to see the most popular landmarks, have the best views, and know which of the world famous golf courses you are passing. The road runs inland past Spanish Bay, then along the beaches, then through the coastal hills. You will see the Lone Cypress tree, which is actually trademarked and the official symbol of Pebble Beach, by itself on a rocky perch with the water beyond. You will drive past Shepherd's Knoll, with views of the Monterey Bay and Gabilan Mountains; Point Joe, where the underwater rocks were the cause of many shipwrecks; Bird Rock, where you can see birds, seals, and sea lions just offshore; Fanshell Overlook, with a view of a white sand beach; the Ghost Tree, which is a bleached Monterey cypress; and the Restless Sea, with its powerful, crashing waves. Golf courses include Del Monte, the Links at Spanish Bay, Spyglass Hill, and of course, the famous Pebble Beach Golf Links.

Classes are held from 9 AM to 1 PM, and all programs include one round at both True Blue and Caledonia golf courses. Three- and five-day programs include an additional round at True Blue. Lunch is included after classes, and students receive a welcome gift, enjoy unlimited practice, take home a CD of their own swing, and receive a copy of Steve Dresser's book, *Golf From the Ground Up.*

The complete schedule with current rates is on the Golf Academy Web site with information on lodging, private lessons, directions, and additional area activities. Pawleys Island is located 70 miles north of Charleston and 25 miles south of Myrtle Beach. Learn more about Pawleys Island at www.townofpawleysisland.com.

Love Game

Gardiner's Resort and Tennis Club (P.O. Box 228, 114 West Carmel Valley Rd., Carmel Valley, CA 93924; 1-800-453-6225; 831-659-2207; fax 831-659-2492; www .gardiners-resort.com; reservations@gardiners-resort.com; 3-day tennis package, Thurs. arrival, $1,800–$1,980 double occupancy, $1,440–$1,590, single occupancy; 3-day tennis package, Sun. arrival, $1,635–$1,735 double occupancy, $1,310–$1,390, single occupancy). Indulge your passion for tennis at one of the top-rated tennis camps in the world. Located in the Carmel Valley, surrounded by the Santa Lucia Mountains, Gardiner's Resort and Tennis Club offers a three-day tennis package that includes 10½ hours of tennis clinics, accommodations, gourmet meals, and use of the resort's facilities.

There is a 3½-hour clinic each morning, with afternoons free and the option of private lessons, working with a ball machine, relaxing at the resort, or sightseeing. You can drive to Big Sur, Carmel-by-the-Sea, or Monterey, golf at a nearby course, visit Carmel Valley wineries, explore Point Lobos State Reserve, or take the 17-Mile Drive in Pebble Beach. Tennis clinics focus on groundstrokes, net play, serve and return of serve, and doubles and singles strategies. There will be a video analysis and review and a round robin.

Accommodations have names like Wimbledon, Grand Slam, Center Court, and Forest Hills, and all rooms have a private patio, fireplace, cable TV, complimentary fruit, beverages, coffees, and teas. Fresh juice and the newspaper will be delivered to your door each morning, with breakfast served in the Clubhouse. Lunch will be served on the Patio, after the conclusion of the clinic, and hors d'oeuvres and dinner will be in the Clubhouse, all part of your inclusive tennis package.

Visit the Resort Web site for driving directions, more information on the resort, and area attractions, as well as Web-only special rates and packages.

Stick Shift

Skip Barber Driving School (P.O. Box 1629, Lakeville, CT 06039; 1-800-221-1131; 860-435-1300; fax 860-435-1321; www.skipbarber.com/driving_school/driving_school.aspx; speed@skipbarber.com; one-day program, $999; two-day program, $1,399; high-performance car one-day program, $1,799; two-day high-performance car program, $2,999; one-day combo program ranges from $1,199 to $1,499). Imagine a getaway to one of the best-known driving and racing facilities in the country: Road Atlanta in Braselton, Georgia; Sebring International Raceway in Sebring, Florida; Lime Rock Park in Lime Rock, Connecticut; Mazda Raceway Laguna Seca in Monterey, California; or Road America in Elkhart Lake, Wisconsin. Master the same skills that professional drivers use to control and handle any car on any road.

With one- and two-day programs at five locations across the country, driving school instructors teach you the fundamentals of safe driving, and racing skills that will make you a better driver, while you experience the thrill of the racetrack. Essential training is given regarding vehicle dynamics and behavior, slides and recoveries, threshold braking, lane-toss exercises, and accident avoidance, in a one-day program. Hone your new skills in a Mazda RX-8, MX-5, and Mazda 3s. Graduates from the one-day class are eligible to enroll in the Advanced Control Program at a later date.

The two-day program builds on the one-day driving school lessons, adding heel and toe downshifting, emergency lane changes, street awareness training, and etiquette and road manners. Graduates are eligible to enroll in the Car Control Clinic at the racing school. Check the Web site for complete program schedules, descriptions of racetracks, a detailed program comparison chart, and registration information.

For racing enthusiasts, there are also one- and two-day high-performance programs, using powerful sports cars such as the Porsche 911, Cayman and Boxster, and the BMW 330i. There is also a One-Day Combo that offers a combination of components from the driving and racing programs. Participants must be able to drive a car with manual transmission and are required to sign a release and waiver and liability, assumption of risk and indemnity agreement. More information on these programs is available on the Web site.

Louis's Driving Story

I attended an all-day program at the Skip Barber Driving School at the Limerock Auto Race Track in upstate Connecticut, near the town of Sharon. In the morning we had a two-hour class with 14 other students ranging in age from late teens to 60s. The classroom gave you an understanding as to the dynamics of driving, including the physics behind steering, accelerating, and stopping. After the class we were divided into three groups.

We took turns driving with an instructor in a pickup truck to learn control skidding, and then we upgraded to driving a Dodge Neon to learn emergency lane change and control braking. Most of the afternoon was spent driving the Neon on a modified racetrack seated next to an instructor. After spending time on the track we each had the opportunity to drive with an instructor in a Dodge Viper. The Viper is probably the fastest factory car built, going from zero to 60 miles per hour in a little over four seconds. Each student, with an instructor, drove the Viper around the track. That was definitely the most exciting part of the day. I felt totally safe the whole time and realized how much concentration is required to race a car, let alone just to drive. Forget listening to music, drinking coffee, or talking on a cell phone! Driving on the track demanded my total attention. By the end of the day I was both exhilarated and exhausted.

Flower Power

New York Botanical Gardens (200th St. and Kazimiroff Blvd., Bronx, NY 10458-5126; 1-800-322-6924; 718-817-8700; www.nybg.org; info@nybg.org; open year-round, Tues. to Sun., 10 AM–6 PM, check for holiday and special events; 20 minutes by train from Grand Central Station on Metro-North Railroad; general fees $13 for adults, $5 for children; program fees vary). The vast offering of courses and programs at the New York Botanical Gardens will amaze you. It's much more than a beautiful place to visit; it's the perfect way to supplement a trip to New York City. Experience botanical art and illustration, floral design, horticulture, botany, gardening, horticultural therapy, landscape design, garden writing, photography, and botanical crafts. Workshops are given on how to design and maintain a naturalistic garden, including plant selection for a wide range of climates and conditions. A favorite course is tree climbing, offered in June for all ages on some fantastic trees.

Climb Every Mountain

Mountain Madness (3018 SW Charleston St., Seattle, WA 98126; 206-937-8389; 1-800-328-5925; fax 206-937-1772; www.mountainmadness.com; info@Mountainmadness .com; Intro to Mountaineering, 4 days, $875; Glacier Mountaineering, 6 days, $1,200; Alpine Mountaineering, 8 days, $1,675, and 13 days, $2,300). Once you master the necessary techniques, you will continue building on your skills to go as high or as far as you choose to go. Mountain Madness Alpine Mountaineering School offers mountaineering courses in the North Cascades and Olympic National Parks, the Alpine Lakes, Glacier Peak, and Mount Baker Wilderness Areas.

Select from the basics to the most advanced skills; level one requires no previous experience and includes an Introduction to Mountaineering, a Glacial Mountaineering course, and both 8- and 13-day Alpine Climbing courses. Level two courses include an Expedition Training course in the North Cascades and Alpine Ice-Climbing courses. Level three offers expeditions to the Pickets Traverse, a sub-range of the North Cascades, and one of the few remaining alpine mountain wildlands in the country. You will find complete course descriptions on the Web site, as well as dates, itineraries, costs, qualifications, equipment needed, client/guide ratios, and climbing grades.

Accredited by the American Mountain Guides Association, Mountain Madness staff have been trained and certified by the Association, and are Wilderness First

Responders. Trips include meals and cooking equipment, tents, and group transportation from Seattle to the mountain and back, some climbing equipment, with the option of renting additional equipment as needed. Mountain Madness also offers courses in rock climbing, backcountry ski programs, an avalanche program, waterfall ice climbing, and women's programs. Check Web site for more information.

Traversing the summit ridge of Mixup Peak in the North Cascades, Washington. *Mountain Madness Collection*

Cathleen's Mountaineering Story

I had been doing some rock climbing and wanted to improve my skills and start getting into mountaineering. I started searching for programs by Googling Mt. Rainier in Washington State, since it's a rather significant peak, and found a number of programs. I liked Mountain Madness because they seemed pretty friendly, they have low guide/climber ratios, and they bring the food—backcountry gourmet!—so you don't have to be bothered preparing your own. I took the basic Glacier Mountaineering course in the North Cascades, in a group of four—two women and two men—with one guide. We learned mountaineering skills, including ice axe and crampon usage, techniques for self and team arrest, crevasse rescue, glacier and roped travel skills, and route finding and navigation. You learn basic skills like how to arrest your own fall or the fall of someone on your rope team, and tips like how much rope you need to leave between climbers. The guide, Geoff, was highly skilled technically and a natural at teaching. I liked the course and learned a lot, so I kept going.

In a group experience, people accomplish different skills at varying rates. I really enjoyed climbing one-on-one with a private guide in Red

Rocks, outside of Las Vegas. With a private guide, I

learned more advanced techniques and he was

able to focus on the particular skills I really

needed to work on.

Each Activity Has Its Season

Carson National Forest (208 Cruz Alta Rd., Taos, NM 87571; 575-758-6200; fax 575-758-6213; www.fs.fed.us/ r3/carson; mailroom_r3_carson@fs.fed.us). One of five national forests in New Mexico, Carson National Forest covers 1.5 million acres, with elevations from 6,000 to 13,161 feet at Wheeler Peak, the highest in New Mexico. You can fish, hike, camp, or hunt, and ski and snowshoe in winter. In the 86,000+ acres of designated wilderness, travel is on foot or horseback only. Wildlife includes mule deer, elk, antelope, black bear, mountain lion, and bighorn sheep. There are 330 miles of trails.

For more information on camping, fishing, trails, winter sports, and wilderness areas, go to Recreational Activities on the Carson National Forest Web site. Consider a trip in the fall, for the views of the golden aspens. Hike, tour by car, or take the train.

The Cumbres & Toltec Scenic Railroad (1-888-CUM-BRES; www.cumbrestoltec.com/scenery; info@cumbres toltec.com) runs from Chama, New Mexico, to Antonito, Colorado, seven days a week from Memorial Day through mid-October. Tucked into a beautiful corner of the southern Rocky Mountains, this is a historic and cultural property owned and run by the states of Colorado and New Mexico. Built in 1880 and hardly changed since, the Cumbres & Toltec Scenic Railroad is an authentic example of steam-era mountain railroading in North America. Its equipment, structures, and landscapes provide an immersion travel experience today quite similar to the way it was during the first half of the 20th century.

Travel in a Basket

Eske's Air Adventures Paradise Balloons (P.O. Box 308, El Prado, NM 87529; 575-751-6098; www.taosballooning.com; ken@taosballooning.com; $225 per person for adults; $100 per child weighing under 100 pounds; includes champagne brunch; call for reservations). Take a beautiful one-and-a-half-hour sunrise flight along the Rio Grande Gorge. Liftoff is at the north end of the gorge, where the Royal Hondo River flows into the Rio Grande and the winds take the balloon through the gorge and then right on down to the river. New Mexico winds are most gentle and predictable in the morning. Flights leave once a day, right after sunrise. Balloon riders often see eagles, hawks, elk, bighorn sheep, and occasionally a

The Rio Grande Gorge

Discovered by Spanish conquistadors in 1519, the Rio Grande flows through a rift valley, a separation of the Earth's crust caused by the Pacific and North American plates scraping against each other millions of years ago. The Rio Grande Rift extends 160,000 square miles, and continued geologic activity is evident in the hot springs along the river. The Rio Grande is one of the longest rivers in the country, starting near the Continental Divide in the San Juan Mountains and running through New Mexico, Texas, and Mexico to the Gulf of Mexico. One of the best views of the Rio Grande Rift is from the Rio Grande Gorge Bridge on US 64 about 13 miles northwest of Taos. Some people find the bridge scary while others think it's the coolest thing going. Know thyself and the people with you.

Two balloons glide through the Rio Grande Gorge down to the Rio Grande River in Taos, New Mexico, for a touch and a splash. *Adam Schallau/www.recapturephoto.com*

bobcat or mountain lion. Balloons can be rented for large groups, multiple flights, or events including weddings.

A Sleeper of a Treehouse

⑤⑤⑤⑤⑤ **The Cedar Creek Treehouse** (Ashford, WA 98304; 360-569-2991; www.cedarcreektreehouse.com; bcompher@centurytel.net; $300 per night for two, $50 additional per person, maximum five guests total). Bill Compher designed, built, and operates this bed & breakfast treehouse 50 feet up in a 200-year-old western red cedar tree, about 10 miles from the Nisqually River entrance to Mount Rainier National Park. You can actually see the top of Mt. Rainier from the bedroom. Oprah featured it as a "Not Your Typical Vacation" destination. *USA Today* called it "one of the ten great places to sleep in a tree." They are both right.

Sheryl's Story

I've never really climbed a tree on my own, up the trunk and limb to limb, but staying overnight in the Cedar Creek Treehouse enabled me to spend a night 50 feet high in a 16-by-16-foot treehouse, with the trunk of the massive cedar growing up through the floor and right out of the roof. Ladders and planks, rocking gently with the wind, make the climb up the tree accessible. Each year, Compher saws away at the floor to accommodate the growing tree.

There's a living room, kitchen, bathroom, sunroom, and second-story sleeping loft. There was no shower, but all of the other needs had been figured out. There was an ice chest for supplies, fresh water in thermos jugs, and a portapotty in the bathroom with the best view in the tree. Solar panels powered the lights. I prepared dinner and breakfast in the kitchen, fascinated by the sound of the water running right through the kitchen sink onto the forest floor. Being level with other trees was the greatest sensation. I couldn't stop taking pictures and sketching images.

Since my visit, Compher has added a Treehouse Observatory, Rainbow Bridge, and Stairway to Heaven 100 feet high in a fir tree. He talks about possibly stringing together a series of catwalks to other trees on the property, connecting a series of treehouses. That would be very cool to stay above the ground and maintain a bird's-eye view throughout the visit.

See Maryland, Delaware, and Virginia by Bike

Bike Inn to Inn (Inn Tours of the Eastern Shore of Maryland & Virginia, 410-632-2722; fax 410-632-2866; www.inntours.com/biking_inn.asp; inquire@inntours.com; weekday tours, $350 per day per two, double occupancy; weekend and holiday tours, $450 per day per two, double occupancy; extra single members of the tour start at $250 per day; children welcome, priced by age, starting at $75; meals and luggage transport included). This is a wonderful biking tour to the Delmarva Peninsula, which includes portions of Delaware, Maryland, and Virginia. It is bordered by the Chesapeake Bay on the west, and the Delaware River and Atlantic Ocean on the east. South of Wilmington, Delaware, is the fall line, a geographic border that separates the Piedmont plateau region from the Atlantic coastal plain, a flat sandy area with very few, or no, hills.

Rides vary from 15 to 45 miles a day, and are flexible to adjust to your capabilities and sightseeing plans. The route follows quiet roads with scenic views and passes through historic villages and farmlands. The Holland House Bed & Breakfast Inn is located in Berlin, Maryland, 8 miles from Ocean City and the Assateague Island National Seashore. The inn, circa 1900 and family-operated, is in a historic district, and the nearby downtown area is included on the National Register of Historic Places.

Assateague Island wild ponies travel the beach near Chincoteague and Ocean City. The island is managed by the National Park Service, and the Chincoteague National Wildlife Refuge is managed by the U.S. Fish & Wildlife Service. The seashore is open to recreational use consistent with maintaining its natural environment. Opportunities for sightseeing, birding, crabbing, and other outdoor activities make this a perfect stop on the tour.

The River House Inn, a National Register Bed & Breakfast, is located on the Pocomoke River in Snow Hill, Maryland. The River House has four guest buildings in a picturesque setting on over 2 acres leading to the river. There are porches to relax on and fireplaces to warm spacious rooms, all with modern amenities. The village of Snow Hill is known for its natural beauty, with antiquing, canoeing, kayaking, fishing, swimming, nature trails, beaches, and wildlife preserves.

The Garden and Sea Inn in New Church, Virginia, built in 1802 as a tavern, is a Victorian bed & breakfast on 4 acres with gardens and ponds, offering modern conveniences, warm hospitality, fine dining, and a peaceful, relaxing atmosphere. You will bike through quaint towns and marinas, in an area rich in history, beautiful architecture, and natural beauty.

Check the Inn Tours Web site for detailed area maps, and call or e-mail to set up your bike tour for an immersion excursion on beautiful Delmarva Peninsula for a trip to remember.

Walk or Hike and Stay Green

Inn to Inn: Country Inns Along the Trail (P.O. Box 55, Forest Dale, VT 05745; 1-800-838-3301; 802-247-3300; www.inntoinn.com; office@inntoinn.com; self-guided hiking/walking trips from 2–7 nights range from $296–$1,075; guided hiking/walking trips from 3–5 nights range from $725–$1,575). Hike or walk from inn to inn, enjoying the beautiful scenery of Vermont. Itineraries are customized for your interests, and both guided and self-guided tours are available for individuals, families, and groups. You choose how many days, the number of inns, and the level of difficulty of trails and terrain. If you select a self-guided trip, you will have a detailed itinerary, and innkeepers will provide you with maps and their suggestions as well. Guided tours for groups no larger than 12 allow Inn to Inn to design a trip that suits your needs.

You will find hospitality, comfort, delicious food, and a chance to relax at the inn chosen for you after a day's hiking or walking. Many guest rooms are furnished with antiques, and all have private bathrooms. Your meals will often be made with local organic vegetables and include home-baked breads and desserts. And you can gather in charming common rooms, sharing your adventures with family, or old or new friends.

Exploring by walking town to town and inn to inn is a true immersion excursion. You'll have the opportunity to get to know the people and places along your way. Learn what it's like to live in this historic part of Vermont. Enjoy the differences between life at home, wherever that may be, and New England values, virtues, and homespun hospitality.

Host inns include Crisanver House, in Shrewsbury; October Country Inn, in Bridgewater Corners; Fox Creek Inn, in Chittenden; The Inn on Park Street, in Brandon; Blueberry Hill Inn, in Goshen; Swift House Inn, in Middlebury; The Inn at Baldwin Creek, in Bristol; Mountain View Inn, in Fayston; and Arbor Inn, in Stowe. There are links to all of the host inns on the Inn to Inn Web site.

All packages include full, hot breakfasts, a hiker's trail lunch, multicourse dinners, door-to-door maps and cue sheets, an orientation at the first inn you visit, taxes and gratuities, hiking suggestions, and an update on trail conditions from your innkeeper. Guided trips include on-trip transportation by van, the service of the guides, and on-trip luggage transfers.

Sample itineraries may be found on the Web site. An interesting choice is the Green Hotel Door-to-Door Hike, a two-day trip that includes accommodations at the only two state-certified green hotels in the 20-inn network, and an 8- to 9-mile hike that connects them. There is also a Vermont Fresh Tour with stays at inns that choose to support local, sustainable, and organic agriculture. Or choose the Hiking Gourmet trip, stopping at inns known for their innovative cuisine.

Try the Appalachian itinerary with portions of the oldest long-distance trails in the country and see ancient ice beds and the Clarendon Gorge. Take a Wildflower Walk in springtime, with guides that have extensive knowledge of wildflowers and birds, or visit both sides of the Green Mountains with planned, guided hikes on Mt. Abraham and Camel's Peak on the Mountain Memories adventure. You may request reservations for all trips on the Inn to Inn Web site.

Bruce and Sue Keep on Walking

My wife and I were looking for someplace to go where we could climb mountains and ride our mountain bikes too. We found Inn to Inn: Country Inns Along the Trail on the Internet and totally enjoyed three nights of hiking, biking, and staying at inns. The next year we decided to bike only.

Then we decided to build upon the experience we had with Inn to Inn and created our own immersion excursions. We wanted to walk the Erie Canal. With a little research and planning, we stayed in B&Bs along the way, and over five week-ends walked 115 miles from Buffalo to Palmyra, New York. We took two cars and left one at the beginning point and the other at our destination. We walked 15 miles a day along the towpaths, and about every 7.5 miles there was a tiny little town with a country store or a place to replenish supplies and get something to eat. It was so much fun meeting people all along the path. Through our experience we realized the song "Fifteen Miles on the Erie Canal" is really true. People walking with their mules and carrying a load could travel about 15 miles a day on the towpaths. That was true then and it was true for us too.

This year Inn to Inn has planned an all-hiking trip for us with my 82-year-old mother-in-law, who is in great shape, and my brother-in-law from Chicago. It's really nice to be asked what you want to do and have it all arranged for you. The inn owners will drive you the 15 or 20 miles you plan to hike that day to drop off your car, and then they'll take you to the trailhead. They've even been known to go to the trail end to wait for their guests. Vermont innkeepers really do deserve their reputation of doing what they do exceptionally well.

Rocks Are for Climbing

Joshua Tree Rock Climbing School (HCR Box 3034, Joshua Tree, CA 92252; 1-800-890-4745; 760-366-4745; www.joshuatreerockclimbing.com; climb@joshuatreerock climbing.com; costs vary by activity, one-day beginner's climb $120). One- and two-day basic rock climbing classes are offered every Saturday and Sunday and on selected weekdays. Intermediate seminars and private guiding are also available. The emphasis is on safety and fun. Joshua Tree National Park is located in Southern California's

Mark Bowling climbing a rock called Trapeze. *Sam Roberts*

Mojave and Colorado Deserts, approximately two to three hours from Los Angeles, San Diego, or Las Vegas, and one hour from Palm Springs. All climbing equipment is provided and included in the cost.

Nancy's Rocky Story

I defy the image of the hardcore rock climber. I'm a slightly overweight, out of shape, older chick (45) from New Jersey. When I was growing up our family sport was going out to dinner and book shopping. I give hope to all people who think they can't possibly go rock climbing. After meeting me they know they can.

When I moved west in my late 20s, it was a whole new world to me. The University of Utah offered a class in rock climbing and a friend asked

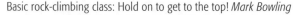

Basic rock-climbing class: Hold on to get to the top! *Mark Bowling*

if I wanted to take it with her. We made an easy climb up a rock and were laying on the ropes, hanging onto a ledge, and the directions were to let go, yell "Falling!" and somebody would catch us. I was hanging on to this ledge with my feet perched on the edge. I yelled, "Falling!" but every fiber of my being did not want to fall, so then I started yelling, "Not falling!"

I finished the course and enjoyed it, but never went climbing again until years later when my friend Carol, who is great at everything she does, invited me to go rock climbing with her. I fell in love with being outside in a beautiful location with friends, the technical gear out on the rocks, and the trust that comes along with it. I've fallen while leading and Carol has caught me a few feet off the ground. This whole other world opened up to me that I didn't get growing up, and I still can't believe I'm doing it.

Filled with Hot Air

Alabama Jubilee Hot Air Balloon Festival (Point Mallard Park, Decatur, AL; for complete information contact the Decatur-Morgan County, Alabama Convention and Visitor's Bureau, 719 6th Ave. SE, Decatur, AL 35602; 1-800-524-6181; 256-350-2028; www.decaturcvb.org; info@decaturcvb.org). Balloonists come from all over the country to participate in the largest and longest-running hot-air balloon festival in Alabama, held annually at Decatur's Point Mallard Park over Memorial Day weekend. The event also hosts the Decatur Arts Guild Arts and Craft Show, Tennessee Valley Tractor and Engine Show, classic car show, and live entertainment by local artists. The event is free and attendees are encouraged to volunteer to help out.

People are needed to chase the flying balloons in cars with two-way radios to assist them. As there are usually about 60 to 70 balloonists, very few of them transport crews with them. There's a volunteer training session at the event and volunteers arriving at all times can approach the stage to request to be placed with someone needing assistance. The balloons fly early in the morning around 6:30 AM and in the afternoon around 5:30 PM. They cannot fly in the heat of the day. The air inside the balloon needs to be hotter than the air outside because heat rises.

Squee's Story

Many years ago there were just two or three balloonists in Decatur who got together and went out for a flight over Memorial Day weekend. People came out to watch, then formed an all-volunteer committee to put on a festival, and it grew and grew, probably because of our Alabama hospitality; the balloonists are all treated very well.

I've been attending the festival for 28 years. It's just so thrilling. You can stand right there by them when they start puffing up the balloons and then they just take off. It's spectacular and hands-on. You just go right up and mingle with the pilots and the crew. My family and I look forward to going every year.

Famous Local Restaurants Not to Be Missed

(S)-(S)(S) **Big Bob Gibson's Bar-B-Q** (1715 6th Ave. SE, Decatur, AL 35601; 256-350-6969; www.bigbobgibson .com; info@bigbobgibson.com). World famous for its slow-cooked meats and award-winning sauces, Big Bob Gibson's barbecue is often featured on cooking shows and he partic-ipates in many national cook-offs. It's a fourth-generation business and the Gibsons created the original white bar-becue sauce. There are three Big Bob Gibson's—two loca-tions in Decatur and one in Monroe, North Carolina.

(S)(S)-(S)(S)(S) **Simp McGhee's** (725 Bank St. NW, Decatur, AL 35601; 256-353-6284). Simp McGhee's is located in the Old Decatur historic district and is named for a riverboat captain who docked there in the 1880s. The Victorian saloon atmosphere lends credence to fascinating stories from the past with Cajun seafood, chicken, and steaks everyone will enjoy.

Eyes to the Sky

Air Combat USA (P.O. Box 2726, Fullerton, CA 92837; 1-800-522-7590; 714-522-7590; fax 714-522-7592; www .aircombatusa.com; Basic Air Combat Maneuvers, $1,195 per person for 2.5–3 hrs., 1 mission, 6 dogfights; Fighter Lead In Program, $1,895 per person for 5–6 hours, 2 mis-sions, 10 dogfights; Top Gun Challenge Package, $11,950 for 10 people, 1 day, 1 mission each; Extreme Biplane ride, Fullerton, CA only, $495 per person for 45-minute flight). Based in Fullerton, Air Combat USA has flight loca-tions across the country. Check the National Deployment

Flight instructor Larry "Worm" Elmore and flying enthusiast J. I. "Skip" Hollingsworth prepare for a flight in Kissimmee, Florida.

Schedule for cities, dates, and airports near you or your destination, and become a fighter pilot for a day. You will fly an authentic military plane with an experienced, licensed fighter pilot in the cockpit with you. Your flight will be recorded by digital cameras for the memory of a lifetime.

Choose your flight suit and helmet and call name, attend your briefing, and be instructed on how to deploy your parachute. You will learn safety, tactics, and maneuvers in ground school, rules of engagement, and the effects of G-force. No flight experience is necessary for this extreme adventure, at the original and oldest civilian dogfighting school in the world, "where everything is real . . . except the bullets." Career naval aviators with 40 or more years experience are the instructors—professional people who know combat, have made hundreds of landings on aircraft carriers, and have stories to tell. Check out the pilot bios and view the specifications of the fighter planes on the Web site, along with answers to frequently asked questions about the program.

One in ten guest pilots is a woman and teenagers age 16 and above may participate. Management reports that women use more finesse with the airplane, demonstrate phenomenal patience and precision, follow directions, and multitask very well.

Available only at their headquarters in Fullerton, California, you can sit at the controls of a biplane, at speeds in excess of 200 mph, performing stunts with an experienced pilot coaching you through loops, rolls, and spins. Briefing, flight, and debriefing total two and a half hours. Videos of these thrilling rides are posted on the Web site, along with videos of actual Air Combat USA fighter flights and a basic training demo.

Skip Loves Flying

You haven't lived until you've flown under 6 Gs and upside down. I fly twice a year with Air Combat and if I had the money I'd fly all over the country with them. After World War I there was a surplus of pilots and equipment. Aviation was a novelty and people everywhere were enamored with it. Barnstormers flew town to town, landing on farms. Pilots would look for barns to locate

what would serve as a grass runway; thus the name
barnstorming.

Air Combat is similar in that they have teams
of retired fighter pilots who leapfrog around the
country and are basically modern barnstormers.
They fly into airports around the country and people come out to go up with them.

I am hooked. The instructors are so good at
what they do and with such precision; I have never
felt that I was in any jeopardy. The trainer controls
the throttles, you have the stick and fly the airplane. You learn the maneuvers, yo-yos and split
S's, aerobatic movements fighter pilots have been

Skip stands triumphantly alongside Air Combat's Marchetti SF260 after a flight in
Norfolk, Virginia.

using since WWI and still use today. Flying with them inspired me to pursue my private pilot's license and a graduate degree in aviation. You can call me a fighter pilot groupie. I absolutely love it.

Is It a Bird or Maybe a Plane?

Kitty Hawk Kites: Hang Gliding (Kitty Hawk Kites/ Carolina Outdoors, P. O. Box 1839, Nags Head, NC 27959; 1-877-FLY-THIS; 252-441-4127; fax 252-441-2498; www.kittyhawk.com; office@kittyhawk.com; 3-hr. beginner lesson, $89; 3-hr. advanced lesson, $79; tandem lesson, 10–15 min., $129; airport mile-high tow, 30 min., $249). Kitty Hawk will forever be associated with the Wright brothers and the birthplace of aviation. You can

A student flies a Kitty Hawk kite over the North Carolina dunes. *Kitty Hawk Kites*

learn to fly at the oldest hang-gliding school on the East Coast, and the largest school of its kind. There are lessons for beginner through advanced students, as well as instruction in foot-launched and tandem hang gliding. Kitty Hawk Kites (KHK), founded in 1974, is located on the Outer Banks in North Carolina, an area known as the "land of beginnings."

Beginner lessons include five solo flights off the dunes at Jockey's Ridge State Park. The fee includes a training film, ground school, log booklet, and all necessary equipment. There is also a beginner's class for children under 85 pounds. There are two instructors for this group, who run with and guide students and gliders. It also includes five solo flights. In a tandem lesson your glider will be towed by an ultralight plane, flying to altitudes of 2,000 feet or higher with an instructor who will glide with you back to the airport where you will land like a plane. Tandem flights are handicapped accessible.

The views will be incredible, and everyone from beginners to advanced students will get the chance to fly. In an advanced lesson you spend your lesson time flying; a beginner dune hang-gliding lesson is a prerequisite. The airport mile-high tow, also a tandem flight, takes you to 5,280 feet for an incredible view of the coastline, and is also handicapped accessible.

KHK also offers hang-gliding camps and clinics. One-week camps include lodging at the KHK beach cottage. There are also clinics for launching and landing, instructor certification, instructional aero-towing, and mountain hang gliding for advanced students. Call for dates, prices, and reservations.

S.E.'s Personal Flight

From personal experience, I can tell you hang gliding is a fantastic feeling! I've done both the foot-launch, dune hang gliding, where you are the one controlling the glider, and the tandem aero-tow hang gliding, where you are in a glider with an instructor and are towed up to 1,500 to 2,000 feet. Both are great! Of course, in the tandem, you have time to talk and really listen, and while participating in that, my instructor stated, "This is as close as we can get to being birds." It was just us and a wing, and then with my agreement, he did the aerobatics. It was like being on a roller-coaster without the rails! Swooping and diving and leaving your stomach behind! That experience encouraged me to get back on the dunes for more practice.

Hang On Rusty

You just never know when hang-gliding knowledge might come in handy. When Rusty worked on top of Mt. Haleakala on Maui he had an unconventional way of going home. He flew. Before leaving he called his wife with his ETA and then took off, hang gliding his way down the mountain. What a relaxing way to end a busy day at the office.

Calling All Astronauts

Zero G, the Weightless Experience (Zero Gravity Corporation, 5275 Arville St., Suite 116, Las Vegas, NV 89118; 1-800-937-6480; www.gozerog.com; Zero G Experience, including flight of 15 parabolas, flight suit, complimentary merchandise, postevent party, photos, and DVD of flight, $3,950 per seat). A once-in-a-lifetime experience; book a flight at Las Vegas, Nevada, or at the Kennedy Space Center near Orlando, Florida. You will achieve zero G, or weightlessness, and have ample room to float and fly in a 90-foot-long padded zone. The aircraft can accommodate 35 flyers and a crew of six. There are usually two to three flights a day starting around 9 AM and leaving as late as 4 PM.

Your weightless (or parabolic) flight, aboard a specially modified Boeing 727 named *G-Force One,* will climb to between 24,000 and 34,000 feet before performing 15 parabolic maneuvers. Each maneuver takes 10 miles of airspace and lasts approximately one minute from start to finish. The plane is pulled up to 45 degrees, and then pushed over the top to reach the zero-gravity segment of the parabola. For about 30 seconds each time, everything in the plane is weightless. At 30 degrees the plane is slowly pulled out of the parabola and stabilized while the G-force is gradually increased. This is the same type of flight that NASA uses to train its astronauts.

The *G-Force One* flight lasts 90–100 minutes, and the entire Zero-G Weightless Experience takes three to four hours, which includes orientation and a safety video, transportation to and from the plane, FAA screening, the

Guests achieve zero gravity, or weightlessness, aboard a specially modified Boeing 727 named *G-Force One,* at Zero G, the Weightless Experience. *Jim Campbell/Aero-News.net*

flight, and the re-gravitational party. The entire plane may be chartered and can be taken to any airport that is able to accommodate a Boeing 727-200. Flight dates and locations for currently scheduled flights can be found on the Web site, along with answers to frequently asked questions, and more information on the Zero Gravity Corporation and the Weightless Experience.

Strike It Rich

Arkansas Crater of Diamonds State Park (Crater of Diamonds State Park, 209 State Park Rd., Murfreesboro, AR 71958; 870-285-3113; www.craterofdiamondsstate park.com; craterofdiamonds@arkansas.com). The Crater of Diamonds State Park is the only diamond-producing site in the world open to the public. The first diamonds were found there in 1906, and remnants of old mining ventures remain: the Mine Shaft Building, the Guard House, mine plant foundations, and mining equipment.

If you forget your prospecting tools, they can be rented at the park. Diamonds found at the site include the 40.23-carat "Uncle Sam" diamond, discovered in 1924, and the 4.25-carat "Kahn Canary" diamond, worn by then First Lady Hillary Clinton at her husband's Presidential Inaugural Galas in 1993 and 1997. The 16.37-carat "Amarillo Starlight" diamond is the largest diamond unearthed by a park visitor, in 1975.

Lucky visitors today can still find diamonds, semiprecious stones, and over 40 types of rocks and minerals. The diamond search area is a 37-acre field that is the eroded surface of a volcanic pipe, a subterranean geological structure formed by the violent eruption of a deep-origin volcano. Park rangers will identify your finds and the policy is "finders, keepers."

Park interpreters offer programs on a regular basis, and there are diamond-mining demonstrations, rock hikes, and history walks offered from Memorial Day through Labor Day. There is also a summer children's program series, which offers hands-on activities for ages 6–12.

In addition to the diamond search area, the park has hundreds of acres of natural forest, and 59 campsites with water and electric hookups. Reservations are accepted 12 months in advance, with a two-night minimum stay on weekends and a three-night minimum stay for a three-day holiday weekend.

Get All Wet

Children of all ages will enjoy Diamond Springs, a 14,700-square-foot aquatic playground, in the park featuring a 4,166-square-foot wading pool with spray geysers, water jets, animated waterspouts, waterfalls, and water slides. The water playground is open from May 26th through August 19th, daily from noon to 6:00 PM, and from August 25th through September 3rd, Saturday and Sunday only.

Wheelchair-Accessible Nature Trail

This is an accessible park for the whole family. Enjoy the River Trail, a 1.5-mile wooded trail from the campground to the Little Missouri River. With a portion of the trail paved, it is the longest wheelchair-accessible trail in southwest Arkansas.

A wildlife observation blind provides the perfect vantage point to observe and photograph a variety of animals and birds in their natural setting. Birders, be sure to bring your binoculars and local bird books. Bank fishing for largemouth bass, catfish, and bream is available on the Little Missouri River, and there is a public boat ramp across from the park. A fishing license is required and is available in Murfreesboro.

Where the Buffalo Roam

Wild Winds Buffalo Preserve (P.O. Box 35, 6975 N. Ray St., Fremont, IN 46737; 260-495-0137; www.wildwinds buffalo.com; wildwindsbuffalo@aol.com; tours Wed.–Sun. hourly beginning at 10 AM, with last tour at 3 PM, $8 per person, $5 children 10 years and under; trail rides, Wed., Fri., and Sun. by reservation, $24 per person, minimum riding age 10; Bed & Breakfast Lodge, first night $119, second night $109; holidays, first night $165, second night, $145; Rendezvous, first night, $205, second night, $195; all rates based on double occupancy). Wild Winds is a privately owned working ranch with over 400 acres of prairie, natural waterways, lakes, birds, and approximately 200 bison. Tour the preserve in an open-air vehicle or choose a guided trail ride.

Special events include a Spring or Fall Rendezvous, with a reenactment of a buckskinners' camp, demonstra-

All in the Neighborhood

Consider a Wild Buffalo, Wine, and Windmills getaway. Visit the Wild Winds Buffalo Reserve in Fremont, Indiana, and sample wine at the nearby Satek Winery (www.satekwinery.com). Stay at the Potawatomi Inn at Pokagon State Park (www.in.gov/dnr/parklake/inns/potawatomi) near Angola, and stop at the nature center to bike, hike, or take a boat tour, then head south to Albion to see the exotic animals at the Black Pine Animal Park (www.blackpineanimal park.com). Visit the Mid-America Windmill Museum in Kendallville (www.mid americawindmillmuseum.com) to see more than 50 restored windmills, and learn about the history of windmills and wind power. Go to the Visit Indiana.com Web site at www.in.gov/visitindiana/index.aspx for more ideas on where to go, what to do, where to stay, and information about Indiana.

tions, storytelling, handmade crafts, fur and blanket traders, and lunch available at the café. Check the Web site or call for dates and schedule of events.

Make reservations at the all-log lodge on the property and enjoy a break from telephones, television, fax machines, and computers. The lodge is also a shoeless zone, so bring your soft slippers. A Buffalo Ranch Breakfast, with ranch staff, is served at 8 AM, and trail rides may be reserved on days other than regularly scheduled ones, with private bison tours available. Visit the Web site for photos of the lodge with its stone fireplace, library, and bathrooms with cast-iron tubs. Enjoy fishing and walking trails during your stay, as well as educational bison tours.

Gold Rush Fever

Gold Prospecting Adventures (18170 Main St., P.O. Box 1040, Jamestown, CA 95327; 209-984-4653; fax 209-984-0711; www.goldprospecting.com; info@goldprospecting.com; call or e-mail for prices). Try your luck at gold prospecting in a gold-mining camp that is an exact replica of the original 1849 camp. Step back in time; see guides dressed in period clothing, and experience 25 Old West attractions as well as your prospecting adventure. You will learn about the California Gold Rush from costumed prospectors, and meet the sheriff and other town characters. Best of all, you will prospect for gold that you can keep.

Join a three- or five-hour gold-panning expedition with your family or group, and a guide, for an average of five pans an hour. Or choose to use a sluice box, a much more effective system that yields about 100 pans an hour. There are a variety of immersion excursions to choose from. On the Bonanza Expedition, the sluice box and water are at your site, so you can average 1,000 pans an hour, and on the Humdinger Trip you get to dredge the bedrock hole after digging out the overburden down to the bedrock, also 1,000 pans an hour. You may also enroll in a three-day electronic prospecting course, and learn skills to take home with you along with all of the gold that you find.

The mining camp is located about two and a half hours north of Yosemite, three hours east of San Francisco, and three hours west of Lake Tahoe. Inquire about courses in prospecting techniques and in staking claims. The Web site also has links to other Gold Country activities including state parks, skiing, golf, water sports, fishing, hiking, theater, and visiting wineries.

Santa Catalina, the Island of Romance

Catalina Island (Catalina Island Chamber of Commerce and Visitors Bureau, P.O. Box 217, Avalon, CA 90704; 310-510-1520; www.catalinachamber.com; info@Catalina Chamber.com). Located 22 miles off the coast of Southern California, Catalina Island, also called Santa Catalina Island, with its great climate and crystal-clear water, is a perfect destination for immersion travelers who love the ocean, water sports, and learning new skills. Choose from scuba diving, snorkeling, kayaking, fishing, parasailing, and other activities on or under the water. Take a day or nighttime trip aboard a semisubmersible vessel, and observe Catalina's marine life (310-510-TOUR), or sign on for a voyage on a glass-bottomed yellow submarine (Catalina Adventure Tours, Inc., special group/senior/combination packages available; 1-877-510-2888 or 562-432-8828; www.catalinaadventuretours.com).

Snorkeling can be enjoyed by anyone comfortable in the water, including young children, and there are scuba-diving programs for the beginner as well as experienced divers. Diving Catalina Island offers introductory dives for those who have never tried scuba, guided scuba tours of the Avalon Underwater Dive Park, and a full range of equipment rentals (1-877-SNORKEL or 1-87-SCUBA DIVE). Catalina Snorkel & Scuba Adventures, onsite at Lover's Cove, a protected marine preserve, offers classes, scuba rentals and tours (www.catalinadiveshop.com).

Decanso Beach Ocean Sports & Catalina Island Kayak Expeditions provides kayak and snorkel rentals with instruction by the hour or day. If you've never kayaked, sign up for a lesson and head for the beach. There are guided history kayak tours that run from one and a half hours to all day. There are also classes for kids, picnic

Catalina Fun Facts

- The Catalina Island Conservancy manages a herd of about 200 bison. A film company brought 14 bison to the island for a movie and left them to roam and procreate.
- Actress Marilyn Monroe lived on Catalina Island with her husband James Dougherty, a Merchant Marine, during WWII.
- The Zane Grey Pueblo Hotel was built in 1924 by author Zane Grey. The rooms are named for his books: *Riders of the Purple Sage* and *The Vanishing American*, among others.
- The Chicago Cubs trained there from 1921 to 1951.
- Former U.S. presidents who have visited the island include Calvin Coolidge, Herbert Hoover, Ronald Reagan, and Richard Nixon.
- Sir Arthur Conan Doyle, author of the Sherlock Holmes mysteries, visited Catalina in 1923.
- In 1929, Winston Churchill visited Catalina Island and caught a marlin.
- Between 1894 and 1898 there was a pigeon mail service between the island and Los Angeles.

and snorkeling tours, corporate programs, and kayak camping, gear provided (310-510-1226).

Call Catalina Adventure Rafting for exciting trips aboard powerful inflatables, exploring Two Harbors, snorkeling, playing with dolphins, and observing bald eagles, sea caves, and flying fish. They also offer corporate team-building activities (www.catalinaoceanrafting.com or 310-510-0211).

Travel to Catalina by boat from San Pedro, Long Beach, Newport Beach, Marina Del Rey, or Dana Point. By air, Island Express Helicopter Service (310-510-2525) departs from Long Beach and San Pedro. For more extensive travel information, hotels, bed & breakfasts, vacation rentals, dining options, events calendar, and activities map, go to www.catalina.com.

Jack and Jason's Snorkeling Experience

I'd heard about so many great places to snorkel, but I wasn't sure if my five-year-old son could handle it. He'd been swimming since he was a year old but I was concerned that he'd get confused with the breathing and choke or panic in the deep water. I just didn't know what to do.

The concierge at our hotel suggested that I try out the snorkeling equipment in the pool. At first Jason balked because he's a good little swimmer and didn't want to wear a life vest. I explained that out in the ocean we needed to wear life jackets. Jason and I practiced floating with the mask on, and then with the breathing tube, and then put on the flippers. He loved it. When I asked him if he wanted to try swimming with the snorkeling equipment at the beach so that he could see all the pretty coral and fish, he said he'd been dreaming about doing that.

We agreed to give it a try and decided to stay together by holding hands. We started off very slow and kept adding a few minutes each time. It was so terrific we snorkeled every day we were there and he decorated his room with photographs he took with an underwater camera. The suggestion to practice first in the safety of the swimming pool is an excellent idea for people of all ages.

Wilderness Recreation near Major Cities

Zoar Outdoor Camping (P.O. Box 245, Charlemont, MA 01339; 1-800-532-7483; fax 413-337-8436; www.zoar outdoor.com/camp.htm; info@zoaroutdoor.com; cabin tents, $20 per person per night, $40 minimum; tent sites, $11 per person per night, $22 minimum; kayak rentals, $40 per person weekday and $42 per person weekend; bike rentals, $35 a day, 10 AM to 5 PM, and $25 a half-day, 1–5 PM). Zoar Outdoor's camping sites are located in the northern Berkshires, in western Massachusetts above the Deerfield River Valley floor. With 80 acres of wilderness hiking trails, it is an ideal camping site. Options include cabin tents that sleep four people, available April 1 to October 31. These are 12-by-14-foot tents set on wooden decks and equipped with cots, a gas lantern, a gas grill, and a porch. Bring along your own sleeping bag or blankets as linens are not included. There are also five tent sites near the Mohawk Trail, each equipped with a picnic table and space for two to four tents. Call for reservations or book online.

Zoar Outdoor offers whitewater rafting trips, kayaking clinics, canoeing instruction, rock-climbing classes, and both kayak and bike rentals. Kayak rentals, available from May 1 through September 30, include singles for those 12 years of age and older and doubles for a child 7 years and older with an adult or for two adults. From May 1 to October 31, rent either sport road bikes or recreational bikes and choose paved or dirt roads to explore the area and view the scenery. You can follow the river up or downstream, bike to a state forest, or head for the hills for rides from an hour to all day. Reservations for rentals are recommended.

Zoar Outdoor's campground is located on MA 2, the Mohawk Trail, approximately two and a half hours from Boston, and three and a half to four hours from New York City. Directions are available on the Web site. For more information about the area, check the Berkshire Visitors Bureau Web site (www.berkshires.org) or contact them at 1-800-237-5747 or e-mail inquiries@berkshires.org. To learn more about the Mohawk Trail, visit the Web site at www.mohawktrail.com.

Ice Sports

Montana Kite Sports (Caird Boat Works, 1308 Orange St., Helena, MT 59601; 406-442-8009; www.montanakite sports.com; info@montanakitesports.com; beginner kite-boarding or ice-boating lessons, two full days, $300). Imagine, it's the middle of winter and you are cutting across the ice on steel runners, under the blue, sunny skies of Montana. If you are an experienced sailor on the water, you might want to try applying your skills to ice boating, snow kiting, or kite surfing on the ice in the winds on Canyon Ferry Lake. These courses are for people who have never sailed at all or for experienced sailors on water.

Snow kiting uses a kite to pull you on skis or a snowboard, which allows you to go uphill as easily as down, and to explore the backcountry of Montana. There are no lift lines and no lifts. You can ski across frozen lakes and farmland, as well as mountains and hills. The season begins in November and runs through late June or early July in parts of the state. Check the Web site for lessons and events, and Montana Kite will match your needs with the right location. In addition to lessons for all levels, there are guided excursions and package retreats available. Kite-surfing lessons are available in summer.

Beginner classes are given over a two-day period, and all kiting equipment is included. You will learn about the wind window, and the difference between neutral and power zones. You will be taught to perform a preflight check and safety precautions. Most importantly you will learn how to launch, land, and actually fly the kite. When you understand the basics you will add skis or a snowboard and be taught to put it all together. Instructors are certified, and there are individualized plans for each student, depending on skill level. For those who already have skills, there are intermediate and advanced classes available. Individual, group and private lessons are available. Call for more information and have a great time.

The Ouray Ice Park (P.O. Box 1058, Ouray, CO 81427; 970-325-4288; www.ourayicepark.com/contact.php; Erin Eddy, Executive Director, oipi@ouraynet.com). Challenge yourself and hone your ice-climbing skills on the sheer walls of the Uncompahgre Gorge. Attend the annual Ice Festival in January and meet other enthusiasts, sign up for ice-climbing clinics for all ability levels, watch thrilling competitions, and see all the latest gear.

The Ice Park, built entirely by volunteers, is a free climbing facility supported by members, sponsors, and private donations. Discounts are available at sponsoring lodges and other businesses listed on the Web site. There is also an interactive map that describes all the climbing areas, along with virtual tours. The views are amazing.

The Ice Festival is the major fund-raiser for the Ice Park and all proceeds are used for the maintenance and operation of the park. The Kids' Climbing College is a free event for all ages, with gear provided and prizes awarded. And there's a new Kids' Wall with nine climbs and marked trails. The annual Ouray Ice Festival is held the second week in January. For more information and a schedule of events, check the Web site at www.ourayicefestival.com.

When visiting the Ice Park, make time to explore the mountain town of Ouray, situated in a river valley at an elevation of 7,700 feet, in the heart of the Rocky Mountains, and nicknamed the Switzerland of America. Once a mining town, Ouray is an outdoor adventurer's paradise. For more information, contact the Ouray Chamber of Commerce at 1-800-228-1876 or log on to their Web site at ouraycolorado.com.

Step into the Wild Side

Texas Speleological Survey (PRC 176/R4000, University of Texas at Austin, Austin, TX 78712; 512-475-8802; www.utexas.edu/tmm/sponsored_sites/tss/wildcave tours/index.html). The Texas Speleological Survey (TSS) collects and maintains information on caves and supports education, conservation, and responsible cave exploration. TSS partners with the Texas Memorial Museum, the Texas Speleological Association, and the National Speleological Society.

Caves are homes to hundreds of ancient species that have adapted to life in permanent darkness. There are salamanders, catfishes, shrimps, snails, spiders, pseudo-scorpions (tiny arachnids that do not have a caudal stinger), beetles, millipedes, centipedes, snails, isopods (aquatic or terrestrial crustaceans with seven thoracic segments each bearing legs), amphipods, and other eyeless troglobites—animals that live in caves and because they have adapted to their environment, cannot live outside of it. Their useful senses (smell, touch, and hearing) have intensified, and many can feel vibrations that help them sense moving objects. Caves also house fossils of vertebrate animals (animals with a spine or backbone) and bat populations.

Texas has both show caves and wild caves. Seven show caves are open to the public and are filled with a variety of amazing speleothems (mineral formations) that line the walls, ceilings, and floors of their passages. Caverns of Sonora (www.cavernsofsonora.com) in Sutton County is thought to be the most beautiful cave in the world; visitors have compared parts of the cave to the inside of a crystal-lined geode. Caverns of Sonora opened to the public in 1960, and long and short tours are available. Check the Web site or call (915-387-3105) for directions, hours, and prices of tours, campgrounds, and RV hookups, and more detailed information on the caverns.

Kickapoo Cavern: A Wild Cave

Wild caves have no trails or electric lights and are remarkable for their native wildlife as well as for their mineral formations. One state-owned cave now open to guided tours is Kickapoo Cavern (www.utexas.edu/tmm/sponsored_sites/tss/wildcavetours/tsskickapoocavern.htm) near Brackettville, which has the largest known speleothems in Texas.

Speleothems are cave deposits most often referred to as cave formations. They result from very slow-moving water that contains dissolving calcium carbonate from the limestone where the cave was formed. The cave formations vary greatly in color, size, and shape. There's a fascinating wild cave vocabulary to learn and use. Stalactites that were immersed in cave pools for a very long time are called bottlebrush. A mushroom-shaped speleothem is called a bell canopy and cave pearls are smooth, rounded speleothem formed by water dripping over and over and over again into a shallow cavity.

Guided Wild Cave Tours

Colorado Bend State Park (www.tpwd.state.tx.us/ spdest/findadest/parks/colorado_bend) in San Sabo County offers guided wild cave tours and self-guided crawling cave explorations on specific days and times. The caves are closed except for scheduled tours or by special permit. Reservations are recommended due to the limited number of people permitted on each tour. Contact the park (325-628-3240) to make reservations and check weather conditions. Hiking boots or substantial footwear is recommended.

Additional activities at Colorado Bend State Park include guided tours to Gorman Falls on Saturdays, which is also accessible by a day-use hiking trail. The trail length is approximately 4 miles round-trip. Reservations are not required for the Gorman Falls tours.

Spelunking Anyone?

If you find that you enjoy spelunking (exploring caves) consider joining a "grotto" (caving club). The Web site of the Texas Speleological Association (www.cavetexas.org /links/grottos.html) provides links to Texas grottos that have training programs to teach you how to cave safely, sponsor caving trips and projects, and are active in scientific study, cave management, education, restoration, and conservation activities.

Inside the Inside Passage

National Geographic Expeditions: Alaska's Inside Passage (1145 17th St. NW, Washington, D.C. 20036; 1-888-966-8687; www.nationalgeographicexpeditions .com/527.html; 8 days aboard a 62-passenger expedition ship, from $5,390 to $7,120 per person, double occupancy; round-trip economy airfare from Seattle to Juneau, return from Sitka, $500, subject to change). The Inside Passage is like a treasure trove of unique towns that were isolated for many years. Today it is heavily traveled by cruise ships, the Alaska Maine Highway, and British Columbia ferries. The Alaskan portion of the Inside Passage stretches 500 miles from north to south and 100 miles from east to west. There are about 1,000 islands and seemingly endless shorelines, coves, caves, and bays. The Inside Passage is a destination for nature lovers, conservationists, photographers, artists, writers, kayakers, and canoeists.

National Geographic calls this a voyage of discovery. Sail on either the *National Geographic Sea Bird* or the *National Geographic Sea Lion,* which depart from Juneau, Alaska. There will be time to explore Juneau, the capital of Alaska, and visit the Mendenhall Glacier and the Alaska State Museum before embarking, on your first day.

On day two, you will enter Tracy Arm, a 22-mile-long fjord, maneuvering between icebergs. The next day you will visit Petersburg, on Mitkof Island, where there will be optional flights over LeConte Glacier. You will cruise LeConte Bay and look for whales. On day four you will explore Frederick Sound and Chatham Strait; watch for whales and sea lions, kayak, or take a walk with naturalists.

On day five you will visit Glacier Bay National Park and
Preserve and watch and hear glaciers calving. Day six will
find you cruising along the northern coast of Chichagof
Island and looking for sea otters. You may also see eagles
in the surrounding Tongass National Forest. On day seven
you will explore more Alaskan islands, hiking or kayaking,
and attend a farewell dinner onboard. After breakfast on
day eight you disembark in Sitka, visit Sitka National Park,
enjoy the Russian cultural influence and architecture in
this remote outpost and then transfer to the airport for the
flight to Seattle.

You may choose an optional seven-day pre- or post-
trip extension to Denali National Park, where you can
explore, hike, bike, and canoe, and visit many cultural
attractions. This trip begins in Fairbanks and includes a
stay at the North Face Lodge and a trip aboard the Alaska
Railroad to Anchorage. The extension cost is $4,390 per
person, double occupancy. For a detailed itinerary or for
more information about the ships, all departure dates, or
to make a reservation, request a catalog, investigate other
National Geographic expeditions, or sign up for an e-mail
newsletter, visit the National Geographic Web site.

A Special Place in the Adirondacks

Great Camp Sagamore (P.O. Box 40, Raquette Lake, NY
13436-0040; 315-354-5311; fax 315-354-5851; www
.sagamore.org; sagamore@telenet.net; Sagagrands, $725
per grandparent, $625 per teen, $525 per child, from
4 PM Sun.–10 AM Fri.; Women-Only Weekend, $249 per
adult, two nights, meals included; Women in the Woods,
$299 per adult per night, two nights, meals included;
Adirondacks Healing and Arts Retreat, $299 per person,
two nights, meals included). Located in the heart of the
Adirondacks, and under the stewardship of the Sagamore
Institute of the Adirondacks, Great Camp Sagamore is a

historic landmark that offers tours, programs, and a spectacular setting. Choose among Grands Camp, Adirondack Women, Culture: Music, History & Arts, and In & Around the Water, and be inspired by your surroundings, the people you meet, and the connections you make.

The Grandparents' and Grandchildren's Camp offers a wide range of activities designed to build connections between people and nature. Share the joys of music, canoeing, swimming, hiking, natural crafts, campfires, a historic walking tour, and more. Grandparents have an opportunity to relax late afternoons while Sagamore staff supervises grandchildren. This program is sponsored in cooperation with Elderhostel (www.elderhostel.org). For program dates and to register call 1-877-426-8056.

Plan a trip with old friends or meet new ones in women-only programs and retreats. A Women-Only Weekend includes a historic walking tour, use of the facilities, and admission to the Adirondack Museum. The Women in the Woods program includes guided canoe outings, a historic tour, and all in-camp activities. The Adirondacks Healing and Arts Retreat, designed for women with cancer and chronic illness, includes music, storytelling, and yoga sessions in addition to the historic walking tour and all in-camp activities. Partial scholarships are available. E-mail or call Camp Sagamore for information, scholarship forms, and registration.

Sign up for Culture: Music, History & Arts, and choose among programs that may include singing, barn dances, theater and concert performances, dance instruction, songwriting, and musical instrument lessons, in addition to a historic tour and in-camp activities. Prices vary depending on program, so consult the calendar of events on the Great Camp Sagamore Web site (www.sagamore .org/courses.htm#calendar) or call for information on current programs.

Boat Building

Camp Sagamore also hosts the Adirondack Boat Building School, offering a variety of 7- to 10-day classes in (non-motorized) boat building and boating instruction. For more information, visit the Adirondack Boat Builder's Web site at www.adkboatschool.com or contact Great Camp Sagamore for a brochure.

North Carolina Recreation Along the Coast

Outer Banks Fishing (North Carolina Charter Fishing, 5411 Old Duffer Ct., Nags Head, NC 27959; 252-619-6655; www.pwsobx.com; mike@pwsobx.com; charter prices for half- and full-day fishing trips, inshore and offshore, range from $700 to $1,775 for up to 6 anglers).

Points of Interest Along the Way

The Outer Banks is a chain of barrier islands along the North Carolina coast. Visit the towns of Duck, Kitty Hawk, Kill Devil Hills, Nags Head, and Roanoke Island to appreciate the history of the area as well as its beaches, wildlife refuges, sportfishing, and other activities. Fort Raleigh National Historic Site, the Wright Brothers National Memorial, and the celebration of the Lost Colony on Roanoke Island are a few of the historic attractions. E-mail the Visitors Bureau at information@outerbanks.org, or call 1-877-629-4386. For further information on Ocracoke, contact the Ocracoke Preservation Society (P.O. Box 1240, Ocracoke, NC 27960; 252-928-7375; www.ocracokepreservation.org; info@membershiporganization.com). Be sure to ask about the summer series of lectures on local history, music, and culture, which are held on the Society's front porch.

Experience North Carolina deep-sea fishing, which includes some of the best fishing destinations on the East Coast. Gannet Sport Fishing Charters has 35 years of experience, and Captain Mike will help make your fishing adventure a memorable one. Big game sportfishing for blue marlin, cobia, yellowfin tuna, and billfish will test your skills and provide an action-packed immersion excursion.

Cape Hatteras is a small fishing village and popular East Coast surfing destination. With its many campgrounds and beautiful beaches, and the best fishing on the Atlantic coast, it is a fishing enthusiast's dream. Everything is about fishing, whether it's commercial fishing or crabbing, boat building, tackle shops, or sportfishing charters. The Oregon Inlet is probably the most popular fishing area for charters, with tourists lining the docks to see the day's catch. Don't just be an observer; charter a boat and find out what sportfishing is all about, or test your skills against a variety of big-game sportfishing species.

After April 1st Captain Mike will be in Hatteras, and from mid-June to November he will be in Oregon Inlet, with trips offshore for tuna, wahoo, dolphin, and other deep-sea species (blue marlin, Atlantic sailfish, swordfish, amberjack, barracuda, shark, and mackerel). When the Outer Banks season closes, Captain Mike heads off for Virginia Beach striper fishing. Virginia stripers, also called rockfish, can top 50 pounds.

Join Captain Mike aboard the *Gannet*, a 46-foot custom sportfishing vessel. The *Gannet* is air-conditioned and has all the latest electronic fishing and safety gear. Captain Mike offers half- and full-day charters and a variety of fishing techniques. The *Gannet* can accommodate six people per trip, and children are welcome. Rates are available by phone and Captain Mike will answer your questions.

Maury and Jane Live Along the Outer Banks

When you're talking Outer Banks, you need to include Ocracoke in your plans. Ocracoke is the crown jewel of the Banks. Accessible only by ferry, air, or private boat, it still has a small population struggling to make a living through commercial fishing and tourism.

If you want to take the ferries, and these are a really exciting part of travel along the Banks, then you need to plan an entire day. From Corolla you would need to drive south to catch the Hatteras ferry, which takes about a half hour to Ocracoke Island.

Along the way you'll often see dolphin, egrets, all kinds of shorebirds, osprey, skimmers, sometimes sea turtles, stingrays, and wild ponies. During the winter months whales migrate along the coast and can sometimes be seen just off the beaches. It's a beautiful place.

Hang Ten

Endless Summer Surf Camp (P.O. Box 414, San Clemente, CA 92674; 949-498-7862; fax 949-388-0193; www.endlesssummersurfcamp.com; info@endless summersurfcamp.com; San Onofre day-only surf camp, Mon.–Fri. from 8 AM to 3 PM, $445; 5-day overnight camp, Mon.–Fri., 8 AM–4 PM, arrival evening before, departure morning after session ends, $895; early sign-up discounts; all sessions June through Sept.). Endless Summer has programs to suit all ages and all levels from beginner to skilled surfer. With instruction on the beach and in the water, video analysis, and emphasis on water safety, Surf Camp is all-inclusive, with meals, surfing equipment, and accommodations included in the price.

The Endless Summer Surf Camp was the first surf school endorsed by Surfing America, the International Surfing Association–recognized national governing body for the sport of surfing in the United States. Founded by professional surfer Jason Senn, Endless Summer has been teaching people to surf for over 14 years, on one of the least crowded beaches in Southern California. The instructors are all adults, CPR certified, and work with students in small groups, with a student-instructor ratio of three to one.

There are three adult-only sessions (both in day and overnight programs) each summer (ages 18 and older), but all ages over 11 are welcome in any program.

Up on the board, no wobbling, confidently riding the wave! *www.endlesssummersurfcamp.com*

Students spend about six hours at the beach each day, with a morning and afternoon instructional session. Private, semiprivate, and group lessons are offered year-round, with surfing equipment provided.

Lodging consists of carpeted tents, with fire rings and a game area. There is also a television and video viewing lounge for nighttime entertainment and reviews of surf sessions. The campground has modern bathrooms, with showers, public telephones, and ranger and lifeguard patrols. Meals and snacks are provided by a full-time cook, with vegetarian alternatives available.

The campsite overlooks the Pacific Ocean in the San Onofre State Park campground, just south of San Clemente. San Clemente is 60 miles south of Los Angeles and 60 miles north of San Diego. A map, directions, and a complete listing of camp programs and sessions can be found on the Surf Camp Web site. The John Wayne/Orange County airport is about 30 minutes from the campsite, and an airport pickup and drop-off service is provided.

Doc's Wave Connection

I'm 74 years old and I started surfing at age 69. My grandson has been riding since age six and insisted this was something his old grandpa could learn how to do, which I doubted because I hadn't swum since my children were young. He took me out for my first time in California for my birthday present and I've been surfing ever since. It's a great sport for overall conditioning. It tones the entire body, particularly the upper torso. The hardest thing about it is learning how to stand up on the board.

The second most difficult part is the energy it takes to swim out against the surf to catch the waves. If you're in overall good health, this is something you can try at almost any age. Before surfing, my only exercise was a nightly walk after supper. I'm in much better shape now than I was five years ago.

The Aloha Spirit

Visit Molokai (Molokai Visitor Association P.O. Box 960, Kaunakakai, Molokai, HI 96748; 1-800-800-6367; 808-553-3876; fax 808-553-5288; local address, The Moore Center, 2 Kamoi St., Suite 200, Kaunakakai, HI 96748; www.molokai-hawaii.com; webmaster@molokai-hawaii.com). *Aloha* and *mahalo* (hello and thank you): To experience what these two words (two of the most important words in the Hawaiian language, representing paramount Hawaiian values) mean, consider an immersion travel adventure to "Moloka'i: The Most Hawaiian Island," full of local charm and its own unique history.

Natives say that the island of Molokai is shaped like a shark. Its head faces east, its tail west, and a dorsal fin points toward the north shore. The dorsal fin is the 10-square-mile Makanalua Peninsula, jutting out into the Pacific below the world's highest sea cliffs.

Molokai, Maui, and Lanai make up the County of Maui, share resources, and promote the three islands as the Magic Isles. Moloka'i (in the traditional spelling and pronunciation) has been the last of the islands to be developed, and that has become the major attraction.

Hawaiian culture is a way of life, and family, or *ohana*, is what is important in daily life. The Molokai Visitor Association (MVA) works closely with the community to

Music on Molokai

Consider attending Aloha Music Camp (Kaupoa Beach Village at Molokai Ranch, 100 Maunaloa Ave, Maunaloa, HI 96770; 808-270-3090; www .AlohaMusicCamp.com; Administration@AlohaMusicCamp.com). The Aloha Music Camps offers an immersion into the music, dance, and culture of Molokai for people of all ages, with or without musical backgrounds. Study the slack guitar or ukulele, learn Hawaiian dances and songs, explore Hawaiian language and culture, traditional crafts, and storytelling. Sessions are offered for one week each in February and June, with registration beginning in mid-April.

offer visitors an immersion experience of a lifetime, without stressing the island's resources.

Outdoor explorers and ocean adventurers can travel to Hawaii's most natural island, experience Hawaiian culture in an unspoiled setting, observe natural habitats with wildlife and plants endangered on most other Hawaiian islands, enjoy secluded beaches, explore growing coral reefs, and appreciate Molokai's rural way of life.

If you are feeling adventurous, you can kayak miles of pristine barrier reefs, hike through the lush Halawa Valley, and ride on horseback along beautiful coastlines and natural rangelands. Land adventures include bicycle tours and rentals, ecotours, hiking and nature walks, guided tours and sightseeing, and excursions to plantations, farms, and gardens. Sixty percent of the food eaten on the island is from the land and waters of Molokai. Learn the native styles of preparing the fresh catch of the day with island staples of mango, pineapple, and macadamia nuts. These recipes and healthful cooking and eating habits can greatly influence you long after your visit.

Water sports include fishing, kayaking, sailing, canoeing, snorkeling, and scuba. Contact Ohana Concierge and Tours at 808-553-8284 or e-mail them at ohanaconcierge @yahoo.com to book activities and make travel arrangements.

Molokai offers a variety of accommodations from small luxury resorts to quaint "old Hawaii" style hotels, condos, bed & breakfasts, vacations rentals, and upscale and more basic camping. Check the MVA Web site for a complete listing, as well as for information on transportation and travel tips. Be sure to consult the calendar of events, also on the MVA Web site, for a comprehensive schedule of activities that includes festivals and celebrations, concerts, and competitions.

Ann's Story: Living History

Bill and I flew from Maui to Molokai for the day, to explore historic Kalaupapa and the sea cliffs of the North Shore. The island seemed extremely remote, very lush yet very simple and rustic. We had arranged to visit the Kalaupapa National Historical Park and take the guided mule ride to visit the settlement where Father Damien devoted his life to caring for people with Hansen's disease (leprosy). It was a very scary ride down. Hugging the nearly perpendicular cliffs, the trail seems never-ending for over 3 miles and descends over 1,600 feet to the Makanalua Peninsula. There are constant switchbacks that corkscrew in and out of canyons and ravines. We were very worried that

one slipped donkey's foot would mean the end of
the donkey and us. But once we arrived, it was definitely worth the trip. Father Damien gave his life
administering to the sick. He built homes and
churches. There were still people with Hansen's
disease living there, but their privacy was
protected.

Music Festival in Charleston, South Carolina

Spoleto Festival USA (P.O. Box 157, Charleston, SC
29402-0157; administration, 843-722-27; box office, 843-
579-3100; fax 843-723-6383; www.spoletousa.org; tickets
generally range from $10 to $130; Charleston Area
Convention and Visitor Bureau Executive Offices, 423 King
St., Charleston, SC 29403; 843-853-8000; www.charleston
cvb.com/about.html). Each spring, this historic and
charming harbor city hosts one of the country's major
arts festivals. For 17 days and nights, Spoleto Festival USA
presents over 120 performances by well-known and
emerging artists in theater, opera, dance, and chamber,
symphonic, choral, and jazz music, as well as the
visual arts.

Charleston has a long tradition of supporting the arts
and is the perfect venue for a festival celebrating the arts.
The city claims the first performance of an opera in the
American colonies (during the first half of the 18th century), the first American ballet company, and the first theater built for public performances. Beyond the historic
downtown area are the Atlantic barrier islands: Isle of
Palms, Sullivan's Island, and Folly Beach, referred to by
locals as "the edge of America," and where George
Gershwin is said to have composed the music for *Porgy
and Bess.*

While visiting Charleston, tour historic sights including Fort Sumter, where the first shots of the Civil War were fired, visit heritage homes, museums, plantations, and gardens. Stop at the South Carolina Aquarium and view exhibits that take you through the five major regions of the Appalachian Watershed. Take a Charleston Harbor ferry tour or rent a kayak and tour the coastline yourself. Charter a fishing boat or head for the water park or beach. And don't forget to try the regional Low Country and coastal cuisine.

Time your visit to Charleston to coincide with the Spoleto Arts Festival and the Piccolo Spoleto, a companion festival sponsored by the City of Charleston that provides low-cost or admission-free events. Check the Spoleto Festival Web site for dates, venues, and performances, and for accommodations and dining suggestions.

Cheese Every Which Way You Please

Wisconsin State Fair (640 South 84th St., West Allis, WI 53214; 1-800-884-FAIR; www.wsfp.state.wi.us/home/ wsfp/; wsfp@wisconsin.gov). State fairs are a great way to enjoy and celebrate the traditions, history, and culture of a community, state, and region. The Wisconsin State Fair is held in August with concerts, contests, 4-H competitions, livestock exhibitions, and presentations extolling everything Wisconsin. In years past 6 calves, 217 piglets, 20 lambs, 30 ducks, 6 goats, and 14 chicks were born in the Birthing Barn and fairgoers donated 98,000 pounds of food to the Hunger Task Force. Two unique Wisconsin events are the cheese and butter contests. There's competition in salted and unsalted butters and cheddar, Colby, Monterey Jack, Swiss, Muenster, Feta, and Provolone, just to name a few. A coveted Grand Master Cheesemaker Trophy is awarded each year.

A Steamboat River Cruise

Mississippi River Cruises (Vacations to Go, 5851 San Felipe, Suite 500, Houston, TX 77057; 1-800-510-4002; www.mississippirivercruises.com; contactriver@vacations togo.com; 7- to 14-day theme cruises range in price from $1,948–$4,278). Take a steamboat tour of the Old South, the American Heartland, or Wilderness Rivers, three diverse regions, each with its own culture, history, and traditions. River ports in the Old South include New Orleans, Louisiana; Natchez, Mississippi; and Little Rock, Arkansas. If you choose the American Heartlands, you will stop in St. Louis, Missouri; Peoria, Illinois; La Crosse, Wisconsin; and Red Wing, Minnesota. The Wilderness Rivers cruise will visit Nashville, Tennessee; Louisville, Kentucky; and Point Pleasant, West Virginia.

Propelled by steam power driving a paddlewheel, steamboats were first used to transport cargo. Passengers booked passage on steamboats as the country expanded westward. Now, steamboat cruises are a great way to see and learn about America. Theme cruises include Big Band Jazz, Civil War, Fall Foliage, Legends of the River, Music of America, and Cajun Culture. A guide will share stories to enhance your experience.

The *Majestic America* is the world's largest steamboat. Relax in the Grand Salon, enjoy the Mark Twain Gallery, or take in the views from the covered "front porch" on its bow. Visit the chart and engine rooms, and spend your evenings listening to music. The *Delta Queen*, built in 1927, is on the National Register of Historic Places and a National Historic Landmark. Learn about its unique history as you enjoy the sights. All staterooms are outside cabins with period furnishings, including patchwork quilts and wood-shuttered windows. The *Mississippi Queen* is modeled after great steamboats of the past, with turn-of-the-century decor. Staterooms are named for Civil War battles, river towns, and authentic riverboats.

Visit the Web site to plan your cruise: select dates, riverboat, and ports, and you will be matched with an appropriate tour. Ship statistics, services and amenities, cabin descriptions, sports, fitness, and kids' facilities, and dining information, as well as special needs accommodations, are also described in detail. Check the Web site for current prices, special deals, and discounts.

Steer Your Own Way Down the Mississippi

Huck's Houseboat Vacations (P.O. Box 73, Neosho, WI 53059; 920-625-3142; www.hucks.com; huck@hucks.com). Explore the Mississippi River on a rented houseboat. The Mississippi begins in northern Minnesota and empties into the Gulf of Mexico. From South Marina Bay in La Crosse, Wisconsin, enjoy miles of calm water, scenic beaches, and excellent fishing. Be a modern-day Huckleberry Finn as you explore historic river towns in three states.

Rent a 15-by-55-foot houseboat for $1,470 for a three-day weekend in spring, April 14th to June 12th; $1,670 in early summer, June 13th to June 26th; $1,970 from June 27th to August 25th; $1,670 from August 25th to September 15th; and for $1,470 in fall, from September 16th to October 20th. Larger boats are available, and there are also four-day midweek and seven-day rentals

Additional Mississippi Cruise Information

A resource for more information on Mississippi River Cruises can be found at www.mississippirivercruises.com or by calling 1-800-510-4002. They have booking information on steamboats, the Majestic America cruise, river ports, and theme cruises.

possible as well. The Web site advertises a 15 percent discount off listed prices before June 11th and after August 25th.

Houseboats sleep 10 people, and you will be the captain of your own boat. A comprehensive training course is provided. You will learn about navigation markers, locks and dams, operating near barges, use of the marine radio, and river etiquette. You will be taught how to approach and beach the boat, as well as how to safely depart the beach. The training cruise usually lasts about an hour and a half, and no boating experience is necessary.

Each boat is equipped with central heat and air-conditioning and has a minimum freshwater capacity of 240 gallons. Navigation maps are provided. All boats have waterslides and operational flybridges and travel at 7 miles an hour upriver and 10 miles an hour downriver. The river is safe for swimming, and all the beaches along the river are public property and are the perfect places to spend nights, enjoy walks along the shore, and the beautiful sunsets. The experience is definitely enhanced by reading Mark Twain's *Huckleberry Finn*.

Get Your Kicks on Route 66

Roadhouse 66 Motorcycle Tour (P.O. Box 1995, Westerville, OH 43086; 614-890-3863; www.roadhouse 66.com/tour.htm; dave@roadhouse66.com; one tour participant, $2,099 double occupancy, and $2,999 single occupancy; extra tour passenger, $1,799 double occupancy). Join a guided 14-day motorcycle tour from Chicago to Los Angeles traveling the legendary Route 66 to see the USA in an exciting new way. You will ride through Illinois, Missouri, Kansas, Oklahoma, Texas, New Mexico, Arizona, and California, and see vintage treasures, quirky landmarks, historic sites, and changing views as you pass through cities, towns, and tallgrass prairies.

The historic Route 66 was intended to link rural and urban communities, so all towns would have access to major transit routes and farmers would be able to transport their grain and produce. The route also appealed to truckers who, by the 1930s, were as significant to the shipping industry as railroads. American writer John Steinbeck called Route 66 the "Mother Road," when writing about the large numbers of people who traveled the route to escape the Dust Bowl of the depression years. The Chicago to Los Angeles highway was completely paved by 1938, and was used during World War II to mobilize military personnel, especially since so many bases were located in the West.

Following WWII, Americans were more mobile than ever, and returning servicemen and women, as well as civilians, were relocating for new jobs and a better lifestyle. With traffic increasing all the time, businesses along Route 66 grew to keep up with the demands for food, lodging, gas, and other services for travelers. Auto camps where people could stop and find facilities for bathing, laundry, and cooking developed into drive-in motels, roadside diners and other eateries, and tourist stops. As you travel the road today, enjoying the scenery and appreciating the role the route played in the country's development and history, you will experience a true piece of Americana while participating in an extraordinary adventure.

Tour prices include hotel/motel accommodations, some with continental breakfast included; a welcome dinner in Chicago; a farewell dinner in Los Angeles; a Texas steak dinner; a pizza and beer party in Missouri; a luncheon in Oklahoma; two other special dining treats; daily briefings by two experienced guides; a support vehicle for luggage, tools, and other equipment; admission fees to museums and national parks; tolls and parking fees; a tour book, itinerary, maps and other travel information;

a group photo; CD of photos from the tour; T-shirt and other mementos of your trip.

Check the Roadhouse 66 Web site for a detailed itinerary, information about motorcycle rentals and motorcycle laws for each state, a checklist of items to pack, a list of frequently asked questions, motorcycle shipping information, touring tips, and a registration application. For more information on Route 66, go to the Legends of America Web site at www.legendsofamerica.com/66-Main page.html.

Kristin's Story from the Rear

I just sit on the back of the bike and absorb nature as we drive across this vast, beautiful country. My husband and I have had a fascinating 15 years on our Honda *Gold Wing* touring bike. We often ride 14-hour days. Many bikers find they can't ride for more than two hours at a time because the bike vibrates too much. Ours is very comfortable. We stop about every hour and a half to stretch. I ride with a GPS on one arm and DVD on the other. We bought fancy padded seats and we ride in style.

It is such a wonderful feeling and I'm so much more observant of the countryside when riding on the motorcycle. A car restricts what you see and feel and smell. I love riding around on the back roads. You don't even realize what's all around you until you sit on the back of a motorcycle; it's a

Habla Usted Español? (Do You Speak Spanish?)

- Spanish is the 4th most spoken language in the world
- There are 332 million Spanish speakers
- Over 40 percent of the population of San Antonio, Texas, speaks Spanish

totally different perspective. I can't wait until summer and to go out riding on Sunday afternoons up the coast.

If You Like Root Beer & BBQ

Be sure to take a little extra spending money for the many gift shops along the way that specialize in Route 66 kitsch, like Route 66 backpacks, salt and pepper shakers, and of course, the complete sets of Route 66 cola glasses with napkins and coasters. Don't miss the culinary delights of the many diners along Route 66. Be sure to arrive hungry at Jiggs Smoke House on Route 66 in Clinton, Oklahoma, and no matter what, stop at Mr. D'z on Route 66 in Kingman, Arizona, for the best homemade root beer on the planet.

Alamo City

San Antonio, Texas (San Antonio Convention and Visitors Bureau, 203 S. St. Mary St., Suite 200, San Antonio, TX 78205; 1-800-447-3372; 210-207-6700; fax 210-207-6768; www.visitsanantonio.com). Experience the history, art, and culture of this unique city, which fuses Spanish, Native American, German, Mexican, Latino, southern, and western influences. San Antonio is best known as the site of the Alamo, where 189 defenders died

Side Trips from San Antonio

Take a drive to Bandera, the "cowboy capital of the world." There are ranch tours, horseback riding, rodeos, historic tours and scenic drives, and special events planned during every month of the year. Check the Bandera Web site at www.banderacowboycapital.com for a schedule of events and festivals, and for lodging and dining information.

Visit Johnson City (www.johnsoncitytexaschamber.com), named for President Lyndon B. Johnson, and tour his childhood home and the Johnson Settlement, and nearby Stonewall, with the LBJ Ranch District. Fredericksburg, Texas (www.fredericksburg-texas.com), is the home of many vineyards and wineries, and also the place to find spas for a day of relaxation.

In San Marcos (www.sanmarcostexas.com) you can fish on the Guadalupe River or go rafting or tubing at one of Canyon Lake's (www.canyonlake chamber.com) eight parks. There is a glass-bottomed boat tour at the Aquarena Texas Rivers Center and an earthquake-formed cave in Wonder World Park. Be sure to check out the monthly market days in Gruene (www.gruenemarketdays.com) where you can see the work of artisans and craftsmen and find German cuisine and Tejano music, made popular by the Hispanic populations of central and southern Texas.

in 1836 after attacks by the Mexican army. The chapel facade and the long barracks are the only remaining parts of the fort. The Long Barracks Museum contains many historic artifacts and offers a narration of the fall of the Alamo. Also visit the other missions, some looking much like they did over two hundred years ago, and the San Fernando Cathedral, built in 1738.

Visit Fort Sam Houston, established in 1845 and the birthplace of military aviation. See the Casa Navarro State

Historic Site, the restored adobe home of Texas patriot Jose Antonio Navarro, and stroll through the King William Historic District, a 25-block area on the banks of the San Antonio River. Be sure not to miss Market Square, known as El Mercado, the largest Mexican market north of the Rio Grande and the site of many festivals.

Plan to walk along the River Walk (Paseo Del Rio) through beautiful 18th-century historic districts, or visit the San Antonio Botanical Gardens or the Zoological Gardens and Aquarium. And be sure to see the Spanish Governor's Palace, called the most beautiful building in San Antonio by the National Geographic Society. For a change of pace, visit the Natural Bridge Caverns, where you can pan for precious stones or take a caving tour.

Cyndi and Gregg join the Wally Byam Caravan to Alaska.

Explore the many museums, art galleries, and cultural centers that celebrate the diversity of Texas, and attend performances at any of the city's theaters and concert venues. Use the links on the San Antonio Web site to view current schedules and pricing information.

Convoy to Alaska

The Wally Byam Caravan Club International (WBCCI Headquarters, P.O. Box 612, Jackson Center, OH 45334; 937-596-5211; fax 937-596-5542; www.wbcci.org; jmorris @wbcci.org). WBCCI is for Airstream RV owners. Cyndi and Gregg traveled to 46 states on their own, but decided

The *Victory Chimes* in full sail alongside the Pemaquid Lighthouse. *Brad Smith*

that for their first trip to Alaska it would be fun and a lot easier to let someone else do the planning. They will be part of an Airstream Caravan of 35 RVs to Alaska on a 55-day trip, attending 40 events including cruises, trains, a flight to the Arctic Circle, and all campsites for $5,800 for two people.

On the World's Top 100 Yachts List

Victory Chimes (P.O. Box 1401, Rockland, ME 04841; 1-800-745-5651; www.victorychimes.com; info@victory chimes.com; fees range from $400–$900, all-inclusive). *Victory Chimes* is an original three-masted Ram Schooner built in 1900. It carries up to 40 passengers on weekly cruises along Maine's coastline. Guests are invited to help hoist and lower the sails, hone their navigational skills, or practice marlinspike seamanship—the art of making splices in a line and knowing how to tie various knots, hitches, and bends—with a crew member. Many opt to relax as pampered guests enjoying the views and birding. Others prefer to engage in more energetic activities such as swimming, rowing, or running on the shore, as well as exploring harbors and ports.

The experience is full of pomp, circumstance, and tradition, with "Morning Colors" at eight bells—that's 8 AM. The mate commands the guests, "On deck, attention to colors." He then rings the ship's bell from the mizzen mast eight times as the National Ensign flag, the Victory Chimes' house flag, and the state of Maine flag rise on

Windjammer Fact

The Maine Windjammer Association (MWA), www.sailmainecoast.com, has 12 owner-operated members that offer Maine sailing vacations.

each of the three masts. They go up "smartly" and come down "stately" at sunset as the cannon fires. Captains Kip and Paul keep audiences mesmerized with stories about the *Victory Chimes's* service in both World Wars.

Accommodations include 21 comfortable and roomy cabins—each has its own porthole and hot and cold running water. Four private suites feature double beds and private heads. Accommodations are made for wheelchairs. Weekly cruises board Sunday night, set sail Monday morning, and return Saturday morning. Special events and four-day cruises are also available.

A Record 66 Cruises: June's Story

Summer 2007 brought me a much appreciated week aboard *Victory Chimes*. The joy never diminishes. September means Wooden Boat Week, visited this year not only by many impressive wooden boats but also by a late-summer rain.

Weather doesn't matter. What matters is appreciating offshore Maine aboard a magnificent 100-plus-year-old schooner. The sailing, the enduring beauty of the coast, sights, sounds, and smells are all part of it. In my 66th trip aboard the *Chimes,* the experience never pales.

Even after all those years, Pretty Marsh on Mt. Desert was a new port for me. Capt. Kip can find them! But I have so many old favorites—they never grow old, only more beautiful and more renewing.

Bryce Canyon. *Chris Kogut*

Helping Photographers Improve Their Images

Close-Up Expeditions (352 Kirk Ave., Brownsville, OR 97327; 541-466-5969; fax 541- 466 5744; www.cuephoto .com; don@cuephoto.com; $250 to $300 per day includes ground transportation by van, double occupancy, AAA-rated motels and lodges, admissions, and a meal budget). Close-Up Expeditions (CUE) travels the country for the best possible photo ops. Popular yearly photo immersion trips are to the Pacific Northwest, Oregon Coast, and Cascade Mountains. Other popular destinations include the Southwest Canyonlands, Slot Canyons, Deserts in Bloom, Death Valley, and the Colorado Rockies. Groups are limited to seven participants. Itineraries are planned around photogenic light, weather conditions, and a deliberately slower photographers' pace.

Chris's Photographic Memory

Most of the time I travel alone to relax, center myself, and work hard at my art without everyday demands and distractions. I like traveling with photographers to meet people with similar interests and feel part of the artists' community. My husband is not a photographer but does enjoy the trips when there is a great deal of history and culture involved.

I've traveled on 20 CUE trips. The photographers' years of experience ensure that you have the opportunities (Mother Nature cooperating, of course) to do your best work. They know where to go at what time of day for the best light and to avoid the crowds. I wouldn't get up at 4 AM to travel to the designated site to hike to the mountaintop before sunrise on my own, but with the group it is fantastic.

I love the Southwest. It is a dramatic, spiritual place. The colors in the early morning and late evening are spectacular on the sandstone. The canyons are indescribable, sensual places. I think my favorite place was in the Vermillion Cliffs. The light was eerie, the sandstone formations incredible, and it was the quietest place I've ever experienced. On my first trip with CUE Photo I knew almost nothing about photography. I have learned all that I know from CUE and fellow travelers. Six years ago I was a nurse with some interest in photography. Now I have a huge photocard business and thought I'd be selling local images, but what I really share are dreams of far-off places.

Fiddlin' Around

Ashokan Fiddle & Dance Camp (P.O. Box 49, Saugerties, NY 12477; 845-246-2121; www.ashokan.org; office@ ashokan.org; about $800 per person includes bunkhouse or camping, all meals, classes, and workshops; work scholarships are available). Here you'll find the perfect combination of summer canoeing and hiking on 300 acres in the Catskill Mountains and three weeks of music and dancing programs. There's eclectic western and swing, contra, Lindy, West Coast country & western, Cajun, barn dances, square dances, two-step partner dances, and much more. Classes are taught by experts from all over the country who enjoy teaching and jamming. Jay Ungar and Molly Mason, performers, composers, and teachers specializing in 19th- and 20th-century American folk songs and dance music, have run the camp for over 20 years.

A Participant's Story

Attending the Fiddle & Dance Camp at Ashokan is sheer joy—a week of intense music-making, dancing, eating, talking, laughing, communing with nature, and listening to some of the finest music around. The Fiddle & Dance Camp is essentially about becoming part of a community.

Participation is intergenerational and it's common to see a young person sitting knee-to-knee playing tunes with someone decades older, and both absorbed and intent on music-making. From beginners to professionals, we learn new things together and build strong connections with each other. I should also mention that the place is absolutely beautiful, the food is fantastic, and after my first camp session there in 1986 I've returned with great enthusiasm every year.

Camping Out in Style

Yosemite High Sierra Camps (Yosemite National Park, P.O. Box 577, Yosemite, CA 95389; 559-253-5674; www.nps.gov/yose/index.htm; www.yosemitepark.com/ Accommodations; about $136 per night includes family-style dinner and breakfast; box lunches $10.50; horseback trips, guided hikes, meals only, and children's rates also available). Hike any part of the backcountry wilderness, 53 miles of the High Sierra Trail accessible by foot or horse, with five campsites about 6 to 10 miles apart. Housing is in canvas-tent cabins with dormitory-style beds with mattresses, pillows, and woolen blankets or comforters provided. Demand is high and trips must be planned ahead. Applications are available until November 30 and must be submitted for a yearly lottery. Hikers provide their own linen, including sleep-sacks and towels. Showers and restroom are dependant upon water levels.

Shelley's Story

I'm sure I hold the record as the slowest hiker ever, but I couldn't have been so bad since I made it from place to place in time for all of my meals. And that was worth it. Since I was a kid I've wanted to hike and camp out in the wilderness by myself. Whenever I set about achieving my goal, naysayers, including myself, worried about my getting lost and my overall safety. We all doubted I could carry a tent, cooking gear, and the required, extremely heavy bear-proof container that needed hoisting into a tree for safekeeping.

Then my grandson read about the campsites.
Yosemite offered me both the freedom and support I needed. I shared cabin space with lovely
people, hiked at my own pace, and joined others
when I wanted company. Next year I plan to hike
with my grandson.

A Sporting Good Time

The Empire State Games (New York State Office of
Parks, Recreation and Historic Preservation, Empire State
Plaza, Agency Building 1, Albany, NY 12238; 518-474-
0456). The Empire State Games is the largest summer
amateur sports competition in the country, with 28 sporting events. Thousands compete in regional trials with
approximately 6,000 finalists at the Summer Games held
annually in July in Westchester County, New York.
Different states and parks sponsor different events. Find
out what's happening in your state.

Competition on a Grand Scale

National Senior Games Association (P.O. Box 82059,
Baton Rouge, LA 70884; 225-766-6800; fax 225-766-9115;
www.nationalseniorgames.org; nsga@nsga.com). The
Senior Games was first held in 1969 in Southern
California. The National Senior Games Association (NSGA)
is a council member of the United States Olympic
Committee (USOC), a nonprofit, community-based organization dedicated to promoting healthy lifestyles for seniors through education, fitness, and sport. The NSGA
serves 51 member organizations and over 250,000
participants.

The NSGA sanctions the National Senior Games that are held every two years in cities around the country. Events are organized for men and women in five-year age segments, from 50 to 100 plus. Athletes must prequalify in authorized competitions at the state level before moving on to the national games.

Louise's Story

I was 58 years old and looking for a team sport to do in the wintertime, and I saw an ad in the newspaper for the formation of a new volleyball league at the local community center. I went to try out and discovered that the vast majority of women were under 30 and they didn't have any openings. But the next day a woman called who had seen me playing and asked if I'd be interested in playing senior volleyball.

Odds and Evens

The Summer National Senior Games are held in odd-numbered years, with competition in 18 sports: archery, badminton, basketball, bowling, cycling, golf, horseshoes, race walk, racquetball, shuffleboard, softball, swimming, table tennis, tennis, track & field, and others. The Winter National Senior Games are held in even-numbered years, with competition in seven sports: alpine skiing, cross-country skiing, curling, figure skating, ice hockey, snowshoeing, and speedskating.

Growing up, I was captain of my high school volleyball team and played at local clubs until the same thing kept happening. I got older and the people I was playing with were much younger, so I'd stopped playing for about 10 years. When I went to meet the women on the senior volleyball team, it was a real tryout. They weren't just looking for the right age, they wanted a good fit. These were 16 women who had been playing together for about 20 years, competing in leagues and representing New England in the Senior Games, and had become like a family. I went to the 2007 Senior Games with them in Kentucky. Our two teams won ribbons when we took 6th and 8th places, which is the best the group had ever done.

In volleyball-speak, I'm a "libero." I'm not tall enough to be effective at spiking or blocking in the front row, but I'm good at returning the other team's serves and spikes back to our setter, which fits my role of a defensive specialist, or libero.

It's important for seniors to know that to compete in the Senior Games, you have to go to a qualifying tournament but you don't necessarily have to be a great athlete. For example, let's say you enjoy swimming and go to your state's qualifying tournament to try out for the 100-meter freestyle and only one other person in your age group shows up, you're in.

Unfortunately it's very hard to find organized senior sports that are competitive, especially for women, but when you do, it's a great experience. And if you can't, you can be creative. I couldn't find a senior woman's softball league, but I did find a men's league that was open to having women join. So I tried out and now I play with them. As George Bernard Shaw said, "You don't play because you get old. You get old because you don't play."

Get Along Little Doggies

Dryhead Ranch (1062 Rd. 15, Lovell, WY 82431; 307-548-6688; fax 307-548-2322; www.dryheadranch.com; dhr@tctweest.net; 6½-day horse drive $1,650, cattle drive $1,400; ranch week $1,350, plus tax and transportation fee). Dryhead Ranch is an authentic working Montana cattle and quarter horse ranch, built in 1898 in Dryhead Canyon, south of Billings. Arrive prepared to work on a real cattle or horse drive, branding calves, halter breaking yearling colts, or whatever else is needed. Guests stay in the bunkhouse except when camping out on the trail, then there are individual tepees with a bedroll and a mattress. You need to be in good physical condition to go out on the trail.

Transport to Dryhead Ranch

If you're driving to Dryhead Ranch, access is only by four-wheel-drive vehicles. The meeting place is the Conoco gas station in Lovell at 4:30 PM on the arriving Sunday; you then follow the truck back to the ranch. Or fly into Billings International Airport. Pickups are at 4 PM on the arriving Sunday. You return to Billings on Saturday by 4 or 5 PM.

Arriving Early or Staying Later

Billings Chamber of Commerce and Visitors Center (815 27th St., Billings, MT 59107; 406-245-4111; www .billingschamber.com; info@billingschamber.com). There are loads of fascinating activities to do and places to see in Billings, including the Montana State Fair, annual rodeo, Yellowstone Art Museum, Moss Mansion, and the not-to-be-missed Yellowstone National Park.

Ⓢ–ⓈⓈ **Rimrock Inn** (1203 North 27th St., Billings, MT 59101; 1-800-624-9770; 406-252-7107; fax 406-252-7107; www.billingsrimrockinn.com; info@billingsrimrockinn .com). A discount is given to guests on their way out to the cattle drive.

ⓈⓈ–ⓈⓈⓈ **Come On Inn** (2020 Overland Ave., Billings, MT 59102; 406-655-1100; www.cmoninn.com; billingsinfo @180com.net). Comfortable rooms, whirlpool, sauna, and swimming pool.

The Not-So-Perfect Horse Ranch: Deborah's Story

Deborah's story reflects her experience at another ranch, not profiled in this book, and reinforces the importance of asking the right questions and checking with others who have actually participated in the same adventure.

Everything sounded absolutely perfect. The girls (twins, age 11 and experienced riders) had such a fabulous week that they made me promise we could go back. And yet it was frustrating in a number of ways because the owner had promised a week of unlimited riding and that the girls could participate in the care of the horses. Then when they wanted to participate in feeding and grooming, the stable hands wouldn't let them.

There were also some safety issues that bothered me. I don't want to recommend them because I don't want people going there and supporting them when I have reservations about the place, and yet they were doing some good things too.

The message is that it's pretty hard to decipher all of the information you need over the Internet and telephone. Since you can't personally check out every detail until you get there with your family in tow, there's no such thing as being overly careful when asking questions and finding out what you need to know.

The only people I could have gotten information from are other mothers with similar standards and expectations for programs that have been recommended by organizations like Mothers of Multiples.

Additional Information

Web sites that promote products and product information for families with multiples include www.nomotc.org and www.twinsmagazine.com. More information on dude ranches can be found at www.duderanch.org and www.ranchweb.com.

Creative Cowboys and Cowgirls

National Cowboy Poetry Gathering (Western Folklife Center, 501 Railroad St., Elko, NV 89801; 1-888-880-5885; fax 775-738-2900; www.westernfolklife.org; tbaer@ westernfolklife.org; day and week guest passes available from $10–$60). The National Cowboy Poetry Gathering is one week of nonstop shows running concurrently on several stages. Poetry, music, stories, video, photography workshops, and demonstrations all celebrate the culture of the West. There are open mikes for people of all ages to perform. There are also education programs, youth workshops, and young buckaroo poetry sessions for kids.

Cowboy Poet Jolynne

My husband and I have been going now for about five years. We'd always wanted to go, but I teach high school English, poetry, and art. It's difficult to take off a whole week. We finally just did it. And once we'd gone, we were hooked.

I'm a cowboy poet and Elko is the very best place to go to meet many poets and musicians. It's stimulating, exciting, and just great! I've met many other poets I'd only heard of before who quickly became old friends. We travel 400 miles to get there and it's worth every minute. (Go to www.westernfolklife.org/site/ to hear Jolynne perform her poem, "The Auction".)

Elko Info

Elko Chamber of Commerce (1405 Idaho St., Elko, NV 89801; 1-800-428-7143; 775-738-7135; fax 775-738-7136; www.elkonevada.com; chamber@elkonevada.com). You'll want a few extra days to see the sights, from visiting ghost towns to modern-day gold mines to trying your luck at the casinos. There are cultural influences from Basque to Bavarian.

Where to Stay

⑤–⑤⑤ **The Stockmen's Hotel Casino** (340 Commercial St., Elko, NV 89801; 1-800-648-2345; 775-738-5141; www.stockmenscasinos.com; reservations@stockmens casinos.com). Stockmen's is a popular place to stay, with newly remodeled rooms, an outdoor pool, and a fitness center.

⑤⑤ **Best Western Gold Country** (2050 Idaho St., Elko, NV 89801; 1-800-621-1332; 775-738-8421; fax 775-738-1798; www.bestwestern.com). Year-round convenience for snowmobiling, hiking, and fishing.

Where to Eat

⑤–⑤⑤⑤ **The Star Hotel** (246 Silver St., Elko, NV 89801; 775-738-9925). The Star is where the locals go for family-style Basque cuisine for lunch or dinner.

Ⓢ–ⓈⓈ **Biltoki** (405 Silver St., Elko, NV 89801; 775-738-9691). Biltoki is a brunch favorite, known for large portions and low prices. The lamb steak dinners come highly recommended.

What's Your Story?

National Storytelling Festival (116 Main St., Jonesborough, TN 37659; 1-800-952-8492; 423-753-2171; fax 423-913-8219; www.storytellingcenter.com; custserv@storytellingcenter.net; adults $155, children $135, seniors $140). Back in 1973, high school journalism teacher Jimmy Neil Smith had an idea to have a local storytelling festival. About 60 people attended that first festival; the festival now hosts more than 10,000 visitors annually in October. Storytellers come from all over the world for the three-day event, with tales of family, travel, history, myth, mystery, and mirth. There are 22 of the best-loved storytellers in residence for the week, along with competitions and open mikes for those who have a story to tell.

The Historic Jonesborough Visitor Center (117 Boone St., Jonesborough, TN 37659; 1-866-401-4223; 423-753-1010; www.jonesboroughtn.org; lisamvc@earthlink.net; Mon.–Fri. 8 AM–5 PM and weekends 10 AM–5 PM). The center provides everything you'll want to know about the storytelling festival and historic Jonesborough, along with maps and trip-planning services.

ⓈⓈⓈ–ⓈⓈⓈⓈ **Historic Eureka Inn** (127 West Main St., Jonesborough, TN 37659; 1-877-734-6100; 423-913-6100; fax 423-913-0429; www.eurekajonesborough.com; eurekainn@earthlink.net). The Historic Eureka Inn is in the heart of downtown Jonesborough, and it's the only historic hotel here in Tennessee's oldest town. This restored turn-of-the century inn is a few doors down from the

International Storytelling Center, antique and craft shops, and the restaurants that line the historic downtown area.

$⑤⑤–⑤⑤⑤$ **Franklin House Bed & Breakfast** (116 Franklin Ave., Jonesborough, TN 37659; 423-753-3819; www.franklinhousebb.com; franklinhousebb@embarq mail.com). A restored home from 1840, the kitchen is the meeting place for guests and friends. Fireplaces through-out create a cozy and informal atmosphere. Three private rooms with baths and a private guest apartment are available. Breakfasts and wireless Internet included.

The Innkeepers' Story: Chuck & Dona Lewis

> Born and raised in New Jersey, we began visiting Jonesborough in 1982 for the Storytelling Festival and fell in love with the town and its residents. After our children were raised, we decided to relocate to Jonesborough. After many months of careful looking we found the Franklin House. We enjoyed restoring it and opened our bed & breakfast in 1997. Since that first season, the same guests return every year to enjoy the Storytelling Festival.

Under the Sea

$⑤⑤⑤–⑤⑤⑤⑤⑤$ **Jules' Undersea Lodge** (51 Shore-land Dr., Key Largo, Florida 33037; 305-451-2353; www .jul.com; info@jul.com; rates vary according to activity and length of stay, from $125 to $675 daily; book ahead, there are only two rooms). Here's a true immersion excursion, just for the thrill of it or to learn in an authentic

The gate that opens up hiking with Adventures in Good Company. *Adventures in Good Company*

underwater research facility. Stay overnight, learn how to dive, or get married and enjoy the honeymoon package, complete with gourmet meals and all diving gear included. There's also the Aquanaut Specialty Program where you can learn about the history and technology of living and working under the sea, and take a night dive. Yes, guests may stay multiple days without surfacing. Can't stay for the night? Scuba dive to Jules' for a three-hour visit and stay for lunch.

Awesome Trips for Women Only

Adventures in Good Company (5913 Brackenridge Ave., Baltimore, MD 21212; 1-877-439-4042; 410-435-1965; www.adventuresingoodcompany.com; marian@good

A group of backpackers learning how to use and pack the newest, lightest equipment.
Adventures in Good Company

adventure.com; 1-week trips, Lightweight Backpacking $1,050 and Havasu Canyon $1,500). Adventures in Good Company specializes in outdoor travel adventures for women of all ages and backgrounds. The Web site has quite a diverse range of selections from all over the United

States. The trips are rated by the level of conditioning participants need to be at to fully enjoy the trip, from moderate good health to top conditioning with endurance or weight training. Both of the trips highlighted here are rated M+, suitable for people who work out vigorously three to four times a week for 30–45 minutes and are comfortable maintaining physical activity the entire day.

Physical Immersion Excursion

Backpacking the Appalachian Trail: An Introduction to Lightweight Backpacking is a great trip for those new to backpacking or who want to learn about the newest lightweight techniques and equipment. This hike is on the Appalachian Trail, from Fox Creek to Wise Mountain (Virginia). Group size is limited to 10.

Cultural Immersion Excursion

Havasu Canyon (Arizona) is a side canyon of the Grand Canyon and outside of the Grand Canyon National Park. Often described as a desert paradise, Havasu is known for its waterfalls and blue-green water. There are no roads leading down to the canyon's floor and everyone must hike in, but the gear goes by mule. Even mail and food delivery is by horse or mule. Stay in the village for five days to get to know and understand the people and the place and to enjoy phenomenal swimming holes like no others anywhere in the world.

Patricia's Story

> I've always enjoyed walking and I realized at some
> point about six years ago that I'd gotten out of the
> hiking mode. Living in Chicago, where there are

forest preserves with a good half-day walk or more on blacktop or concrete, and city views rather than wilderness areas, I had to make an effort to find a hiking group. I signed up for Adventures in Good Company's five-day hike on what's called the Superior Hiking Trail, along Lake Superior, Minnesota, which starts in Duluth and goes north from there.

I wasn't sure I was going to like being with a group, but it worked out great. I like the philosophy and design of the trips. I specifically seek out hiking trips and that's what I can count on getting—trips with the emphasis on hiking and backpacking.

I want to come back changed from my travels. It isn't that it has to be anything drastic, sometimes it's just observing what someone else does to create less waste, or learning about a different seasoning, how to use a new spice. Interacting with others and learning about where I go makes me rethink the ordinary in my life and the things I take for granted. I watch others to see how they live, how their city is structured, how traffic flows, and attitudes in the wilderness, or behavior in traffic jams, and they all provide perceptions to improve how I live.

Combine Hiking Fitness with Spa Luxury

SpaFari (P.O. Box 325, Old Snowmass, CO 81654; 970-927-2882; 1-800-488-TRIP; www.globalfitnessadventures.com; hike@spafari.com; scheduled SpaFari adventures: 7 days, Aspen, CO, $3,600 per person, double occupancy; 7 days, Sedona, AZ, $3,600 per person, double occupancy; 7 days, Santa Barbara, CA, $3,700 per person, double occupancy; 7 days, Jackson Hole, WY, $3,800 per person, double occupancy). Combine mountain hiking and fitness adventures in Aspen, Colorado; Sedona, Arizona; Santa Barbara, California; and Jackson Hole, Wyoming, locations chosen for their natural beauty as well as their proximity to cultural attractions.

The spa component of the adventure includes yoga and meditation, massage, weight loss, and healthy cuisine. For an immersion experience that nurtures mind, body, and spirit, choose either a scheduled group SpaFari or a custom SpaFari with your choice of up to five companions, accommodations, dates, and activities. SpaFari also offers active adventures for seniors age 65 and older.

In Aspen you will stay at the Aspen Sky Hotel, and your adventure will include whitewater rafting, a riverside bike ride, and privileges at the Aspen Athletic Club. In Sedona, accommodations are at the Creekhouses at Junipines, in Oak Creek Canyon. You will be able to explore Oak Creek and hike breathtaking canyons of red rocks and cliffs, with time for meditation. In Santa

The Wilderness Southeast Mission

To develop appreciation, understanding, and enjoyment of the natural world and to instill a strong sense of environmental stewardship.

Barbara you will stay at the Santa Barbara Inn, near the beach, and enjoy organic, healthy dinners in town. Optional evening activities may include inspirational and motivational talks on a variety of subjects or evenings out at cultural activities.

Healthy menus may be viewed on the Web site, and complete trip itineraries and activities with dates and current costs, and a typical day's schedule, are also available. Physical activities are adjusted for each individual's ability and fitness level. Check-in/out varies with location, but is generally 2 PM Sunday with an 11 AM departure on Saturday for seven-day trips.

Walk Georgia

Wilderness Southeast (P.O. Box 15185, Savannah, GA 31416; 912-236-8115; www.wilderness-southeast.org; info@wilderness-southeast.org; fees vary from $37.50 to $185, including lunch on a full-day trip; group rates available). Explore Savannah or Georgia's coastline on very short (from two hours) to longer day trips led by area nature and wildlife specialists. Tours include a salt marsh walk, alligators and anhingas, native plants, birding, wild island explorations, and a downtown Savannah stroll. Great activities for all ages.

Magnificent Moab

Canyonlands Field Institute (P.O. Box 68, 1320 South Hwy. 191, Moab, UT 84532; 1-800-860-5262; 435-259-7750; fax 435-259-2335; www.canyonlandsfieldinst.org; info@canyonlandsfieldinst.org; fees vary according to activity). Thousands of adults, families, and students have participated in these brief or multiday ecotours in Arches and Canyonlands National Parks, rafting the

Colorado River, or exploring southeastern Utah with a naturalist-guide. There are one- to six-day field and river camp programs, including outdoor learning, hiking, and rafting day trips, half-day Moab nature tours, and professional guide courses for wilderness medicine, river rescue, and leave-no-trace naturalists.

Perfect Addition to a Road Trip

Global Positioning Systems (GPS) are satellite-based navigation systems created by a network of satellites placed into orbit by the U.S. Department of Defense for military use. The system was made available to the public in the 1980s. GPS satellites circle the earth daily, transmitting information to GPS receivers to calculate the user's exact location in latitude and longitude, which is displayed on the unit's electronic map.

GPS devices have become commonplace in cars, and are often standard equipment on some models. The car model is helpful but the portable, handheld GPS units provide great fun for the entire family, turning ordinary days into great adventures.

Just Sign Up

FREE Geocaching (www.geocaching.com; www.gpsmaze .com). This is a high-tech, outdoor scavenger hunt that anyone can join. Choices for thousands of Geocaches are free on the Internet. Sign up and you'll have access to caches in different locales. Select one that interests you and print out the directions, which have latitude and longitude specifics that you feed into your GPS. It's like following a modern-day pirate's map with rules, guidelines, and geographic puzzles to figure out.

For example: Walk forward 100 feet and look below the pointing branch to the hosting log. There, tucked into a recess in the log, is a long thin tube with directions to another spot.

Players are expected to return the cache to exactly where it was with all of the parts intact. Sometimes there are favors inside the treasure chest. You can also apply to create your own clever caches. It's great fun and all you'll need is a GPS unit, walking gear, water, sunscreen, and a sense of adventure. (Note: Geocaching is prohibited in some natural areas. Check with the parks service or the organization that maintains the area you intend to explore first.)

The Ax: Ray Shares His Story

I started Geocaching about four years ago. So far I have created 36 caches and found 675. As I love music and play guitar and bass, I decided on the name The Ax, which is a nickname for a guitar or bass. A good friend of mine uses the name CT Trampers, and my daughter calls herself kiddKerouac. My favorite caches are Smith Identity by The Wilkens (GCP373), which is the first of a series of caches where you are a detective trying to solve a murder mystery in order to find the cache. Another favorite is The Pit by Yodadog (GCTKAT), which takes you on a hike through the woods to an abandoned quarry. Both of these caches are located in Connecticut, but caches are literally all over the world. Whenever I'm traveling anywhere, I always check out sites along the way.

One of the nice things I like about Geocaching is many of the caches are hidden in beautiful parks and preserves that I would not normally visit. One I found was in a park I'd passed daily for years and never entered. Now it's one of my favorite places to go to relax. Geocaching is a great excuse to get out of the house, exercise a bit, and enjoy the outdoors.

Calling All Mothers

Mountain Mother Contest (Talkeetna Chamber of Commerce, P.O. Box 334, Talkeetna, AK 99676; 907-733-2330). The Mountain Mother Contest is an annual Moose Droppings Festival event, held at the Veterans of Foreign Wars (VFW) in Talkeetna, Alaska, the second Saturday and Sunday in July. It is limited to 12 participants; sign up one hour before starting time. The contest is a tribute to the strength and ingenuity it takes to be a mountain mother. Women of all ages flock to compete in this display of mountain mother talents:

- Cross a stream wearing hip waders, balancing on a log, carrying groceries, with a baby in a backpack.
- Chop firewood into four even quarters.
- Blow up a balloon for a target and pop it with an arrow shot 30 feet away.
- Cast a line 100 feet between two markers to hook a fish.
- Hammer a nail flush into a chunk of wood.
- Change a diaper, wash it out, and hang it on the line.
- Prepare a cherry pie.

- Ring the dinner bell to call the kids in for supper and stop the timer.
- A record winning time is 2 minutes, 40 seconds to accomplish all of these feats. Prizes often include a massage, manicure, and mountain mother clothing.

Pat's Return Trip

My husband and I were here last year and we attended the Moose Droppings Festival and the Mountain Mother Contest. I was so intrigued by the competition that I wanted to see if I could do it. I'm 64 years old and wanted the thrill of accomplishing this goal.

I returned to Kentucky and went into training for the year. I started lifting weights and running to build up my stamina. I focused on building strength and losing weight. The toughest part was learning how to chop wood into even pieces, and shooting the bow and arrow. Casting the fishing line to place the hook within that small space wasn't easy either. We returned this year just so I could compete and it was worth every minute. I completed the course in 3 minutes and 20 seconds to come in second place. I might have to come back next year and try it again.

Mush! with Wintermoon Summersun.

Mush!

Wintermoon Summersun Adventures (3388 Petrell Rd., Brimson, MN 55602; www.wintermoonsummersun.com; wintermoon@brimson.com; intermoonsummersun@hot mail.com; dogsledding 2 to 5 days, $175–$450 per person; 2- to 3-night stay sea kayaking, $225–$300, includes all meals, per person). Wintermoon Summersun is owned and run by an avid outdoorswoman who teaches women dogsledding in winter and kayaking in summer. If you are bringing your own group of 6 to 10 people it's possible to reserve the lodge, and participants can be women, men, or children over eight years old. The mother-and-daughter trips sell out quickly.

Sled-Dog Breeder and Trainer Kathleen Anderson's Story

I went on a weekend's dogsledding adventure and fell in love with dogs, the outdoors, and bonding with the women. That was 20 years ago and I was 37 then and aware that I had slowly been changing my life, but I had no intention of owning 37 dogs and running trips for women!

Growing up in the age when there weren't any sports for women and we were not encouraged to go out and do physical activity, we need the opportunity now to experience taking risks. It's important to try some activities that take us out of our comfort zone. Here we create a community of support and camaraderie to safely try things out and expand ourselves emotionally and physically. I believe that when women take risks doing physical activity that transfers into other parts of their lives.

My 37 Alaskan huskies are part of a team working together and they respond to verbal commands. Guests develop an immediate bond and rapport with the dogs. It's really neat to connect with another species and have that respect and total involvement for each other. Part of the experience is teaching people how to mush. They help in all the care: watering, feeding, hooking the dogs up to the gangline, and driving the sled.

I live totally off the grid, with solar power, wood heat, an organic garden, and a Finnish sauna for bathing. Sharing this environment and the joy of mushing with other women is very important to me. Connecting with the natural world is a very healing, healthful, and helpful way to live.

Teamwork

Mountain Workshops and Trailmark Expeditions (9 Brookside Ave., West Redding, CT 06896; 203-544-0555; fax 203-544-0333; www.mountainworkshop .com/companies/index.shtml; corporate@mountain workshop.com). Here's an immersion excursion that can radically improve life at work. You and your coworkers can share an adventure and develop new leadership skills when you choose an immersion excursion that will build teamwork, improve communication and decision-making, and encourage both personal and group achievement. There are team challenges that involve using a map and compass to navigate your way, building a raft and paddling across a lake, racing through a slalom course in 10-person canoes, and engaging in a treasure hunt at a museum and zoo. These are full-day activities for groups between 15 and 50 people that are held at Bear Mountain State Park, New York, and other locations.

Choose a half-day excursion to Croton Point State Park, Croton-on-Hudson, New York, for 15 to 250 people, and build your own raft from materials you've collected. Or spend a full day searching for Captain's Kidd's treasure using teamwork, navigation, paddling, and communication skills at Calf Pasture Beach in South Norwalk, Connecticut. An island picnic is included. Other options include a PVC Road Rally, and Charting the Course, a day of hiking, orienteering, and an exercise in group dynamics. Challenge yourself and your teammates and enjoy the thrill of healthy competition and the excitement of outdoor adventure.

Mountain Workshops will also plan company picnics and adventure outings for groups of 25 to 500 people. Corporate Team Building partners with corporate event and travel planners to provide team-building activities and can design programs that meet the goals of your group. Whether for a half-day or longer adventure, or to complement a conference or meeting, this will be an experience that will never be forgotten. View a partial client list on the Mountain Workshops Web site, download a brochure, check out employment possibilities, or submit an e-mail sign-up form.

Down on the Farm

Hobson's Bluffdale Vacation Farm (Rt. 1 Box 145, Eldred, IL 62027; 217-983-2854; www.bluffdalevacation farm.com; bluffdale@irtc.net; open mid-Mar.–mid-Nov.; guest house: adults $99 per night, $629 per week, with adjusted rates for children; cabins and cottage accommodations slightly higher). Arriving at Bluffdale is like stepping back in time into another world. Bill and Lindy Hobson own and work this 320-acre farm with their son, Ken, growing corn and soybeans 280 miles southwest of Chicago. Children and adults help with the farm chores; feeding the chickens, tending to the larger animals, and collecting eggs. There's horseback riding, fishing, and swimming. Evening activities include ice-cream socials, bonfires, hayrides, cookouts, or square dances.

The farm is located 4 miles north of Eldred, Illinois, and about a 4.5-hour drive from Chicago. Specific directions will be given with your reservation. It's a beautiful drive through farm country.

Lindy's Story

I grew up in Oak Park, Illinois, and Bill and I met when we were in college at the University of Illinois at Urbana–Champaign. Bill's family has owned Bluffdale Farm since 1820. When we first moved here, my friends and family from the city visited and called it heaven with a fence around it. It occurred to me that we were onto something very good, that city folk needed a place to come to relax and enjoy the finer points of living in the country.

There's a lot of wonderful history in this house. Bill's great-great-grandmother was just a girl when she attended George Washington's funeral at Mount Vernon, Virginia, on December 14, 1799. Both Charles Dickens and Ernest Hemingway visited here. It's a beautiful place and we love sharing it with so many people from around the world who visit and return. I'm 80 now and have some trouble with the computer, but I cook all the meals and bake all my own breads, rolls, and pies from scratch.

I Was Waltzin' with My Darlin'

Nashville, Tennessee (Nashville Convention and Visitors Bureau, One Nashville Pl., 150 4th Ave., N., Suite G-250, Nashville, TN 37219; 615-259-4730; 1-800-657-6910, fax 615-259-4126; www.visitmusiccity.com/visitors/index; Nashcvb@visitmusiccity.com; Grand Ole Opry performances are on Fridays at 8 PM; Saturdays at 6:30 and 9:30 PM; and on Tuesdays at 7 PM (March 6 through December 18; adults $31.50–$46.50, children's pricing available). Experience Nashville and an incredible immersion excursion to Music City. Music is what this city is all about. Walk through Nashville and stop in any of the many clubs offering live performances. Visit the famous Grand Ole Opry (1-800-SEE-OPRY; www.opry.com), the "home of American music" and "country's most famous stage," to hear music legends and rising new stars. The best of country, bluegrass, gospel, and comedy can be found here, as well as the Grand Ole Opry Museum, which honors country greats like Patsy Cline, Marty Robbins, Roy

Acuff, Minnie Pearl, and Little Jimmy Dickens. There are exhibits featuring today's chart-topping artists as well.

Check out the calendar of events and weekly schedule on the Web site, call ahead to inquire about backstage tours, and bring your camera as still photography is encouraged during stage performances.

Be sure to visit the Country Music Hall of Fame and Museum (615-416-2001; www.countrymusichalloffame .com), open daily from 9 AM to 5 PM, closed Tuesdays in January and February, as well as Thanksgiving, Christmas, and New Year's Day. There's something for everyone here, with rhinestone costumes, instruments and lyrics, interactive exhibits, films featuring county music's top performers, and private sessions with professional songwriters.

Next on your musical agenda should be a stop at Historic RCA Studio B, on Music Row (615-416-2001; www.countrymusichalloffame.com). Tours depart from 10:30 AM to 2:30 PM daily from the Country Music Hall of Fame, every hour from Sunday to Thursday, and every half hour on Friday and Saturday. Tickets are available only in conjunction with museum admission. Historic RCA Studio B, "The Home of 1,000 Hits," was once the second home of Elvis Presley, Chet Atkins, Dolly Parton, and other music legends. Over 35,000 songs were recorded there by many of the greatest performers from the 1950s through the 1970s.

You can't miss the 40-foot-high musical sculpture at the Music Row roundabout. This group of nine huge bronze figures celebrates the energy and diversity of the music industry in Nashville and is the largest figure group in America, located at the entry to Music Row. Take a stroll down the Music City Walk of Fame on Nashville's Music Mile and see the platinum-and-granite, star-and-guitar sidewalk markers that honor those who have made a significant contribution to the music industry with a connection to Music City. The Music Mile connects downtown Nashville to Music Row.

Nashville may be Music City, but history and the visual and performing arts are represented as well. Explore historic Nashville, founded as a fort in 1779, home to two U.S. presidents and site of Civil War battles, with its graceful architecture and riverfront sites of interest. For art galleries, theater, sports and outdoor activities, science and nature attractions, and historical sites, log on to the Visitors Bureau Web site and plan your Nashville adventure.

Where to Stay

⑤⑤⑤⑤ **Hyatt Place Opryland** (220 Rudy's Circle, Nashville, TN 37214; 615-872-0422; 1-800-833-1516; www.hyatt-place.com). This is a newly renovated, all-suite property located 1 mile from the Grand Ole Opry. Its spacious guest rooms feature an oversized sleep sofa that is separated from the main sleeping area, data port, and high-speed wireless Internet. Continental breakfast is included, and there is 24-hour room service as well as a restaurant, fitness center, outdoor pool, and complimentary airport shuttle. Hyatt Place offers special weekend deals, AAA and senior citizen rates, seasonal specials, and a variety of program discounts.

⑤⑤⑤ **Daisy Hill Bed & Breakfast** (2816 Blair Blvd., Nashville, TN 37212; 615-297-9795; fax 615-298-1482; www.daisyhillbedandbreakfast.com; daisyhil@bellsouth .net). This charming B&B is located only minutes from downtown and is next door to Music Row. A Tudor Revival home built in 1925 in historic Hillsboro Village, it has three themed guest rooms with a common living room, library, sunroom, and observatory. The dining room has family-style seating for breakfast, with beverages and snacks available all day. There is free wireless Internet access as well.

ⓈⓈ **Fiddler's Inn** (2410 Music Valley Dr., Nashville, TN 37214; 615-885-1440; 1-877-223-7621; fax 615-883-6477; www.fiddlers-inn.com; inquiries@fiddlers-inn.com). A locally owned and operated inn with down-home charm and a great location on Music Valley Drive in the Opryland area, comfortable, modern rooms, wireless high-speed Internet, free coffee and pastry each morning, and an out-door pool. Special discount coupon offered to Web site visitors.

Where to Dine, Southern Style

ⓈⓈ–ⒺⓈⓈ **Ellendale's Restaurant** (2739 Old Elm Pike, Nashville, TN 37214; 615-884-0171). An oversized bunga-low with traditional furnishings, Ellendale's offers a cre-ative menu for the entire family. The lunchtime buffet is a local favorite, at $10.95 for the full buffet and $6.95 for soup and salad. Weekend brunch is $13.95 on Saturday and $15.95 on Sunday. There is patio dining, live music, and a kids' menu available. Hours: Monday through Thursday, 11 AM–10 PM; Friday, 11 AM–11 PM; Saturday, 10 AM–11 PM; Sunday 10 AM–10 PM.

ⓈⓈ **South Street Original Crab Shack & Authentic Dive Bar** (907 20th Ave. S., Nashville, TN 37212; 615-320-5555; fax 615-327-0696). Decorated like a treehouse, with rolled-up garage-door windows, South Street is open for breakfast/brunch, dinner, and late-night dining, with outdoor seating. The menu is American, with barbecue, seafood, and Gulf Coast cuisine as well as lighter fare. Try the steamer bucket or split a crab and slab (of ribs). Hours: Monday to Saturday, 11 AM–3 AM; Sunday, 11 AM–12 AM.

ⓈⓈ–ⓈⓈⓈ **Sperry's Restaurant** (5109 Harding Pike, Nashville, TN 37205; 615-353-0809; fax 615-353-0814). A Nashville tradition of steak and seafood, Sperry's opened in 1974 and is now serving second- and third-generation customers. The atmosphere is warm and comfortable, with three stone fireplaces and decorative stained glass. Customers often ask about the tabletops and bar, which were built on the premises from Liberty ship hatch covers used in World War II. The bar top is carved from this wood. For a treat, try the bananas Foster, prepared tableside, for dessert. Hours: Friday to Saturday, 5:30 PM–11 PM; Sunday to Thursday, 5:30 PM–10 PM.

Go Fish

Teton Valley Lodge: Fly-Fishing (Teton Valley Lodge, Inc., 379 Adams Rd., Driggs, ID 83422; 1-800-455-1182; 208-354-2386; fax 1-866-417-2323; tetonvalleylodge.com; info@tetonvalleylodge.com; 2 nights, 1 day fishing, $1,485 for 1 person, $1,670 for 2 people; 3 nights, 2 days fishing, $2,600 for 1 person, $2,870 for 2 people; 4 nights, 3 days fishing, $3,695 for 1 person, $4,070 for 2 people; 5- and 6-night packages available, all packages are inclusive; day trip, including terminal tackle, lunch, and drinks, $150 per person). Teton Valley is a full-service fishing lodge with magnificent views of the Teton Mountain Range and seasoned guides. And it is located in what is called the Golden Three of Fly-Fishing in the West: the best dry-fly river, the South Fork of the Snake River, as well as spring creek and canyon fishing on the Teton River, and the Henry's Fork of the Snake.

Cabins are situated on the banks of the Teton River, and accommodations are first class, with gourmet meals included. You will be served breakfast at 8 AM and select your lunch items from a lunch buffet. You leave for South

This proud fisherman caught a native cutthroat trout in the South Fork of the Snake.
Teton Valley Lodge

Fork, Teton, or Henry's Fork at 9 AM with your guide, and return around 7:30–8 PM, for a 9 PM dinner with the other guests. Day trips are available if you are staying in nearby Jackson Hole or Island Park, or anywhere else within commuting distance.

All fishing packages include meals, lodging, guides, terminal tackle, transportation to and from rivers, and beverages. Guides carry all available tackle and a complete selection of custom fly patterns. People come from all over the country and well beyond to experience fly-fishing at its best in this particular Idaho location. To find out more about the lodge, equipment rentals, rivers, or trout species, check out the links on the Teton Valley Lodge Web site.

Deep-Sea Fishing

Driftwood Charters (135 West Bunnell Ave, Homer, AK 99603; 907-235-9744; www.thedriftwoodinn.com; driftwoodinn@alaska.com; seasonal prices June 1–Aug. 31, $235 per person, $1,300 to charter boat; half-day and combination trips available). There are halibut and salmon charter fishing boats up and down Homer Spit. Plan to reserve ahead during the summer season. Homer is the world's capital for great halibut fishing and the trips sell out.

Driftwood Charters has two boats, the *Misty* for halibut fishing on Kachemak Bay, and the *Mari* for salmon fishing in Cook Inlet. Experienced, licensed, and friendly fishermen, the Walli family know their fishing. Full-day charters leave about 6 AM. Bring a packed lunch, layered clothing, raingear, and a fishing license, which must be bought the day of the fishing expedition at the local Safeway for $20 per person or ahead of time online at www.admin.adfg .state.ak.us/license.

Bill's Story

> I had never been halibut fishing and I was never a big fishing enthusiast, so I wasn't too thrilled about it, but my girlfriend really wanted to go so we made the plans and woke up at 4:30 AM to meet the boat at 5:30. Finding the dock was tense. The directions were to an obscure parking lot north of Homer. The weather seemed awfully nasty for a day out on the water. If I hadn't prepaid over $200 for the day's activities I would have turned around, but at the moment of throwing in the towel two

of the most stunning bald eagles flew right down the length of the Kachemak Bay and I knew somehow it would turn out to be a great day.

Unfortunately the seas were rough and for hours the halibut were not biting. Finally the captain said, "Heard the salmon are jumping over in the cove. Let's go see what's happening." After a bumpy, rolling ride the sun came out over this beautiful little cove and the silver salmon were literally jumping out of the water so close to the boat I felt like I could put out my hand and catch them. They were beautiful. Within minutes each fisherman on board had caught the allotted six fish and we were headed back to clean up our catch. It was a great day I wouldn't have traded for anything. I went halibut fishing and came home with 25 pounds of salmon and halibut, too. The captain called his wife to meet us on the road to

Halibut Facts

- The North Pacific halibut's scientific name is *Hippoglossus stenolepis,* which has been translated as "horsetongue tinyscale."
- A record Alaska halibut catch is 459 pounds.
- Kodiak, Alaska, is the state's largest fishing port.

Ninilchik with halibut from their home freezer. It was all quite delicious.

The Fish Fly Home

Deep Creek Custom Packing (P.O. Box 229, Mile 137 Sterling Hwy., Ninilchik, AK 99639; 1-800-764-0078; 907-567-3395; fax 907-567-1041; www.DeepCreekCustom Packing.com; dccp@ptialaska.net). After the fish catch is cleaned by the crew, take it to Deep Creek Custom Packing for processing and shipping. Have your salmon smoked, canned, or filleted to your specifications and shipped frozen overnight. Go hungry so you can taste all of the different options. A freezer full of Alaskan halibut and salmon is the greatest souvenir of a true Alaskan immersion adventure.

Do the Derby

Homer Chamber of Commerce (201 Sterling Hwy., Homer, AK 99603; 907-235-7740; www.homerhalibut derby.com; halibutderby@homeralaska.org). The Homer Jackpot Halibut Derby is an annual event, open from May 1 to September 30 each year. Entry tickets sell for $10 each. A recent winning halibut weight was 376 pounds for a jackpot prize of $37,243. The cash prize is based on the number of derby tickets sold. Additional prizes are given for the monthly big fish and there are lady angler and kids' prizes.

Where to Stay

⑤⑤⑤ **The Driftwood Inn** (135 West Bunnell Ave., Homer, AK 99603; 1-800-478-8019; 907-235-8019; www.thedriftwoodinn.com; driftwoodinn@alaska.com). The Driftwood Inn is a hotel, motel, and RV park on

Things to Know

The MILEPOST® (www.themilepost.com) is the everything-you-need-to-know Alaskan trip planner and travel guide, well worth the $24.95 investment. The Web site includes discussion boards and other valuable trip tidbits from people who have been there.

Bishop's Beach in downtown Homer with views of Kachemak Bay's mountains, glaciers, and coves.

⑤⑤⑤ **Brigitte's Bavarian Bed & Breakfast** (P.O. Box 2391, 59800 Tern Ct., Homer, AK 99603; 907- 235-6620; call for rates and reservations). Brigitte's home is high above Homer, with soaring views of the area and beautifully maintained gardens, walkways, and bridges. Accommodations include very roomy bedrooms and modern bathrooms. The breakfasts are homemade and accompanied by delightful conversation.

Where to Eat

⑤⑤ **The Boardwalk Coffee House and Café** (Beach Access Rd., Ninilchik, AK; 907-567-3388). This is a hidden gem with a phenomenal view of Cook Inlet. Mt. Augustine, Mt. Iliamna, Mt. Redoubt, and Mt. Spur are all within view on a clear day. Local fish prepared fresh with home-baked desserts. Take the beach access road at the Ninilchik River bridge and stay to the left until you get to the beach, then turn right.

Whitewater Rafting for People and Pets

Adventure Bound River Expeditions (2392 H Rd., Grand Junction, CO 81505; 1-800-423-4668; 970-245-

Negotiating through whitewater on the Colorado River in an inflatable kayak, surrounded by Canyonlands National Park. *Adventure Bound–Colorado*

5428; fax 970-241-5633; www.adventureboundusa.com; info@adventureboundusa.com; 1-day trips begin at $95, and 2- to 7-day trips from $340 to $1,310). Adventure Bound offers whitewater rafting and inflatable kayaking trips in Colorado and Utah. These professionally guided trips begin and end in Grand Junction or Steamboat Springs, Colorado, and explore remote wilderness areas including Canyonlands National Park, Dinosaur National Monument, and Desolation and Westwater Canyons.

Adventure Bound offers a variety of craft: oar rafts, large pontoon boats, and inflatable kayaks. Trips can combine crafts and are suitable for a range of skill levels. In addition to knowledgeable guides, your crew will be experienced in river running, licensed, and certified in first aid. The crew will handle the rafts and gear and prepare meals. You will learn about the history and geography of the region, observe wildlife, and have the opportunity to engage in activities of your choice, including swimming, hiking, exploring canyons, or relaxing at campsites.

Take your own sleeping bag, sleeping pad, and tent, or rent or purchase these items from Adventure Bound and they will be delivered to the launch site. Some trips include a sleeping pad and tent at no additional charge. A complete packing list with clothing, personal items, and gear is available on the Web site, along with rapids ratings and transportation and lodging (for the nights before and after your trip) information.

There are also specialty river-rafting trips that include Yoga and River Rafting, a joint venture with Life Is Great LLC., for yoga and life-coaching retreats, Full Moon Float, and Dogs Go Free Ruby Mondays (all dogs are required to wear a life jacket) on the Colorado River through scenic (no rapids) Horsethief and Ruby Canyons. Check the Web site for all trips and detailed itineraries, dates, costs, and activities.

A Special Place off the Beaten Path

Otter Bay Lodge Kayak School (14026 Salmon River Rd., Forks of Salmon, CA 96031; 530-462-4772; fax 530-462-4788; www.otterbar.com; otterbar@gmail.com; open from mid.-Apr. to mid-Sept.; 7-day classes, all inclusive, $2,190; discounts available first 3 weeks of season). Otter Bay is surrounded by the Trinity Alps and Marble Mountain Ranges in the Klamath National Forest in California's far northwest corner. The lodge generates its own power, and the surrounding area has beaches and swimming holes along the Salmon River, as well as walking trails and wildlands. The Salmon and Klamath Rivers are part of the National Wild and Scenic Rivers System.

Spend a week by yourself, or with family or friends, and learn to kayak in this magnificent setting. The lodge has a fireplace, an outdoor hot tub, wood-fired sauna, and decks off each room. With gourmet food prepared with many ingredients from the lodge's organic garden, and a massage cabin with incredible views, this is an adventure that will provide the time, place, and awareness to allow change and growth.

Otter Bay offers beginner, basic intermediate, and intermediate advanced programs. There is also a boating and advanced river-running skills course, a kids' kayaking camp for ages 10–14, a teen leadership camp, and an annual Grand Canyon trip in the fall. All equipment for beginner and basic intermediate programs is provided, but you may use Otter Bay equipment and a kayak, free of charge, in all programs with prior arrangements. New gear is purchased every year. There is a "what to bring" list on the Otter Bay Web site, as well as course descriptions and dates, and a sign-up form.

Ride Your Horse to the Painting Site

Mountain Sky Guest Ranch (P.O. Box 1219, Emigrant, MT 59027; 1-800-548-3392; www.mtnsky.com; info@mtnsky.com). In the Montana Rockies, 30 miles from Yellowstone National Park and southeast of Bozeman, you'll find the Mountain Sky Guest Ranch on 8,000 acres. It is perfect for walking, hiking, mountain biking, kayaking, fly-fishing, whitewater rafting, and simply reconnecting with yourself and the land.

Fall Special Horseback Riding and Painting

Enjoy the full fall beauty of Montana in September on horseback, riding out for a day of painting for beginning or more advanced painters. Master teacher Cassandra James offers instruction and critique, along with spectacular horseback rides to and from preselected painting sites. Supplies and meals are transported separately to the day's painting location. The fee of $1,980 includes meals, lodging for six nights and five days in a private room with bath, instruction, horseback riding, and airport transfer from Bozeman. Taxes, purchases, and massages not included.

For Cowgirls Only

Wild West Women Adventures have become so popular at the Mountain Sky Guest Ranch that they have been expanded. Each guest is assigned a horse to groom and tack during her stay. Activities include learning spring cow roundup techniques, lassoing, western music, and two-stepping. It's a cowgirl week or extended weekend filled with hiking, riding, and gourmet meals. The four-night package is $1,100, excluding taxes, purchases, and spa services.

See Through Painting

Art Treks (P.O. Box 1103, Bolinas, CA 94924; 1-888-522-2652; 415-868-9558; www.arttreks.com; carol@arttreks.com; Art Trek California:1-day class, $95; 2-day class, $180; private 3-hr. class, $150; private 6-hr. class, $300; Art Trek Santa Fe: 6 nights/7 days, $1,395 per person, double occupancy). Carol Duchamp has been teaching outdoor watercolor classes here and abroad for 20 years. In the United States she leads classes in northern California; Santa Fe, New Mexico; and Ketchum, Idaho.

Art Treks offers one-day and weekend Watercolor for Self Expression excursions to Duchamp's Studio on the Mesa, in Bolinas, Marin County, California. These courses are for all skill levels and are limited to six participants. There are demonstrations and discussions of technique, with individualized instruction. Both courses would be ideal for beginners, teachers, art therapists, or artists. Students are encouraged to use a variety of techniques to create what Duchamp calls a personal visual language. There are also three- and six-hour private watercolor classes available.

Art Treks to Santa Fe, New Mexico, at Casa Nambé Retreat, include six nights' lodging, workshop tuition, Santa Fe transfers to Casa Nambé and all ground transportation, meals, excursions to Chimayo, Ojo Caliente, and Taos Pueblo, and visits to the Georgia O'Keeffe and Folk Art Museums, and galleries. Class size is limited to seven participants. The watercolor workshop is for all skill levels, and the spectacular landscape and light in Santa Fe will add to your immersion experience and inspiration.

Classes are also offered at Sun Valley Art Center in Ketchum, Idaho. Check the Art Treks Web site for dates and schedule to be announced, as well as for a current schedule of California and New Mexico Art Treks. You can also learn more about Carol Duchamp, a watercolor artist and teacher, and view her work, see detailed descriptions of classes, read students' comments, and make reservations.

A Horseback-Riding Cultural Immersion

Equitours (P.O. Box 807; Dubois, WY 82513; www.ridingtours.com; info@ridingtours.com; 1-800-545-0019; Navajo Land Ride, Canyon de Chelly, 7 nights, begins and ends in Page, Arizona; intermediate riding ability, good physical condition, maximum body weight 210 pounds; $1,840 camping and all meals included). Canyon de Chelly is one of the most beautiful canyons in

Ear of the Wind in Monument Valley, Arizona. *www.ridingtours.com*

Riding in Canyon de Chelly and Canyon del Muerto, Arizona. *www.ridingtours.com*

the Southwest. Soaring red sandstone walls set the stage, from the compelling history of the Anasazi to the current Navajo inhabitants. You will spend the week accompanied by a traditional Navajo guide riding for four full days and three half days. This experience is for seasoned and skilled riders. This immersion excursion will give you a personal perspective on a wondrous place. You are responsible for tacking, grooming, and caring for your horse, and assisting with some chores like helping to set up and pack up the tents.

Equitours: The Navajo Land Ride Itinerary Speaks Volumes

Day 1: It's about a four-hour drive from Page, Arizona, to the Canyon de Chelly. Spend the first night at Navajo Camp on the south rim of the canyon.

Day 2: Saddle up and ride down the Bat Trail into Canyon de Chelly. Riders will see Spider Rock, Anasazi ruins, petroglyphs, and Navajo hogans.

Day 3: Continue up Canyon del Muerto, named for the massacre of Navajos in 1804, to view Anasazi ruins and Navajo farms along the route. Follow a switchback trail up and out of Canyon del Muerto. Camp on the rim of Monument Valley.

Day 4: Ride through the buttes and mesas of Little Monument Valley, then back to camp on the rim. The sunsets and sunrises are spectacular.

Day 5: Ride more Monument Valley trails in the morning. Stop at the visitor's center and the rows of stalls selling Navajo Indian jewelry before driving to Navajo Mountain, sacred to the Navajo. This is very rough terrain, which is how some Navajo people escaped capture during the Kit Carson era. There are hogans still standing from that era.

Day 6: Take the day to explore on horseback the rock formations and canyons of this remote corner of the reservation. The red, pink, and white sandstone is a labyrinth of drainages, domes, and hidden arches.

Day 7: Explore a maze of canyons while riding toward the Colorado River. Enjoy vistas for hundreds of miles across the Colorado River Plateau into Utah and Colorado.

Day 8: Ride the final miles down Paiute Canyon to Lake Powell to board boats to Rainbow Bridge, a phenomenal rock formation. The arch is 278 feet wide and 309 feet high. Elevation at the base is 3,708 feet, and it is accessible only by boat, a strenuous hike, or by horseback down a precipitous trail.

Vermont Family Fun

Smugglers' Notch (4323 VT 108 South, Smugglers' Notch, VT 05464-9537; 1-800-419-4615; fax 802-644-8580; www.smuggs.com; smuggs@smuggs.com; costs vary according to package). This resort actually has a family-fun guarantee that guests will have a great time, and learn or improve upon skills they arrived with if taking lessons. That's quite a statement and reinforces the service-oriented qualities they look for in the people they hire and train. There are excellent facilities, and the

Map Fact

An interactive map of adaptive ski and sport programs in every state can be found at www.sitski.com/pg3.htm.

diverse programs include dogsledding, skiing, spa amenities, air-boarding, and cross-country skiing, along with award-winning children's ski and snowboard programs, lessons, and activities.

The Smugglers' Notch Adaptive Program (SNAP) is for special-needs individuals of all ages. They offer a one-on-one experience with specifically trained counselors. In addition to the traditional methods of skiing and riding, adaptive equipment is also available for those who might not otherwise have access to the mountains. Reservations are needed a minimum of four weeks in advance for this program.

Caitlin Sarubbi follows her guide down the slalom course in the adaptive ski competition.
Ken Watson

Legally blind, Caitie (left) won gold medals in each of her four events at the 2008 National Championships. *Ken Watson*

Adaptive Skiing Enables Everyone to Hit the Slopes

The Adaptive Sports Foundation (P.O. Box 266, 100 Silverman Way, Windham, NY 12496; 518-734-5070; fax 518-734-6740; www.adaptivesportsfoundation.org; asf windham@mhcable.com). The Adaptive Sports Foundation (ASF) provides services to children and adults with cognitive and physical disabilities. Their sports center is a completely accessible 8,000-square-foot building located slopeside to Windham Mountain and is serviced by a beginner triple chairlift.

Since its start in 1984 with 20 students and fewer than 10 volunteer instructors, it has grown to 1,300 student visits a year with more than 200 volunteer instructors. It is the largest adaptive ski program on the East Coast. Activities include skiing and snowboarding every day of the week from December through March and summer camp programs.

Caitie's Skiing Achievements

Following the events of September 11, 2001, members of Wounded Warrior Disabled Sports Project invited World Trade Center firefighters with disabled children to attend their December event. John Sarubbi, a New York City fireman, his wife Cathy, daughter Caitlin, and their three other children (they have since added a fifth child to their family) were flown out to Colorado and they've all been on skis ever since.

Caitlin (known as Caitie to friends and family), then age 11, was on skis for the first time in December 2001. After that first Ski Spectacular, the Sarubbis became hooked on skiing and started taking Caitie to the adaptive ski program in Windham, New York. Born with Ablepharon Macrostomia Syndrome, a rare genetic condition that results in a deformed facial appearance, Caitie has had 50 reconstructive surgeries. She is also legally blind and hearing impaired.

She began racing in 2003 and teamed up with guide and coach Kim Seevers in 2004. "Caitie skis on her own a few feet behind me," explains Seevers. "I am talking to her all the way down the mountain through the combinations of gates."

At the 2006 Disabled Sports USA Eastern Regional Championships, Caitie won a gold medal in level-two giant slalom and slalom titles. She also won the junior national disabled giant slalom title, and was the only junior athlete who competed in and finished the U.S. Disabled Championship Slalom. At the 2008 National Championships she won four gold medals and National Championship titles in all events. Following that accomplishment, Caitie said, "It was a good week."

"Caitie is working hard toward earning a spot on the United States Disabled Ski Team for the next Olympic Team competing in Vancouver 2010," says Seevers.

Before Caitie began skiing, there were many family rules put into place for her safety. She wasn't even allowed to cross a busy street on her own near her house. Since she started skiing, Caitie travels all over the United States to compete and flew solo to Chile to ski in the off-season.

"I can do everything everyone else does: attend mainstream classes, work in a restaurant cooking and serving, and volunteer with my brother's soccer team," says Caitie. "Skiing is the only time I'm disabled and being disabled has opened up exciting doors for me and given me an outlet to be far more independent."

Not the End: Where to Next?

Great things are done by a series of small things brought together.

—VINCENT VAN GOGH

Congratulations! You ventured out to achieve something new in a different way and you did it. Now you can hardly wait to get back out there for the next great adventure. The successful conclusion of an immersion excursion is a momentous occasion. Take a step back to consider your accomplishments and appreciate what went into planning and implementing your immersion travel achievement. Every immersion travel excursion has an impact on you. The experience changes you, and when you return home you're not necessarily the same person who left. The change might be subtle or more obvious. Reentry is not always easy and may require some readjustment. Be prepared for some surprises when returning home, getting back into the groove, and making new spaces in old places. Note the changes in your own behavior patterns. While on your adventure, perhaps you took time to meditate in the morning to prepare yourself for your day, or write and reflect on your experiences in your journal at night. Consciously continue new habits that fit into and complement your daily life.

The first thing to do is to recognize your achievement. You needed to depend on yourself in challenging situations and you came through with flying colors.

The second is to applaud yourself for taking chances, meeting new people, trying new things, and learning that life isn't always lived in the ways you're used to.

The third thing to do is to realize that you took time to value yourself and those you met. You refueled and regenerated in ways that will stay with you forever. Good for you!

Four Stages to Returning Home

There are four stages to returning home: initial excitement, disillusionment, gradual readjustment, and adaptation. Seasoned adventurers take what they've learned about themselves and apply that knowledge to a new way of life following the immersion excursion. With each adventure people learn something new to build on and fit into an evolving lifestyle.

You return home on a high, excited about the new you. Yes, it's great to be back, but the real pleasure lies in what you've learned and accomplished. Then reality sets in and you enter stage two, disillusionment, where you feel a bit like a round peg in a square hole.

Disillusionment sets in as you try to fit back into the same old routines. People at home may feel threatened because you returned with a broadened outlook on life while nothing changed for them. Old friends might seem a bit tentative and boring. Perhaps they are threatened by your newly discovered strengths. Give yourself and others the time and space needed to understand and appreciate the new you.

In step three, as you make gradual readjustments to life at home, stay cognizant of your strides forward without giving up what you've achieved while you were away. *Keep dreaming, planning, and moving forward.*

Give yourself the time you need to decompress from the intensity of your immersion experience, which is more meaningful, more emotional, and has a greater impact on you than your average vacation. Plan a day or two to gradually readjust. Rather than arriving home on Sunday night for work on Monday, reach your destination Friday night or Saturday to ease into your reentry.

Step four is adaptation. That's when what you've learned and accomplished is assimilated into your daily life. You've reached a comfort level with who you are and how you do things in a slightly new and different way. This could very well signal that it's time for another immersion travel adventure.

Abraham Maslow (1908–1970) was an American psychologist and founding father of humanistic psychology, known for his work on the hierarchy of human needs. He said, "If you plan on being anything less than you are capable of being, you will probably be unhappy all the days of your life." I prefer to paraphrase his statement and say: To be happy all the days of your life, plan to be everything you are capable of being and choose to be.

Where to Next?

Use your achievements from your last immersion excursion to plan your next challenge. Take what you've learned about yourself to apply to your next great adventure. Use your journal to reflect on what you enjoyed most about your experience. Perhaps it was your first green trip and you decide to make all of your future travels green. Perhaps you volunteered with an organization that you want to fundraise for and educate others about.

Share Your Experiences

Phrases like "My Fantastic Summer Job" or "You'll Never Guess What I Did Last Summer" might remind you of what you did in elementary school, but they are actually very interesting topics for speaking engagements with local interest groups. Jaycees, hospital auxiliaries, and mountain-climbing clubs all look for interesting speakers. There's also the possibility that local businesses and organizations will help sponsor your next trip, particularly if it is to a destination of interest to them.

You might be very surprised to learn that your new approach to travel takes you into new territory. Web site links, blogs, or endorsements on a car or clothing work as advertising for local businesses and can help you save on expenses. Inquire if your employer offers any sabbatical packages that would be applicable or if there are educational, research, or private grants available.

Better Than Ever Before

Adventures nourish the soul. I believe we return from each trip with more of ourselves clearly in front of us. Immersion excursions give us new and improved versions of ourselves. It's a gift to break away from having other people set your priorities and return home a more focused and confident you. No one can give that gift to you but you.

Between adventures I'm itchy in my own body, yearning to be somewhere new, pushing myself into another persona, finding out what I just don't know yet. When the awareness of how much is accomplished with immersion travel fully hits, you just can't wait to go back out to experience another great adventure.

I keep a running master list of trips I absolutely must take. I want to learn how to rock climb, have immersion experiences in the four U.S. states I haven't visited yet, start backpacking, live off-grid for two weeks on my own, and learn how to play a fiddle. My list for what I want to do for others includes help someone learn how to read, enable someone to travel who wouldn't ordinarily have that luxury, and plant a garden in a public place for others to enjoy.

What's on your list? Where to next? Whatever and wherever it is, cherish, enjoy, and celebrate the you who embarks on the adventure and the new you who returns ready to plan the next one. Happy immersion traveling to all immersion travelers.

Index